CAMBRIDGE LIBRARY COLLECTION

Books of enduring scholarly value

Mathematics

From its pre-historic roots in simple counting to the algorithms powering modern desktop computers, from the genius of Archimedes to the genius of Einstein, advances in mathematical understanding and numerical techniques have been directly responsible for creating the modern world as we know it. This series will provide a library of the most influential publications and writers on mathematics in its broadest sense. As such, it will show not only the deep roots from which modern science and technology have grown, but also the astonishing breadth of application of mathematical techniques in the humanities and social sciences, and in everyday life.

Diophantos of Alexandria

The Greek mathematician Diophantos of Alexandria lived during the third century CE. Apart from his age (he reached eighty-four), very little else is known about his life. Even the exact form of his name is uncertain, and only a few incomplete manuscripts of his greatest work, *Arithmetica*, have survived. In this impressive scholarly investigation, first published in 1885, Thomas Little Heath (1861–1940) meticulously presents what can be gleaned from Greek, Latin and Arabic sources, and guides the reader through the algebraist's idiosyncratic style of mathematics, discussing his notation and originality. This was the first thorough survey of Diophantos' work to appear in English. Also reissued in this series are Heath's two-volume *History of Greek Mathematics*, his treatment of Greek astronomy through the work of Aristarchus of Samos, and his edition in modern notation of the *Treatise on Conic Sections* by Apollonius of Perga.

T0382514

Cambridge University Press has long been a pioneer in the reissuing of out-of-print titles from its own backlist, producing digital reprints of books that are still sought after by scholars and students but could not be reprinted economically using traditional technology. The Cambridge Library Collection extends this activity to a wider range of books which are still of importance to researchers and professionals, either for the source material they contain, or as landmarks in the history of their academic discipline.

Drawing from the world-renowned collections in the Cambridge University Library and other partner libraries, and guided by the advice of experts in each subject area, Cambridge University Press is using state-of-the-art scanning machines in its own Printing House to capture the content of each book selected for inclusion. The files are processed to give a consistently clear, crisp image, and the books finished to the high quality standard for which the Press is recognised around the world. The latest print-on-demand technology ensures that the books will remain available indefinitely, and that orders for single or multiple copies can quickly be supplied.

The Cambridge Library Collection brings back to life books of enduring scholarly value (including out-of-copyright works originally issued by other publishers) across a wide range of disciplines in the humanities and social sciences and in science and technology.

Diophantos
of Alexandria

A Study in the History of Greek Algebra

T.L. HEATH

CAMBRIDGE
UNIVERSITY PRESS

CAMBRIDGE
UNIVERSITY PRESS

University Printing House, Cambridge, CB2 8BS, United Kingdom

Published in the United States of America by Cambridge University Press, New York

Cambridge University Press is part of the University of Cambridge.
It furthers the University's mission by disseminating knowledge in the pursuit of
education, learning and research at the highest international levels of excellence.

www.cambridge.org
Information on this title: www.cambridge.org/9781108062930

© in this compilation Cambridge University Press 2014

This edition first published 1885
This digitally printed version 2014

ISBN 978-1-108-06293-0 Paperback

This book reproduces the text of the original edition. The content and language reflect
the beliefs, practices and terminology of their time, and have not been updated.

Cambridge University Press wishes to make clear that the book, unless originally published
by Cambridge, is not being republished by, in association or collaboration with, or
with the endorsement or approval of, the original publisher or its successors in title.

DIOPHANTOS OF ALEXANDRIA.

𝕷𝖔𝖓𝖉𝖔𝖓: C. J. CLAY AND SON,
CAMBRIDGE UNIVERSITY PRESS WAREHOUSE,
AVE MARIA LANE.

CAMBRIDGE: DEIGHTON, BELL, AND CO.
LEIPZIG: F. A. BROCKHAUS.

DIOPHANTOS OF ALEXANDRIA;

A STUDY IN THE HISTORY

OF

GREEK ALGEBRA.

BY

T. L. HEATH, B.A.

SCHOLAR OF TRINITY COLLEGE, CAMBRIDGE.

EDITED FOR THE SYNDICS OF THE UNIVERSITY PRESS.

Cambridge:

AT THE UNIVERSITY PRESS.

1885

𝕮𝖆𝖒𝖇𝖗𝖎𝖉𝖌𝖊:

PRINTED BY C. J. CLAY, M.A. AND SON,
AT THE UNIVERSITY PRESS.

PREFACE.

THE scope of the present book is sufficiently indicated by the title and the Table of Contents. In the chapter on "Diophantos' notation and definitions" several suggestions are made, which I believe to be new, with regard to the origin and significance of the symbols employed by Diophantos. A few words may be necessary to explain the purpose of the Appendix. This is the result of the compression of a large book into a very small space, and claims to have no independent value apart from the rest of my work. It is intended, *first*, as a convenient place of reference for mathematicians who may, after reading the account of Diophantos' methods, feel a desire to see them in actual operation, and, *secondly*, to exhibit the several instances of that variety of peculiar devices which is one of the most prominent of the characteristics of the Greek algebraist, but which cannot be brought under general rules and tabulated in the same way as the processes described in Chapter V. The Appendix, then, is a. necessary part of the whole, in that there is much in Diophantos which could not be introduced elsewhere ; it must not, however, be considered as in any sense an alternative to the rest of the book : indeed, owing to its extremely condensed form, I could hardly hope that, by itself, it would even be comprehensible to the mathematician. I will merely add that I have twice carefully worked out the solution of

every problem from the proof-sheets, so that I hope and believe that no mistakes will be found to have escaped me.

It would be mere tautology to enter into further details
here. One remark, however, as to what the work does not,
and does not profess to, include may not be out of place.
No treatment of Diophantos could be complete without a
thorough revision of the text. I have, however, only cursorily
inspected one MS. of my author, that in the Bodleian Library,
which unfortunately contains no more than a small part of
the first of the six Books. The best MSS. are in Paris and
Rome, and I regret that I have had as yet no opportunity of
consulting them. Though this would be a serious drawback
were I editing the text, no collation of MSS. could affect my
exposition of Diophantos' methods, or the solutions of his
problems, to any appreciable extent; and, further, it is more
than doubtful, in view of the unsatisfactory results of the
collation of three of the MSS. by three different scholars in
the case of one, and that the most important, of the few obscure passages which need to be cleared up, whether the text
in these places could ever be certainly settled.

I should be ungrateful indeed if I did not gladly embrace
this opportunity of acknowledging the encouragement which
I have received from Mr J. W. L. Glaisher, Fellow and Tutor
of Trinity College, to whose prospective interest in the work
before it was begun, and unvarying kindness while it was
proceeding, I can now thankfully look back as having been
in a great degree the "moving cause" of the whole. And,
finally, I wish to thank the Syndics of the University Press
for their liberality in undertaking to publish the volume.

T. L. HEATH.

11 *May*, 1885.

LIST OF BOOKS OR PAPERS READ OR REFERRED TO, SO FAR AS THEY CONCERN OR ARE USEFUL TO THE SUBJECT.

1. *Books directly upon Diophantos.*

XYLANDER, Diophanti Alexandrini Rerum Arithmeticarum Libri sex......
Item Liber de Numeris Polygonis. Opus incomparabile......Latine
redditum et Commentariis explanatum...... Basileae, 1575.
BACHET, Diophanti Alexandrini Arithmeticorum Libri sex, et de numeris
multangulis liber unus. Lutetiae Parisiorum, 1621.
Diophanti Alexandrini Arithmeticorum libri sex, et de numeris multangu-
lis liber unus. Cum commentariis C. G. BACHETI V.C. et obserua-
tionibus D. P. de FERMAT Senatoris Tolosani. Tolosae, 1670.
SCHULZ, Diophantus von Alexandria arithmetische Aufgaben nebst dessen
Schrift über die Polygon-zahlen. Aus dem Griechischen übersetzt
und mit Anmerkungen begleitet. Berlin, 1822.
POSELGER, Diophantus von Alexandrien über die Polygon-Zahlen.
Uebersetzt, mit Zusätzen. Leipzig, 1810.
CRIVELLI, Elementi di Fisica......ed i Problemi arithmetici di Diofanto
Alessandrino analiticamente dimostrati. In Venezia, 1744.
P. GLIMSTEDT, Första Boken af Diophanti Arithmetica algebraisk Oefver-
sättning. Lund, 1855.
STEVIN and GIRARD, "Translation" in Les Oeuvres mathématiques de
Simon Stevin. Leyde, 1684.

2. *Works indirectly elucidating Diophantos.*

BOMBELLI, L'Algebra......diuisa in tre Libri...... Bologna, 1579.
FERMAT, Opera Varia mathematica. Tolosae, 1679.
BRASSINNE, Précis des Oeuvres mathématiques de P. Fermat et de l'Arith-
métique de Diophante. Paris, 1853.
COSSALI, Origine, trasporto in Italia, primi progressi in essa dell' Algebra
......Storia critica....... Parma, 1797.
NESSELMANN, Die Algebra der Griechen. Berlin, 1842.
JOHN KERSEY, Elements of Algebra. London, 1674.
WALLIS, Algebra (in Opera Mathematica. Oxoniae, 1695—9).
SAUNDERSON, N., Elements of Algebra. 1740.

3. *Books which mention or give information about Diophantos,
    including histories of mathematics.*

COLEBROOKE, Algebra with Arithmetic and Mensuration from the Sanscrit
of Brahmagupta and Bháscara. London, 1817.
SUIDAS, Lexicon (ed. G. Bernhardy). Halis et Brunsvigae, 1853.
FABRICIUS, Bibliotheca Graeca (ed. Harless).
ABULFARAJ, History of the Dynasties (tr. Pococke). Oxon. 1663.
CH. TH. V. MURR, Memorabilia Bibliothecarum publicarum Norimbergen-
sium et Universitatis Altdorfinae. Norimbergae, 1786.
DOPPELMAYR, Historische Nachricht von den Nürnbergischen Mathema-
ticis und Künstlern. (Nürnberg, 1730.)
VOSSIUS, De universae mathesios natura et constitutione......
Amstelaedami, 1660.
HEILBRONNER, Historia matheseos universae. Lipsiae, 1742.
MONTUCLA, Histoire des Mathématiques. Paris, An 7.
KLUEGEL, Mathematisches Wörterbuch. Leipzig, 1830.
KAESTNER, Geschichte der Mathematik. Göttingen, 1796.
BOSSUT, Histoire Générale des Mathematiques. Paris, 1810.
HANKEL, Zur Geschichte der Mathematik in Alterthum und Mittelalter.
Leipzig, 1874.
CANTOR, Vorlesungen über Geschichte der Mathematik, Band I.
Leipzig, 1880.
Dr HEINRICH SUTER, Gesch. d. Mathematischen Wissenschaften.
Zürich, 1873.
JAMES GOW, A short History of Greek Mathematics.
Camb. Univ. Press, 1884.

4. *Papers or Pamphlets read in connection with Diophantos.*

POSELGER, Beiträge zur Unbestimmten Analysis.
(Berlin *Abhandlungen*, 1832.)
L. RODET, L'Algèbre d'Al-Khārizmi et les methodes indienne et grecque.
(*Journal Asiatique*, Janvier, 1878.)
WOEPCKE, Extrait du Fakhrî, traité d'Algèbre par Aboú Bekr Mohammed
ben Alhaçan Alkarkhî, précédé d'un memoire sur l'algèbre indéterminée
chez les Arabes. Paris, 1853.
WOEPCKE, Mathématiques chez les Orientaux.
1. *Journal Asiatique*, Février-Mars, 1855.
2. *Journal Asiatique*, Avril, 1855.
P. TANNERY, "À quelque époque vivait Diophante ?" (*Bulletin des Sciences
Mathém. et Astronom.* 1879.)
P. TANNERY, L'Arithmétique dans Pappus...... (*Bordeaux Memoirs*, 1880.)
ROSEN, The Algebra of Mohammed ben Musa. London, 1831.
HEIBERG, Quaestiones Archimedeae. Hauniae, 1879.

CONTENTS.

CHAPTER I.

HISTORICAL INTRODUCTION.

PAGES

§ 1. Diophantos' name and particulars of his life 1
§ 2. His date. Different views 3
     (a) Internal evidence considered . . . . 4—8
     (b) External evidence . . . . 8—16
§ 3. Results of the preceding investigation . . . . . . 16—17

CHAPTER II.

THE WORKS OF DIOPHANTOS; THEIR TITLES AND GENERAL CONTENTS; THE PORTIONS WHICH SURVIVE.

§ 1. Titles: no real evidence that 13 books of *Arithmetics* ever existed
     corresponding to the title . . . . 18—23
     No trace of lost books to be restored from Arabia. Corruption
     must have taken place before 11th cent. and probably before
     950 A.D. . . . . 23—26
     Porisms lost before 10th cent. A.D. 26
§ 2. What portion of the *Arithmetics* is lost? The contents of the
     lost books. The *Polygonal Numbers* and *Porisms* may have
     formed part of the complete *Arithmetics*. Objections to this
     theory . . . . 26—35
     Other views of the contents of the lost Books . . . . 35—37
     Conclusion 37

CHAPTER III.

THE WRITERS UPON DIOPHANTOS.

§ 1. Greek . . . . 38—39
§ 2. Arabian . . . . 39—42
§ 3. European generally . . . . 42—56

CHAPTER IV.

NOTATION AND DEFINITIONS OF DIOPHANTOS.

PAGES

§ 1. Introduction 57
§ 2. Sign for the unknown quantity discussed . . . . . 57—67
§ 3. Notation for powers of the unknown . . . . . 67—69
§ 4. Objection that Diophantos loses generality by the want of
more algebraic symbols answered 69
Other questions of notation: operations, fractions, &c. . . 69—76
§ 5. General remarks on the historical development of algebraic
notation: three stages exhibited . . . . . . 76—80
§ 6. On the influence of Diophantos' notation on his work . . 80—82

CHAPTER V.

DIOPHANTOS' METHODS OF SOLUTION.

§ 1. General remarks. Criticism of the positions of Hankel and
Nesselmann . . . . 83—88
§ 2. Diophantos' treatment of equations . . . . . . 88—114
(A) Determinate equations of different degrees.
(1) Pure equations of different degrees, i.e. equations containing only one power of the unknown . . . 88—90
(2) Mixed quadratics . . . . 90—93
(3) Cubic equation . . . . 93—94
(B) Indeterminate equations.
I. Indeterminate equations of the first and second degrees.
(1) Single equation (second degree) . . . . 95—98
1. Those which can always be rationally solved . 95
2. Those which can be rationally solved only
under certain conditions . . . . 95—98
(2) Double equations.
1. First general method (first degree) . . . 99—105
Second method (first degree) . . . . 105—107
2. Double equation of the second degree . . 107
II. Indeterminate equations of higher degrees.
(1) Single equations (first class) . . . . 108—111
,, (second class) . . . . 111—112
(2) Double equations . . . . 112—113
§ 3. Summary of the preceding investigation . . . . . 113—114
§ 4. Transition . . . . 114—115
§ 5. Method of limits . . . . 115—117
§ 6. Method of approximation to limits . . . . . . 117—120

CHAPTER VI.

PAGES
§ 1. The *Porisms* of Diophantos . . . . . . 121—125
§ 2. Other theorems assumed or implied . . . . . 125—132
   (a) Numbers as the sum of two squares . . . . . 127—130
   (b) Numbers as the sum of three squares . . . . . 130—131
   (c) Numbers as the sum of four squares . . . . . 131—132

CHAPTER VII.

HOW FAR WAS DIOPHANTOS ORIGINAL ?

§ 1. Preliminary . . . . 133—134
§ 2. Diophantos' algebra not derived from Arabia . . . . 134—135
§ 3. Reference to Hypsikles . . . . 135—136
§ 4. The evidence of his language . . . . 136—138
§ 5. Wallis' theory of Greek Algebra 138
§ 6. }
§ 7. } Comparison of Diophantos with his Greek predecessors . . 139—142
§ 8. Discussion in this connection of the *Cattle-problem* . . . 142—147

CHAPTER VIII.

DIOPHANTOS AND THE EARLY ARABIAN ALGEBRAISTS.

§ 1. Preliminary 148
§ 2. Comparison of Diophantos with Mohammed ibn Mūsā . . 149—155
§ 3. Diophantos and Abu'l-Wafā 155
§ 4. An anonymous Arabic MS. . . . . 155—156
§ 5. Abu Ja'far Mohammed ibn Alhusain 156
§ 6. Alkarkhī . . . . 156—159

APPENDIX.

ABSTRACT OF DIOPHANTOS.

Arithmetics. Book I. . . . . 163—171
    Book II. . . . . 172—181
    Book III. . . . . 181—189
    Book IV. . . . . 189—208
    Book V. . . . . 209—224
    Book VI. . . . . 225—237
Polygonal Numbers . . . . 238—244

DIOPHANTOS OF ALEXANDRIA.

CHAPTER I.

HISTORICAL INTRODUCTION.

§ 1. THE doubts about Diophantos begin, as has been remarked by Cossali[1], with his very name. It cannot be positively decided whether his name was Diophan*tos* or Diophan*tes*. The preponderance, however, of authority is in favour of the view that he was called Diophan*tos*.

(1) The title of the work which has come down to us under his name gives us no clue. It is $\Delta\iota o\phi\acute{a}\nu\tau o\upsilon$ $'A\lambda\epsilon\xi a\nu\delta\rho\acute{\epsilon}\omega\varsigma$ $'A\rho\iota\theta\mu$-$\eta\tau\iota\kappa\hat{\omega}\nu$ $\beta\iota\beta\lambda\acute{\iota}a$ $\overline{\iota\gamma}$. Now $\Delta\iota o\phi\acute{a}\nu\tau o\upsilon$ may be the Genitive of either $\Delta\iota\acute{o}\phi a\nu\tau o\varsigma$ or $\Delta\iota o\phi\acute{a}\nu\tau\eta\varsigma$. We learn however from this title that he lived at Alexandria.

(2) In Suidas under the article $'\Upsilon\pi a\tau\acute{\iota}a$ the name occurs in the Accusative and in old editions is given as $\Delta\iota o\phi\acute{a}\nu\tau\eta\nu$; but Bachet[2] in the Preface to his edition of Diophantos assures us that two excellent Paris MSS. have $\Delta\iota\acute{o}\phi a\nu\tau o\nu$. Besides this, Suidas has a separate article $\Delta\iota\acute{o}\phi a\nu\tau o\varsigma$, $\acute{o}\nu o\mu a$ $\kappa\acute{\upsilon}\rho\iota o\nu$. Moreover Fabricius mentions several persons of the same name $\Delta\iota\acute{o}\phi a\nu\tau o\varsigma$, but the name $\Delta\iota o\phi\acute{a}\nu\tau\eta\varsigma$ nowhere occurs. It is on this ground probable that the correct form is $\Delta\iota\acute{o}\phi a\nu\tau o\varsigma$. We may compare it with $'' E\kappa\phi a\nu\tau o\varsigma$, but we cannot go so far as to say, with Bachet, that $\Delta\iota o\phi\acute{a}\nu\tau\eta\varsigma$ is not Greek; for we have the analogous forms $'I\epsilon\rho o\phi\acute{a}\nu\tau\eta\varsigma$, $\sigma\upsilon\kappa o\phi\acute{a}\nu\tau\eta\varsigma$.

---

[1] "Su la desinenza del nome comincia la diversità tra gli scrittori" (p. 61).

[2] "Ubi monendus es imprimis, in editis Suidae libris male haberi, $\epsilon\iota\varsigma$ $\Delta\iota o$-$\phi\acute{a}\nu\tau\eta\nu$, ut ex duobus probatissimis codicibus manu exaratis qui extant in Bibliotheca Regia, depraehendi, qui veram exhibent lectionem $\epsilon\iota\varsigma$ $\Delta\iota\acute{o}\phi a\nu\tau o\nu$."

(3) In the only quotation from Diophantos which we know Theon of Alexandria (fl. 365—390 A.D.) speaks of him as Διόφαντος.

(4) On the other hand Abu'lfaraj, the Arabian historian, in his *History of the Dynasties,* is thought to be an authority for the form Diophan*tes,* and certainly in his Latin translation of the two passages in which D. is mentioned by Abu'lfaraj, Pococke writes Diophantes. But, while in the first of the two passages in the original the vowel is doubtful, in the second the name is certainly Diophan*tos.* Hence Abu'lfaraj is really an authority for the form Diophan*tos.*

(5) Of more modern writers, Rafael Bombelli in his Algebra, published 1572, writes in Italian " Diofan*te*" corresponding to Διοφάντης. But Joannes Regiomontanus, Joachim Camerarius, James Peletarius, Xylander and Bachet all write Diophan*tus.*

We may safely conclude, then, that Diophan*tos* was the name of our author. Far more perplexing than the doubt as to his name is the question of the time at which he lived. As no certainty can even now be said to have been reached on this point, it will be necessary to enumerate the indications which bear on the question. Before proceeding to consider in order the internal and external evidence, it will be well to give the only facts which are known of his personal history, and which can be gathered from an arithmetical epigram upon Diophantos. This epigram, the probable date of which it will be necessary to consider later along with the question of its authorship, is as follows :

Οὗτός τοι Διόφαντον ἔχει τάφος, ἃ μέγα θαῦμα,
   Καὶ τάφος ἐκ τέχνης μέτρα βίοιο λέγει.
῞Εκτην κουρίζειν βιότου θεὸς ὤπασε μοίρην,
   Δωδεκάτῃ δ' ἐπιθεὶς μῆλα πόρεν χλοάειν.
Τῇ δ' ἄρ' ἐφ' ἑβδομάτῃ τὸ γαμήλιον ἥψατο φέγγος,
   'Εκ δὲ γάμων πέμπτῳ παῖδ' ἐπένευσεν ἔτει.
Αἲ αἲ τηλύγετον δειλὸν τέκος, ἥμισυ πατρός,
   Τοῦ δὲ καὶ ἡ κρυερὸς μέτρον ἑλὼν βιότου.
Πένθος δ' αὖ πισύρεσσι παρηγορέων ἐνιαυτοῖς
   Τῇδε πόσου σοφίῃ τέρμ' ἐπέρησε βίου.

The solution of this epigram-problem gives 84 as the age at which Diophantos died. His boyhood lasted 14 years, his beard grew at 21, he married at 33; a son was born to him 5 years later and died at the age of 42, when his father was 80 years old. Diophantos' own death followed 4 years later at the age of 84. Diophantos having lived to so great an age, an approximate date is all that we can expect to find for the production of his works, as we have no means of judging at what time of life he would be likely to write his *Arithmetics*.

§ 2. The most important statements upon the date of Diophantos which we possess are the following:

(1) Abu'lfaraj, whom Cossali calls "the courageous compiler of a universal history from Adam to the 13th century," in his *History of the Dynasties* before mentioned, places Diophantos, without giving any reason, under the Emperor Julian (361—363 A.D.). This is the view which has been ordinarily held. It is that of Montucla.

(2) We find in the preface to Rafael Bombelli's Algebra, published 1572, a dogmatic statement that Diophantos lived under Antoninus Pius (138—161 A.D.). This view too has met with considerable favour, being adopted by Jacobus de Billy, Blancanus, Vossius, Heilbronner, and others.

Besides these views we may mention Bachet's conjecture, which identifies the Diophantos of the *Arithmetics* with an astrologer of the same name, who is ridiculed in an epigram attributed to Lucilius; whence Bachet concludes that he lived about the time of Nero (54—68) (not under Tiberius, as Nesselmann supposes Bachet to say). The three views here mentioned will be discussed later in detail, as they are all worthy of consideration. The same cannot be said of a number of other theories on the subject, of which I will quote only one as an example. Simon Stevin[1] places Diophantos later than the Arabian algebraist Mohammed ibn Mūsā

---

[1] *Les Oeuvres Mathém. de Sim. Stevin, augm. par Alb. Girard*, Leyden, 1634. "Quant à Diophant, il semble qu'en son temps les inventions de Mahomet ayent seulement esté cognues, comme se peult colliger de ses six premiers livres."

Al-Khārizmi who lived in the first half of the 9th century, the absurdity of which view will appear..

We must now consider in detail the

(a) Internal evidence of the date of Diophantos.

(1) It would be natural to hope to find, under this head, references to the works of earlier or contemporary mathematicians. Unfortunately there is only one such reference traceable in Diophantos' extant writings. It occurs in the fragment upon *Polygonal Numbers,* and is a reference to a definition given by a certain *Hypsikles*[1]. Thus, if we knew the date of Hypsikles, it would enable us to fix with certainty an upper limit, before which Diophantos could not have lived. It is particularly unfortunate that we cannot determine accurately at what time Hypsikles himself lived. Now to Hypsikles is attributed the work on *Regular Solids* which forms Books XIV. and XV. of the Greek text of Euclid's Elements. In the introduction to this work the author relates[2] that his father knew a treatise of Apollonios only in an incorrect form, whereas he himself afterwards found it correctly worked out in another book of Apollonios, which was easily accessible anywhere in his time. From this we may with justice conclude that Hypsikles' father was an elder contemporary of Apollonios, and must have died before the corrected version of Apollonios' treatise was given to the world. Hypsikles' work itself is dedicated to a friend of his father's, Protarchos by name. Now Apollonios died about 200 B.C.; hence it follows that Hypsikles' treatise

---

[1] *Polyg. Numbers,* prop. 8.

"καὶ ἀπεδείχθη τὸ παρὰ Ὑψικλεῖ ἐν ὅρῳ λεγόμενον."

"συναποδειχθέντος οὖν καὶ τοῦ Ὑψικλέους ὅρου, κ. τ. λ."

[2] "καί ποτε διελοῦντες (sc. Basileides of Tyre and Hypsikles' father) τὸ ὑπὸ Ἀπολλωνίου γραφὲν περὶ τῆς συγκρίσεως τοῦ δωδεκαέδρου καὶ τοῦ εἰκοσαέδρου τῶν εἰς τὴν αὐτὴν σφαῖραν ἐγγραφομένων, τίνα λόγον ἔχει πρὸς ἄλληλα, ἔδοξαν ταῦτα μὴ ὀρθῶς γεγραφέναι τὸν Ἀπολλώνιον. αὐτοὶ δὲ ταῦτα διακαθάραντες ἔγραψαν ὡς ἦν ἀκούειν τοῦ πατρός. ἐγὼ δὲ ὕστερον περιέπεσον ἑτέρῳ βιβλίῳ ὑπὸ Ἀπολλωνίου ἐκδεδομένῳ, καὶ περιέχοντι ἀπόδειξιν ἡγιῶς (?) περὶ τοῦ ὑποκειμένου. καὶ μεγάλως ἐψυχαγωγήθην ἐπὶ τῇ προβλήματος ζητήσει. τὸ μὲν ὑπὸ Ἀπολλωνίου ἐκδοθὲν ἔοικε κοινῇ σκοπεῖν. καὶ γὰρ περιφέρεται, κ. τ. λ."

on *Regular Solids* was probably written about 180 B.C. It was clearly a youthful production. Besides this we have another work of Hypsikles, of astronomical content, entitled in Greek ἀναφορικός. Now in this treatise we find for the first time the division of the circumference of a circle into 360 degrees, which Autolykos, an astronomer a short time anterior to Euclid, was not acquainted with, nor, apparently, Eratosthenes who died about 194 B.C. On the other hand Hypsikles used no trigonometrical methods : these latter are to some extent employed by the astronomer Hipparchos, who made observations at Rhodes between the years 161 and 126. Thus the discovery of trigonometrical methods about 150 agrees well with the conclusion arrived at on other grounds, that Hypsikles flourished about 180 B.C.

We must not, however, omit to notice that Nesselmann, an authority always to be mentioned with respect, takes an entirely different view. He concludes that we may with a fair approach to certainty place Hypsikles about the year 200 of our era, but upon insufficient grounds. Of the two arguments used by Nesselmann in support of his view one is grounded upon the identification of an Isidoros whom Hypsikles mentions[1] as his instructor with the Isidoros of an article in Suidas : Ἰσίδωρος φιλόσοφος ὃς ἐφιλοσόφησε μὲν ὑπὸ τοῖς ἀδελφοῖς, εἴπερ τις ἄλλος, ἐν μαθήμασιν : and, further, upon a conjecture of Fabricius about it. Assuming that the two persons called Isidoros in the two places are identical we have still to determine his date. The question to be answered is, what is the reference in ὑπὸ τοῖς ἀδελφοῖς? Now Fabricius makes a conjecture, which seems hazardous, that the ἀδελφοί are the brothers M. Aurelius Antoninus and L. Aurelius Verus, who were joint-Emperors from 160 to 169 A.D. This date being assigned to Isidoros, it would follow that Hypsikles should be placed about A.D. 200.

In the second place Nesselmann observes that according to Diophantos Hypsikles is the discoverer of a proposition respecting polygonal numbers which we find in a rather less perfect

[1] Eucl. xv. 5. "ἡ δὲ εὕρεσις, ὡς Ἰσίδωρος ὁ ἡμέτερος ὑφηγήσατο μέγας διδάσκαλος, ἔχει τὸν τρόπον τοῦτον."

form in Nikomachos and Theon of Smyrna; from this he argues that Hypsikles must have been later than both these mathematicians, adducing as further evidence that Theon (who is much given to quoting) does not quote him. Doubtless, as Theon lived under Hadrian, about 130 A.D., this would give a date for Hypsikles which would agree with that drawn from Fabricius' conjecture; but it is not possible to regard either piece of evidence as in any way trustworthy, even if it were not contradicted by the evidence before adduced on the other side.

We may say then with certainty that Hypsikles, and therefore *a fortiori* Diophantos, cannot have written before 180 B.C.

(2) The only other name mentioned in Diophantos' writings is that of a contemporary to whom they are dedicated. This name, however, is *Dionysios*, which is of so common occurrence that we cannot derive any help from it whatever.

(3) Diophantos' work is so unique among the Greek treatises which we possess, that he cannot be said to recal the style or subject-matter of any other author, except, indeed, in the fragment on *Polygonal Numbers;* and even there the reference to Hypsikles is the only indication we can lay hold of.

The epigram-problem, which forms the last question of the 5th book of Diophantos, has been used in a way which is rather curious, as a means of determining the date of the *Arithmetics*, by M. Paul Tannery[1]. The enunciation of this problem, which is different from all the rest in that (*a*) it is in the form of an epigram, (*b*) it introduces numbers in the concrete, as applied to things, instead of abstract numbers (with which alone all the other problems of Diophantos are concerned), is doubtless borrowed by him from some other source. It is a question about wine of two different qualities at the price respectively of **8** and **5** drachmae the χοῦς. It appears also that it was wine of inferior quality as it was mixed by some one as drink for his servants. Now M. Tannery argues (*a*) that the numbers 8 and 5 were not hit upon to suit the metre, for, as these are the only numbers which occur in the epigram, and both are found in

---

[1] *Bulletin des Sciences mathematiques et astronomiques*, 1879, p. 261,

the same line in the compounds ὀκταδράχμους and πεντεδράχμους, some other numerals would serve the purposes of metre
equally well. (b) Neither were they taken in view of the solution of the problem, for each number of χόες which it was
required to find are found to contain fractions. Hence (c) the
basis on which the author composed his problem must have
been the price of wines at the time. Now, says M. Tannery[1],
it is evident that the prices mentioned for wines of poor quality
are famine prices. But wine was not dear until after the time
of the Antonines. Therefore the composer of the epigram, and
hence Diophantos also, is later than the period of the Antonines.

This argument, even if it is correct, does no more than give
us a later date than we before arrived at as the upper limit.
Nor can M. Tannery consistently assert that this determination
necessarily brings us at all near to the date of Diophantos; for
in another place he maintains that Diophantos was no original
genius, but a learned mathematician who made a collection of
problems previously known; thus, if so much had already been
done in the domain which is represented for us exclusively by
Diophantos, the composer of the epigram in question may well
have lived a considerable time before Diophantos. It may be
mentioned here, also, that one of the examples which M. Tannery quotes as an evidence that problems similar to, and even
more difficult than, those of Diophantos were in vogue before
his time, is the famous Problem of the Cattle, which has been
commonly called by the name of Archimedes; and this very
problem is fatal to the theory that arithmetical epigrams must
necessarily be founded on fact. These considerations, however,
though proving M. Tannery to be inconsistent, do not necessarily preclude the possibility that the inference he draws from
the epigram-problem solved by Diophantos is correct, for (a) the
date of the Cattle-problem itself is not known, and may be
later even than Diophantos, (b) it does not follow that, if
M. Tannery's conclusion cannot be proved to be necessarily
right, it must therefore be wrong.

---

[1] "Il est d'ailleurs facile de se rendre compte que ces prix n'ont pas été
choisis en vue de la solution: on doit donc supposer qu'ils sont réels. Or ce
sont évidemment, pour les vins de basse qualité, de prix de famine."

On the vexed question as to how far Diophantos was original
we shall have to speak later. We pass now to a consideration of the

(b)   *External evidence as to the date of Diophantos.*

(1)   We have first to consider the testimony of a passage of
Suidas, which has been made much of by writers on the question of Diophantos, to an extent entirely disproportionate to its
intrinsic importance. As however it does not bear solely upon
the question of date, but upon another question also, it cannot
be here passed over. The passage in question is Suidas' article
Ὑπατία[1]. The words which concern us apparently stood in
the earliest texts thus, ἔγραψεν ὑπόμνημα εἰς Διοφάντην
τὸν ἀστρονομικόν. Κανόνα εἰς τὰ κωνικά· Ἀπολλωνίου
ὑπόμνημα. With respect to the reading Διοφάντην, we have
already remarked that Bachet asserts that two good Paris MSS.
have Διόφαντον.

The words as found in the text cannot be right. Διοφάντην
τὸν ἀστρονομικόν should (if the punctuation were right) be
Διοφάντην τὸν ἀστρονόμον, the former not being Greek.

Kuster's conjecture[2] is that we should read ὑπόμνημα εἰς
Διοφάντου ἀστρονομικὸν κανόνα· εἰς τὰ κωνικὰ Ἀπολλωνίου
ὑπόμνημα. If this is right the Diophantos here mentioned must
have been an astronomer. In that case the person in question
is not our Diophantos at all, for we have no ground whatever to
imagine that he occupied himself with Astronomy. It is certain that he was famous only as an arithmetician. Thus John
of Jerusalem in his life of John of Damascus[3] in speaking of
some one's skill in Arithmetic compares him to Pythagoras and

---

[1] Ὑπατία ἡ Θέωνος τοῦ Γεωμέτρου θυγάτηρ τοῦ Ἀλεξανδρέως φιλοσόφου καὶ αὐτὴ
φιλόσοφος, καὶ πολλοῖς γνώριμος· γυνὴ Ἰσιδώρου τοῦ φιλοσόφου· ἤκμασεν ἐπὶ τῆς
βασιλείας Ἀρκαδίου· ἔγραψεν ὑπόμνημα εἰς Διοφάντην τὸν ἀστρονομικόν. Κανόνα εἰς
τὰ κωνικά· Ἀπολλωνίου ὑπόμνημα.

[2] *Suidae Lexicon*, Cantabrigiae, 1705.

[3] Chapter XI. of the Life as given in *Sancti patris nostri Joannis Damasceni,
Monachi, et Presbyteri Hierosolymitani, Opera omnia quae exstant et ejus nomine
circumferuntur. Tomus primus.* Parisiis, 1712. Ἀναλογίας δὲ Ἀριθμητικὰς οὕτως
ἐξησκήκασιν εὐφυῶς, ὡς Πυθαγόραι ἢ Διόφαντοι.

Diophantos, as representing that science. However, Bachet has proposed to identify our Diophantos with an astrologer of the same name, who is ridiculed in an epigram¹ supposed to be written by Lucilius. Now the ridicule of the epigram would be clearly out of place as applied to the subject of the epigram mentioned above, even supposing that Lucilius' ridiculous hero is not a fictitious personage, as it is not unreasonable to suppose.

Bachet's reading of the passage is ὑπόμνημα εἰς Διόφαντον, τὸν ἀστρονομικὸν κανόνα, εἰς τὰ κωνικὰ 'Απολλωνίου ὑπόμνη-μα². He then proceeds to remark that it shows that Hypatia wrote a Canon Astronomicus, so that she evidently was versed in Astronomy as well as Geometry (as shown by the Commentary on Apollonios), two of the three important branches of Mathematics. It is likely then, argues Bachet, that she was acquainted with the third, Arithmetic, and wrote a commentary on the *Arithmetics* of Diophantos. But in the first place we know of no astronomical work after that of Claudius Ptolemy, and from the way in which ὁ ἀστρονομικὸς κανών is mentioned it would be necessary to suppose that it had been universally known, and was still in common use at the time of Suidas, and yet was never mentioned by any one else whom we know : an inexplicable hypothesis.

---

¹   'Ερμογένη τὸν ἰατρὸν ὁ ἀστρολόγος Διόφαντος
        Εἶπε μόνους ζωῆς ἐννέα μῆνας ἔχειν.
        Κἀκεῖνος γελάσας, Τί μὲν ὁ Κρόνος ἐννέα μηνῶν,
        Φησί, λέγει, σὺ νόει· τἀμὰ δὲ σύντομά σοι·
        Εἶπε καὶ ἐκτείνας μόνον ἥψατο· καὶ Διόφαντος
        Ἄλλον ἀπελπίζων, αὐτὸς ἀπεσκάρισεν.

"Ludit non inuenustus poëta tum in Diophantum Astrologum, tum in medicum Hermogenem, quem et alibi saepe falsè admodum perstringit, quòd solo attactu non aegros modò, sed et benè valentes, velut pestifero sidere afflatos repentè necaret. Itaque nisi Diophantum nostrum Astrologiae peritum fuisse negemus, nil prohibet, quo minus eum aetate Lucillij extitisse dicamus."

Bachet, *Ad lectorem.*

² From this reading it is clear that Bachet did not rest his view of the identity of our Diophantos with the astrologer upon the passage of Suidas. M. Tannery is therefore mistaken in supposing this to be the case, "Bachet, ayant lu dans Suidas qu'Hypatia avait commenté le Canon astronomique de notre auteur..."; that is precisely what Bachet did *not* read there.

Next, the expression εἰς Διόφαντον has been objected to by Nesselmann as not being Greek. He maintains that the Greeks never speak of a book by the name of its author, and therefore we ought to have Διοφάντου ἀριθμητικά, if the reference were to Diophantos of the *Arithmetics*. M. Tannery, however, defends the use of the expression, on the ground that similar ones are common enough in Byzantine Greek. M. Tannery, accordingly, to avoid the difficulties which we have mentioned, supposes some words to have dropped out after Διόφαντον, and thinks that we should read εἰς Διόφαντον...τὸν ἀστρονομικὸν κανόνα. εἰς τὰ κωνικὰ Ἀπολλωνίου ὑπόμνημα, suggesting that before τὸν ἀστρονομικὸν κανόνα we might supply εἰς and understand Πτολεμαίου.

It will be seen that it is impossible to lay any stress upon this passage of Suidas. We cannot even make sure from this that Hypatia wrote a commentary upon Diophantos, though it has been very generally asserted by historians of mathematics as an undoubted fact, even by Cossali, who in speaking of the corrupt state into which the text of Diophantos has fallen remarks that Hypatia was the most fortunate of the commentators who have ever addressed themselves to his writings.

(2) I have already mentioned the epigram which in the form of a problem gives us the only facts we know of Diophantos' life. If we only knew the exact date of the author of this epigram, our difficulties would be much lessened. It is commonly assigned to Metrodoros, but even then we are not sure whether Metrodoros of Skepsis or Metrodoros of Byzantium is meant. It is now generally supposed that the latter was the author; and of him we know that he was a grammarian and arithmetician who lived in the reign of Constantine the Great.

(3) It is satisfactory in the midst of so much uncertainty to find a most certain reference to Diophantos in a work by Theon of Alexandria, the father of Hypatia, which gives us a *lower* limit for the date, more approximate than we could possibly have derived from the article of Suidas. The fact that Theon quoted Diophantos was first noted by Peter Ramus[1]: "Diophantus,

---

[1] *Schola Mathematica*, Book I, p. 35,

cujus sex libros, cum tamen author ipse tredecim polliceatur, graecos habemus de arithmeticis admirandae subtilitatis artem complexis, quae vulgo Algebra arabico nomine appellatur : cum tamen ex authore hoc antiquo (*citatur enim a Theone*) antiquitas artis appareat. Scripserat et Diophantus harmonica." This quotation was known to Montucla, who however draws an absurd conclusion from it[1] which is repeated by Klügel in his Wörterbuch[2]. The words of Theon which refer to Diophantos are καὶ Διόφαντός φησιν ὅτι, τῆς μονάδος ἀμεταθέτου οὔσης καὶ ἑστώσης πάντοτε, τὸ πολλαπλασιαζόμενον εἶδος ἐπ' αὐτὴν αὐτὸ τὸ εἶδος ἔσται. We have only to remark that these words are identically those of Diophantos' sixth definition, as given in Bachet's text, with the sole difference that πάντοτε stands in the place of the equivalent ἀεί, in order to see that the reference is certain beyond the possibility of a doubt. The name of Diophantos is again mentioned by Theon a few lines further on. Here then we undoubtedly have a lower limit to the time of Diophantos, supplied by the date of Theon of Alexandria, and one which must obviously be more approximate than we could have arrived at from any information about his daughter Hypatia, however trustworthy. Theon's date, fortunately, we can determine with accuracy. Suidas[3] tells us that he was contemporary with Pappos and lived in the reign of Theodosius I. The statement that he was contemporary with Pappos is almost

[1] "Théon cite une autre ouvrage de cet analyste, où il étoit question de la pratique de l'arithmétique. Je soupçonnerois que c'étoit là qu'il expliquoit plus au long les règles de sa nouvelle arithmétique, sur quoi il ne s'étoit pas assez étendu au commencement de ses questions." Montucla.
Apparently translated word for word in Rosenthal's *Encyclopädie d. reinen Mathem.* III. 195.

[2] I. 177, under *Arithmetik*: "Diophantus hab ausser seinem grossen arithmetischen Werke auch ein Werk über die praktische Arithmetik geschrieben, das aber verloren ist."
To begin with, Montucla quotes the passage as occurring in the 5th Book of Theon's Commentary, instead of the first. The work of Diophantos which Theon quotes is *not* another work, but is identically the *Arithmetics* which we possess.

[3] Θέων ὁ ἐκ τοῦ Μουσείου, Αἰγύπτιος, φιλόσοφος, σύγχρονος δὲ Πάππῳ τῷ φιλοσόφῳ καὶ αὐτῷ Ἀλεξανδρεῖ· ἐτύγχανον δὲ ἀμφότεροι ἐπὶ Θεοδοσίου βασιλέως τοῦ πρεσβυτέρου· ἔγραψε Μαθηματικά, Ἀριθμητικά, κ. τ. λ.

certainly incorrect and due to a confusion on the part of Suidas, for Pappos probably flourished under Diocletian (A. D. 284— 305); but the date of a certain Commentary of Theon has been definitely determined[1] as the year 372 A. D. and he undoubtedly flourished, as Suidas says, in the reign of Theodosius I. (379— 395 A. D.).

(4) The next authority who must be mentioned is the Arabian historian Abu'lfaraj, who places Diophantos without remark under the emperor Julian. This statement is important in that it gives the date which has been the most generally accepted. The passage in Abu'lfaraj comes after an enumeration of distinguished men who lived in the reign of Julian, and is thus translated by Pococke: "Ex iis Diophantes, cuius liber A. B. quem Algebram vocat celebris est."

It is a difficult question to decide how much weight is to be allowed to Abu'lfaraj's dogmatic statement. Some great authorities have unequivocally pronounced it to be valueless. Cossali attributes it to a confusion by Abu'lfaraj of our author with another Diophantos, a rhetorician, who is mentioned in another article[2] of Suidas as having been contemporary with the emperor Julian (361—363); and assumes that Abu'lfaraj made the statement solely on the authority of Suidas, and confused two persons of the same name. Cossali remarks at the same time upon a statement of Abu'lfaraj's translator, Pococke, to the effect that the Arabian historian did not know Greek and Latin. Colebrooke too[3] (*Algebra of the Hindus*) takes the same view. Now it certainly seems curious that Cossali should remark upon Abu'lfaraj's ignorance of Greek and yet suppose that he made a statement merely upon the authority of Suidas; and the question suggests itself: had Abu'lfaraj no other authority? We

---

[1] "On the date of Pappus," &c., by Hermann Usener, *Neues Rheinisches Museum*, 1873, Bd. xxviii. 403.

[2] Λιβάνιος, σοφιστὴς Ἀντιοχεύς, τῶν ἐπὶ τοῦ Ἰουλιανοῦ τοῦ Παραβατοῦ χρόνων, καὶ μέχρι Θεοδοσίου τοῦ πρεσβυτέρου, Φασγανίου πατρός, μαθητὴς Διοφάντου.

[3] Note M. p. lxiii. "The Armenian Abu'lfaraj places the Algebraist Diophantus under the emperor Julian. But it may be questioned whether he has any authority for that date, besides the mention by Greek authors of a learned person of the name, the instructor of Libanius, who was contemporary with that emperor."

must certainly, as was remarked by Schulz, admit that he must
have had ; for he gives yet another statement about Diophantos,
which certainly comes from another source, that his work was
translated into Arabic, or commented upon, by Mohammed
Abu'l-Wafā. There would seem however to be but one possibility
which would make Abu'lfaraj's statement trustworthy. Is it
possible that the two persons, whom he is supposed to have
confused, are identical? Is it a sufficient objection that Libanius distinguished himself chiefly as a rhetor and not as a
mathematician? In fact, in the absence of any evidence to the
contrary, why should the arithmetician Diophantos not have
been a rhetorician also? This question has given occasion to
some jests on the compatibility of the two accomplishments.
M. Tannery, for example, quotes Fermat, who was "Conseiller
de Toulouse"; and Nesselmann mentions Aristotle, arriving
finally at the conclusion that the two may be identical, and so,
while Abu'lfaraj's statement has nothing against it, it has a
great deal in its favour. But M. Tannery thinks he has made
the identification impossible by finding Suidas' authority, namely
Eunapios in the *Lives of the Sophists*, who mentions this other
Diophantos as an Arabian, not an Alexandrian, and professing
at Athens[1]. Certainly if this supposition is correct, we cannot
identify the two persons, and therefore cannot trust the statement of Abu'lfaraj. There is a further consideration—that the
reign of Julian (361—363) could certainly only have been the
end of Diophantos' life, as we see by comparing Theon's date,
above mentioned, to whom Diophantos is certainly anterior;
he may indeed have been much earlier, because (1) Theon
quotes him as a classic, and (2) the absence of quotations before
Theon does not necessarily show that the two were nearly
contemporary, for of previous writers to Theon who would have
been likely to quote Diophantos?

(5) In the preface to his Algebra, published A.D. 1572,
Rafael Bombelli gives the bare statement that Diophantos lived

---

[1] "Il nous donne ce Diophante, qu'il a connu et dont il ne fait d'ailleurs
pas grand cas, comme né, non pas à Alexandrie, ainsi que le mathématicien,
mais en Arabie (Διόφαντος ὁ Ἀράβιος), et, d'autre part, comme professant à
Athènes."

in the reign of Antoninus Pius[1], giving no proof or evidence of it. From the demonstrated incorrectness of certain other statements of Bombelli concerning Diophantos we may infer that we ought not hastily to give credence to this; on the other hand it is scarcely conceivable that he would have made the assertion without any ground whatever. The question accordingly arises, whether we can find any statement by an earlier writer, which might have been the origin of Bombelli's assertion. M. Tannery thinks he has found the authority while engaged in another research into the evidence on which Peter Ramus ascribes to Diophantos a treatise on Harmonics[2], an assertion repeated by Gessner and Fabricius[3]. As I cannot follow M. Tannery in his conjectures—for they are nothing better, but are rather conjectures of the wildest kind,—I will give the substance of his remarks without much comment, to be taken for what they are worth. According to M. Tannery Ramus' source of information was a Greek manuscript on music; this there is no reason to doubt; and in the edition of *Antiquae musicae auctores* by Meibomius we read, in the treatise by Bacchios ὁ γέρων, that there were five definitions of *rhythm*, attributed to Phaidros, Aristoxenos, Nikomachos, Λεόφαντος and Didymos. Now the name Λεόφαντος is not Greek; the form Λεώφαντος however is, but M. Tannery argues that a confusion between Λεο and Λεω is much less likely than a confusion between Λεο and Διο. (I may be allowed to remark here that I cannot agree with this view. Of course Λ and Δ are extremely likely to be confounded, but that ι should have been at the same time changed into ε seems to me anything but probable. Besides, this involves two changes, whereas the change of Λεω into Λεο involves only one variation. This latter change then is the smaller one, and why should it

---

[1] "Questi anni passati, essendosi ritrouato una opera greca di questa disciplina nella libraria di Nostro Signore in Vaticano, composta da un certo Diofante Alessandrino Autor Greco, *il quale fù à tempo di Antonin Pio...*"
[I quote from the edition published in 1579, which is in the British Museum. I have not seen the original edition of 1572.]

[2] "Scripserat et Diophantus harmonica."

[3] "Harmonica Diophanti, *quae Gesnerus et alii memorant*, intellige de harmonicis numeris, non de scripto quodam musici argumenti," though what is meant by "harmonic numbers," as Nesselmann remarks, is not quite clear.

be less likely than the other ? I confess that it seems to me by
far the more likely of the two; for the long and short vowels o,
ω must have been closely associated, as is proved by the fact
that in ancient inscriptions[1] we find O written for both O and Ω
indiscriminately, and in others Ω used for both sounds.) Then,
according to M. Tannery, Ramus probably took the name for
Διόφαντος, and was followed by other writers. Admitting that
the identification with the arithmetician Diophantos is hypo-
thetical enough, M. Tannery goes on to say that it is confirmed
by finding the name of Nikomachos next to Λεόφαντος, and by
observing that Euclid and Ptolemy also were writers on music,
which formed part of the μαθήματα. Now in enumerations of
this sort the chronological order is generally followed, and the
dates of many authors have been decided on grounds no more
certain than this. (It is an obvious remark to make to M.
Tannery that "two wrongs do not make a right": it does not
follow that, because other dates have been decided on insufficient
grounds, we should determine Diophantos' date in the same
manner; we ought rather to take warning by such unsatisfactory
determinations. But to proceed with M. Tannery's remarks)—
In the present case we know that Aristoxenos was a disciple of
Aristotle, and that Nikomachos was posterior to Thrasyllos who
lived in the reign of Tiberius. Thus we can prove the chronological order for two of the five names. Again, Nikomachos
must be anterior to his commentator Apuleius who was contemporary with Ptolemy, and Ptolemy speaks in his Harmonics
of a tetrachord due to a neo-Pythagorean Didymos. Of Phaidros
we know nothing. Hence if we admit that the names are given
in chronological order, and remember that Diophantos lived to
be 84 years of age, we might say that, coming between Nikomachos and Didymos, he lived in the reign of Antoninus Pius,
as Bombelli states, i.e. 138—161 A.D.

M. Tannery, however, is conscious of certain objections to
this theory of Diophantos' date. This determination would, he
says, have great weight if Bacchios ὁ γέρων had been an author

---

[1] I mean, of course, inscrr. later than the introduction of Ω, before which
time one sign was necessarily used for both letters. Further, I lay no stress
upon this fact except as an *illustration*.

sufficiently near in point of time to Diophantos and the rest in order to know their respective ages. Unfortunately, however, that is far from certain, Bacchios' own date being very doubtful. He is generally supposed to have lived in the time of Constantine the Great; this is however questioned by M. Tannery who thinks that the epigram given by Meibomius, in which Bacchios is associated with a certain Dionysios, refers to Constantine Porphyrogenetes, who belongs to the sixth century. Next, grave doubts may be raised concerning the determination by means of the supposed chronological order; for the definitions of rhythm given by Nikomachos and Diophantos (?) are very nearly alike, that of Diophantos being apparently a development of that of Nikomachos: κατὰ δὲ Νικόμαχον, χρόνων εὔτακτος σύνθεσις· κατὰ δὲ Διόφαντον (?), χρόνων σύνθεσις κατ' ἀναλογίαν τε καὶ συμμετρίαν πρὸς ἑαυτούς. The similarity of the two definitions might itself account for their juxta-position, which might then after all be an inversion of chronological order. Again the age of Didymos must be fixed differently. By "Didymos" is meant the son of Herakleides Ponticus, grammarian and musician, whom Suidas places in the reign of Nero. Thus, if we assume Bacchios' order to be chronological, we must place Diophantos in the reign of Claudius, and Nikomachos in that of Caligula.

§ 3. *Results of the preceding investigation.*

I have now reviewed all the evidence we have respecting the time at which Diophantos lived and wrote, and the conclusions arrived at, on the basis of this evidence, by the greatest authorities upon the subject. It must be admitted the result cannot be called in any sense satisfactory; indeed the *data* are not sufficient to determine indisputably the question at issue. The latest determination of Diophantos' date is that of M. Tannery, and there has been no theory propounded which seems on the whole preferable to his, though even it cannot be said to have been positively established; it has, however, the merit that, if it cannot be proved, it cannot be impugned; as therefore it seems open to no objection, it would seem best to accept it provisionally, as the least unsatisfactory theory. We shall therefore be not improbably right in placing Diophantos in the second half of the third century of our era, making him thus a contemporary of Pappos, and anterior by a century to Theon of Alexandria and his daughter Hypatia.

One thing is quite certain: that Diophantos lived in a period when the Greek mathematicians of great original power had been succeeded by a number of learned commentators, who confined their investigations within the limits already reached, without attempting to further the development of the science. To this general rule there are two most striking exceptions, in different branches of mathematics, Diophantos and Pappos. These two mathematicians, who would have been an ornament to any age, were destined by fate to live and labour at a time when their work could not check the decay of mathematical learning. There is scarcely a passage in any Greek writer where either of the two is so much as mentioned. The neglect of their works by their countrymen and contemporaries can be explained only by the fact that they were not appreciated or understood. The reason why Diophantos was the earliest of the Greek mathematicians to be forgotten is also probably the reason why he was the last to be re-discovered after the Revival of Learning. The oblivion, in fact, into which his writings and methods fell is due to the circumstance that they were not understood. That being so, we are able to understand why there is so much obscurity concerning his personality and the time at which he lived. Indeed, when we consider how little he was understood, and in consequence how little esteemed, we can only congratulate ourselves that so much of his work has survived to the present day.

CHAPTER II.

THE WORKS OF DIOPHANTOS; THEIR TITLES AND GENERAL
CONTENTS; THE PORTIONS OF THEM WHICH SURVIVE.

§ 1. We know of three works of Diophantos, which bear
the following titles.

(1) Ἀριθμητικῶν βιβλία ῑγ.

(2) περὶ πολυγώνων ἀριθμῶν.

(3) πορίσματα.

With respect to the first title we may observe that the
meaning of "ἀριθμητικά" is slightly different from that assigned
to it by more ancient writers. The ancients drew a marked
distinction between ἀριθμητική and λογιστική, both of which
were concerned with numbers. Thus Plato in *Gorgias* 451 B[1]
states that ἀριθμητική is concerned with the abstract properties
of numbers, odd even, and so on, whereas λογιστική deals with
the same odd and even, but *in relation to one another*. Geminos
also gives us definitions of the two terms. According to him
ἀριθμητική deals with abstract properties of numbers, while
λογιστική gives solutions of problems about concrete numbers.
From Geminos we see that enunciations were in ancient times
concrete in such problems. But in Diophantos the calculations

---

[1] εἴ τίς με ἔροιτο...Ὦ Σώκρατες, τίς ἐστιν ἡ ἀριθμητικὴ τέχνη; εἴποιμ' ἂν
αὐτῷ, ὥσπερ σὺ ἄρτι, ὅτι τῶν διὰ λόγου τις τὸ κῦρος ἐχουσῶν. καὶ εἴ με ἐπανέροιτο Τῶν περὶ τί; εἴποιμ' ἄν, ὅτι τῶν περὶ τὸ ἄρτιόν τε καὶ περιττὸν ὅσ' ἂν
ἑκάτερα τύγχανει ὄντα. εἰ δ' αὖ ἔροιτο, Τὴν δὲ λογιστικὴν τίνα καλεῖς τέχνην;
εἴποιμ' ἂν ὅτι καὶ αὕτη ἐστὶ τῶν λόγῳ τὸ πᾶν κυρουμένων. καὶ εἰ ἐπανέροιτο Ἡ
περὶ τί; εἴποιμ' ἂν ὥσπερ οἱ ἐν τῷ δήμῳ συγγραφόμενοι, ὅτι τὰ μὲν ἄλλα καθάπερ
ἡ ἀριθμητικὴ ἡ λογιστικὴ ἔχει· περὶ τὸ αὐτὸ γάρ ἐστι, τό τε ἄρτιον καὶ τὸ περιττόν·
διαφέρει δὲ τοσοῦτον, ὅτι καὶ πρὸς αὐτὰ καὶ πρὸς ἄλληλα πῶς ἔχει πλήθους ἐπισκοπεῖ
τὸ περιττὸν καὶ τὸ ἄρτιον ἡ λογιστική. *Gorgias*, 451 B,C.

take an *abstract* form, so that the distinction between λογιστική and ἀριθμητική is lost. We thus have 'Αριθμητικά given as the title of his work, whereas in earlier times the term could only properly have been applied to his treatise on *Polygonal Numbers*. This broader use by Diophantos of the term *arithmetic* is not without its importance.

Having made this preliminary remark it is next necessary to observe that of these works which we have mentioned some have been lost, while probably the form of parts of others has suffered considerably by the ravages of time. The *Arithmetics* should, according to the title and a distinct statement in the introduction to it, contain thirteen Books. But all the six known MSS.[1] contain only six books, with the sole variation that in the Vatican MS. 200 the same text, which in the rest forms six books, is divided into *seven*. Not only do the MSS. practically agree in the external division of the work; they agree also in an equally remarkable manner—at least all of them which have up to the present been collated—in the lacunae and the mistakes which occur in the text. So much is this the case that Bachet, the sole editor of the Greek text of Diophantos, asserts his belief that they are all copied from one original[2]. This can, however, scarcely be said to be established,

[1] The six MSS. are:

    1—3. Vatican MSS. No. 191, XIII. c., charta bombycina.
                         No. 200, XIV. c., charta pergamena.
                         No. 304, XV. c., charta.
    4. MS. in Nat. Library at Paris, that used by Bachet for his text.
    5. MS. in Palatine Library, collated for Bachet by Claudius Salmasius.
    6. Xylander's MS. which belonged to Andreas Dudicius.
Colebrooke considers that 5 and 6 are probably identical.

[2] "Etenim neque codex Regius, cuius ope hanc editionem adornavimus; neque is quem prae manibus habuit Xilander; neque Palatinus, vt doctissimo viro Claudio Salmasio referente accepimus; neque Vaticanus, quem vir summus Iacobus Sirmondus mihi ex parte transcribendum curauit, quicquam amplius continent, quam sex hosce Arithmeticorum libros, et tractatum de numeris multangulis imperfectum. Sed et tam infeliciter hi omnes codices inter se consentiunt, vt ab vno fonte manasse et ab eodem exemplari descriptos fuisse non dubitem. Itaque parum auxilij ab his subministratum nobis esse, verissimè affirmare possum." *Epistola ad Lectorem.*

It will be seen that the learned Bachet spells here, as everywhere, Xylander's name wrongly, giving it as Xilander.

for Bachet had no knowledge of two of the three Vatican MSS. and had only a few readings of the third, furnished to him by Jacobus Sirmondus. It is possible therefore that the collation of the two remaining MSS. in the Vatican might even now lead to important results respecting the settling of the text. The evidence of the existence in earlier times of all the *thirteen* books is very doubtful, some of it absolutely incorrect. Bachet says [1] that Joannes Regiomontanus asserts that he saw the thirteen books somewhere, and that Cardinal Perron, who had recently died, had often told him that he possessed a MS. containing the thirteen books complete, but, having lent it to a fellow-citizen, who died before returning it, had never re-covered it. Respecting this latter MS. mentioned by Bachet we have not sufficient data to lead us to a definite conclusion as to whether it really corresponded to the title, or, like the MSS. which we know, only *announced* thirteen books. If it really corresponded to the title, it is remarkable how (in the words of Nesselmann) every possible unfortunate circumstance and even the "pestis" mentioned by Bachet seem to have conspired to rob posterity of at least a part of Diophantos' works.

Respecting the statement that Regiomontanus asserts that he saw a MS. containing the thirteen books, it is clear that it is founded on a misunderstanding. Xylander states in two passages of his preface [2] that he found that Regiomontanus

---

[1] "Ioannes tamen Regiomontanus tredecim Diophanti libros se alicubi vidisse asseverat, et illustrissimus Cardinalis Perronius, quem nuper extinctum magno Christianae et literariae Reipublicae detrimento, conquerimur, mihi saepe testatus est, se codicem manuscriptum habuisse, qui tredecim Diophanti libros integros contineret, quem cùm Gulielmo Gosselino conciui suo, qui in Diophantum Commentaria meditabatur, perhumaniter more suo exhibuisset, paullo post accidit, ut Gosselinus peste correptus interiret, et Diophanti codex eodem fato nobis eriperetur. Cum enim precibus meis motus Cardinalis amplissimus, nullisque sumptibus parcens, apud heredes Gosselini codicem illum diligenter exquiri mandasset, et quouis pretio redimi, nusquam repertus est." *Ad lectorem.*

[2] "Inueni deinde tanquam exstantis in bibliothecis Italicis, sibique uisi mentionem a Regiomontano (cuius etiam nominis memoriam ueneror) factam." Xylander, *Epistola nuncupatoria.*

"Sane tredecim libri Arithmeticae Diophanti ab aliis perhibentur exstare in bibliotheca Vaticana; quos Regiomontanus ille uiderit." *Ibid.*

mentioned a MS. of Diophantos which he had seen in an Italian library; and that others said that the thirteen books were extant in the Vatican Library, "which Regiomontanus saw." Now as regards the latter statement, Xylander was obviously wrongly informed; for not one of the Vatican MSS. contains the thirteen books. It is necessary therefore to inquire to what passage or passages in Regiomontanus' writings Xylander refers. Nesselmann finds only one place which can be meant, an *Oratio habita Patavii in praelectione Alfragani*[1] in which Regiomontanus remarks that "no one has yet translated from the Greek into Latin the thirteen books of Diophantos[2]." Upon this Nesselmann observes that, even if Regiomontanus saw a MS., it does not follow that it had the thirteen books, except on the title-page; and the remarks which Regiomontanus makes upon the contents show that he had not studied them thoroughly; but it is not usually easy to see, by a superficial examination, into how many sections a MS. is divided. However, this passage is interesting as being the first mention of Diophantos by a European writer; the date of the *Speech* was probably about 1462. The only other passage, which Nesselmann was acquainted with and might have formed some foundation for Xylander's conclusion, is one in which Regiomontanus (in the same *Oratio*) describes a journey which he made to Italy for the purpose of learning Greek, with the particular (though not exclusive)

[1] Printed in the work *Rudimenta astronomica Alfragani*. "Item Albategnius astronomus peritissimus de motu stellarum, ex observationibus tum propriis tum Ptolemaei, omnia cum demonstrationibus Geometricis et Additionibus Joannis de Regiomonte. *Item Oratio introductoria in omnes scientias Mathematicas Joannis de Regiomonte, Patavii habita, cum Alfraganum publice praelegeret.* Ejusdem utilissima introductio in elementa Euclidis. Item Epistola Philippi Melanthonis nuncupatoria, ad Senatum Noribergensem. Omnia jam recens prelis publicata. Norimbergae anno 1537. 4to."

[2] The passage is: "Diofanti autem tredecim libros subtilissimos nemo usquehac ex Graecis Latinos fecit, in quibus flos ipse totius Arithmeticae latet, ars videlicet rei et census, quam hodie vocant Algebram Arabico nomine."

It does not follow from this, as Vossius maintains, that Regiomontanus supposed Dioph. to be the inventor of algebra.

The "ars rei et census," which is the solution of determinate quadratic equations, is not found in our Dioph.; and even supposing that it was given in the MS. which Regiomontanus saw, this is not a point which would deserve special mention.

object of turning into Latin certain Greek mathematical works[1]. But Diophantos is not mentioned by name, and Nesselmann accordingly thinks that it is a mere conjecture on the part of Cossali and Xylander, that among the Greek writers mentioned in this passage Diophantos was included; and that we have no ground for thinking, on the authority of these passages, that Regiomontanus saw the thirteen books in a complete form. But Nesselmann does not seem to have known of a passage in another place, which is later than the *Oration* at Padua, and shows to my mind most clearly that Regiomontanus never saw the complete work. It is in a letter to Joannes de Blanchinis[2], in which Regiomontanus states that he found at Venice "Diofantus," a Greek arithmetician who had not yet been translated into Latin; that in the proëmium he defined the several powers up to the sixth, but whether he followed out all the combinations of these Regiomontanus does not know; *"for not more than six books are found, though in the proëmium he promises thirteen. If this book, a wonderful and difficult work, could be found entire, I should like to translate it into Latin, for the knowledge of Greek I have lately acquired would suffice for this[3],"* &c. The date of this occurrence is stated

---

[1] After the death of his teacher, Georg von Peurbach, he tells us he went to Rome &c. with Cardinal Bessarion. "Quid igitur reliquum erat nisi ut orbitam viri clarissimi sectarer? coeptum felix tuum pro viribus exequerer? Duce itaque patrono communi Romam profectus more meo literis exerceor, ubi scripta plurima Graecorum clarissimorum ad literas suas discendas me invitant, quo Latinitas in studiis praesertim Mathematicis locupletior redderetur."

Peurbach died 8 April, 1461, so that the journey must have taken place between 1461 and 1471, when he permanently took up his residence at Nürnberg. During this time he visited in order Rome, Ferrara, Padua (where he delivered the *Oration*), Venice, Rome (a second time) and Vienna.

[2] Given on p. 135 of Ch. Th. v. Murr's *Memorabilia*, Norimbergae, 1786, and partly in Doppelmayr, *Historische Nachricht von der Nürnbergischen Mathematicis und Künstlern*, p. 5. Note *y* (Nürnberg, 1730).

[3] The whole passage is:

"Hoc dico dominationi uestrae me reperisse nunc uenetiis Diofantum arithmeticum graecum nondum in latinum traductum. Hic in prohemio diffiniendo terminos huius artis ascendit ad cubum cubi, primum enim uocat numerum, quem numeri uocant rem, secundum uocat potentiam, ubi numeri dicunt censum, deinde cubum, deinde potentiam potentiae, uocant numerum censum de censu, item cubum de censu et tandem cubi. Nescio tamen si omnes com-

in a note to be **1463**. Here then we have a distinct contradiction
to the statement that Regiomontanus speaks of having seen thirteen books ; so that Xylander's conclusions must be abandoned.
No conclusion can be arrived at from the passage in Fermat's
letter to Digby (15 August 1657) in which he says: The name
of this author (Diophantos) " me donne l'occasion de vous faire
souvenir de la promesse, qu'il vous a pleu me faire de recouvrer
quelque manuscrit de cét Autheur, qui contienne tous les treize
livres, et de m'en faire part, s'il vous peut tomber en main."
This is clearly no evidence that a complete Diophantos existed
at the time.

Bombelli (1572) states the number of books to be *seven*[1],
showing that the MS. he used was Vatican No. 200.

To go farther back still in time, Maximus Planudes, who
lived in the time of the Byzantine Emperors Andronicus I. and
II. in the first half of the 14th century, and wrote Scholia to
the two first books of the *Arithmetics*, given in Latin in
Xylander's translation of Diophantos, knew the work in the
same form in which we have it, so far as the first two books
are concerned. From these facts Nesselmann concludes that
the corruptions and lacunae in the text, as we have it, are due
to a period anterior to the 14th or even the 13th century.

There are yet other means by which lost portions of Diophantos might have been preserved, though not found in the original
text as it has come down to us. We owe the recovery of some
Greek mathematical works to the finding of Arabic translations
of them, as for instance parts of Apollonios. Now we know

binationes horum prosecutus fuerit. non enim reperiuntur nisi 6 eius libri qui
nunc apud me sunt, in prohemio autem pollicetur se scripturum tredecim. Si
liber hic qui reuera pulcerrimus est et difficilimus, integer inueniretur [Doppel-
mayr, inuen*iatur*] curarem eum latinum facere, ad hoc enim sufficerent mihi
literae graecae quas in domo domini mei reuerendissimi didici. Curate et uos
obsecro si apud uestros usquam inueniri possit liber ille integer, sunt enim in
urbe uestra non nulli graecarum litterarum periti, quibus solent inter caeteros
tuae facultatis libros huiusmodi occurrere. Interim tamen, si suadebitis, sex
dictos libros traducere in latinum occipiam, quatenus latinitas hoc nouo et
pretiosissimo munere non careat."

[1] "Egli e io, per arrichire il mondo di cosi fatta opera, ci dessimo à tradurlo
e cinque libri (*delli sette che sono*) tradutti ne abbiamo." Bombelli, pref. to
Algebra.

that Diophantos was translated into Arabic, or at least studied and commented upon in Arabia. Why then should we not be as fortunate in respect of Diophantos as with others? In the second part of a work by Alkarkhī called the *Fakhrī*[1] (an algebraic treatise) is a collection of problems in determinate and indeterminate analysis which not only indicate that their author had deeply studied Diophantos, but are, many of them, directly taken from the *Arithmetics* with the change, occasionally, of some of the constants. The obligations of Alkarkhī to Diophantos are discussed by Wöpcke in his *Notice sur le Fakhrī*. In a marginal note to his MS. is a remark attributing the problems of section IV. and of section III. *in part* to Diophantos[2]. Now section IV. begins with problems corresponding to the last 14 of Diophantos' Second Book, and ends with an exact reproduction of Book III. Intervening between these two parts are twenty-five problems which are not found in our Diophantos. We might suppose then that we have here a lost Book of our author, and Wöpcke says that he was so struck by the gloss in the MS. that he hoped he had discovered such a Book, but afterwards abandoned the idea for the reasons : (1) That the first twelve of the problems depend upon equations of the first or second degree which lead, with two exceptions, to irrational results, whereas such were not allowed by Diophantos. (2) The thirteen other problems which are indeterminate problems of the second degree are, some of them, quite unlike Diophantos ; others have remarks upon methods employed, and references to the author's commentaries, which we should not expect to find if the problems were taken from Diophantos.

It does not seem possible, then, to identify any part of

---

[1] The book which I have made use of on this subject is: "Extrait du Fakhrî, traité d' Algèbre par Abou Bekr Mohammed ben Alhaçan Alkarkhî (manuscrit 952, supplément arabe de la bibliothèque Impériale) précédé d'un mémoire sur l'Algèbre indéterminée chez les Arabes, par F. Woepcke, Paris, 1853."

[2] Wöpcke's translation of this gloss is: "J'ai vu en cet endroit une glose de l'écriture d'Ibn Alsirâdj en ces termes: Je dis, les problèmes de cette section et une partie de ceux de la section précédente, sont pris dans les livres de Diophante, suivant l'ordre. Ceci fut écrit par Ahmed Ben Abi Beqr Ben Ali Ben Alsirâdj Alkelâneci."

the *Fakhrī* as having formed a part of Diophantos' work now lost. Thus it seems probable to suppose that the form in which Alkarkhī found and studied Diophantos was not different from the present. This view is very strongly supported by the following evidence. Bachet has already noticed that the solution of Dioph. II. 19 is really only another solution of II. 18, and does not agree with its own enunciation. Now in the *Fakhrī* we have a problem (IV. 40) with the same enunciation as Dioph. II. 19, but a solution which is not in Diophantos' manner. It is remarkable to find this followed by a problem (IV. 41) which is the same as Dioph. II. 20 (choice of constants always excepted). It is then sufficiently probable that II. 19 and 20 followed each other in the redaction of Diophantos known to Alkarkhī; and the fact that he gives a non-Diophantine solution of II. 19 would show that he had observed that the enunciation and solution did not correspond, and therefore set himself to work out a solution of his own. In view of this evidence we may probably assume that Diophantos' work had already taken its present mutilated form when it came into the hands of the author of the *Fakhrī*. This work was written by Abu Bekr Mohammed ibn Alhasan Alkarkhī near the beginning of the 11th century of our era; so that the corruption of the text of Diophantos must have taken place before the 11th century.

There is yet another Arabic work even earlier than this last, apparently lost, the discovery of which would be of the greatest historical interest and importance. It is a work upon Diophantos, consisting of a translation or a commentary by Mohammed Abu'l-Wafā, already mentioned incidentally. But it is doubtful whether the discovery of his work entire would enable us to restore any of the lost parts of Diophantos. There is no evidence to lead us to suppose so, but there is a piece of evidence noted by Wöpcke[1] which may possibly lead to an opposite conclusion. Abu'l-Wafā does not satisfactorily deal with the possible division of any number whatever into four squares. Now the theorem of the possibility of such division

[1] *Journal Asiatique.* Cinquième série, Tome v. p. 234.

is assumed by Diophantos in several places, notably in IV. 31. We have then two alternatives. Either (1) the theorem was not distinctly enunciated by Diophantos at all, or (2) It was enunciated in a proposition of a lost Book. In either case Abu'l-Wafā cannot have seen the statement of the theorem in Diophantos, and, if the latter alternative is right, we have an argument in favour of the view that the work had already been mutilated before it reached the hands of Abu'l-Wafā. Now Abu'l-Wafā's date is 328—388 of the Hegira, or 940—988 of our Era.

It would seem, therefore, clear that the parts of Diophantos' *Arithmetics* which are lost were lost at an early date, and that the present lacunae and imperfections in the text had their origin in all probability before the 10th century.

It may be said also with the same amount of probability that the *Porisms* were lost before the 10th century A.D. We have perhaps an indication of this in the title of another work of Abu'l-Wafā, of which Wöpcke's translation is "Démonstrations des théorèmes employés par Diophante dans son ouvrage, et de ceux employés par (Aboul-Wafâ) lui-même dans son commentaire." It is not possible to conclude with certainty from the title of this work what its contents may have been. Are the "theorems" those which Diophantos assumes, referring for proofs of them to his *Porisms?* This seems a not unlikely supposition; and, if it is correct, it would follow that the proofs of these propositions, which Diophantos must have himself given, in fact, the *Porisms*, were no longer in existence in the time of Abu'l-Wafā, or at least were for him as good as lost. It must be admitted then that we have no historical evidence of the existence at any time subsequent to Diophantos himself of the *Porisms*.

Of the treatise on *Polygonal Numbers* we possess only a fragment. It breaks off in the middle of the 8th proposition. It is not however probable that much is wanting; practically the treatise seems to be nearly complete.

§ **2.** The next question which naturally suggests itself is : As we have apparently six books only of the *Arithmetics* out of thirteen, where may we suppose the lost matter to have been placed in the treatise? Was it at the beginning, middle, or end? This question can only be decided when we have come to a conclusion about the probable contents of the lost portion. It has, however, been dogmatically asserted by many who have written upon Diophantos—often without reading him at all, or reading him enough to enable them to form a judgment on the subject—that the Books, which we have, are the *first six* and that the loss has been at the end; and such have accordingly wondered what could have been the subject to which Diophantos afterwards proceeded. To this view, which has no ground save in the bare assertions of incompetent or negligent writers, Nesselmann opposes himself very strongly. He maintains on the contrary, with much reason, that in the sixth Book Diophantos' resources are at an end. If one reads carefully the last four Books, from the third to the sixth, the conclusion forces itself upon one that Diophantos moves in a rigidly defined and limited circle of methods and artifices, that any attempts which he makes to free himself are futile. But this fact can only be adequately appreciated after a perusal of his entire work. It may, however, be further added that the sixth Book forms a natural conclusion to the whole, in that it is made up of exemplifications of methods explained and used in the preceding Books. The subject is the finding of right-angled triangles in rational numbers, such that the sides satisfy given conditions, Arithmetic being applied to Geometry in the geometrical notion of the right-angled triangle. As was said above, we have now to consider what the contents of the lost Books of the *Arithmetics* may have been. Clearly we must first inquire what is actually wanting which we should have expected to find there, either as promised by the author himself in his own work, or as necessary for the elucidation or completion of the whole. We must therefore briefly indicate the general contents of the work as we have it.

The first book contains problems leading to determinate equations of the first degree[1]; the remainder of the work being

---

[1] As a specimen of the rash way in which even good writers speak of Diophantos, I may instance here a remark of Vincenzo Riccati, who says: "De problematibus determinatis quae resolutis aequationibus dignoscuntur, nihil

a collection of problems which, with scarcely an exception, lead
to indeterminate equations of the second degree, beginning with
simpler cases and advancing step by step to more complicated
questions. These indeterminate or semideterminate problems
form the main feature of the collection. Now it is a great step
from determinate equations of the first degree to semideterminate and indeterminate problems of the second; and we must
recognise that there is here an enormous gap in the exposition.
We ought surely to find here (1) determinate equations of the
second degree and (2) indeterminate equations of the first.
With regard to (2), it is quite true that we have no definite
statement in the work itself that they formed part of the
writer's plan; but that they were discussed here is an extremely
probable supposition. With regard to (1) or determinate
quadratic equations, on the other hand, we have certain
evidence from the writer's own words, that the solution of the
adfected or complete quadratic was given in the treatise as it
originally stood; for, in the first place, Diophantos promises a
discussion of them in the introductory definitions (def. 11)
where he gives rules for the reduction of equations of the
second degree to their simplest forms; secondly, he uses his
method for their solution in the later Books, in some cases
simply giving the result of the solution without working it out,
in others giving the irrational part of the root in order to find
an approximate value in integers, without writing down the
actual root[1]. We find examples of *pure* quadratic equations

omnino Diophantus (!); agit duntaxat de eo problematum semideterminatorum
genere, quae respiciunt quadrata, aut cubos numerorum, quae problemata ut
resolvantur, quantitates radicales de industria sunt vitandae." Pref. to *ana-
litiche istituzioni*.
    [1] These being the indications in the work itself, what are we to think of a
recent writer of a History of Mathematics, who says: "Hieraus und aus dem
Umstand, dass Diophant nirgends die von ihm versprochene Theorie der
Auflösung der quadratischen Gleichungen gibt, schloss man, er habe dieselbe
nicht gekannt, und hat desshalb den Arabern stets den Ruhm dieser Erfindung
zugetheilt," and goes on to say that "nevertheless Nesselmann after a thorough
study of the work is convinced that D. knew the solution of the quadratic"?
It is almost impossible to imagine that these remarks are serious. The writer
is Dr Heinrich Suter, *Geschichte d. Mathematischen Wissenschaften*. Zweite
Auflage. Zürich, 1873,

even in the first Book : a fact which shows that Diophantos regarded them as in reality simple equations, taking, as he does, the positive value of the root only. Indeed it would seem that Diophantos adopted as his ground for the classification of these equations, not the index of the highest power of the unknown quantity contained in it, but the *number of terms* left in it when it is reduced to its simplest form. His words are[1]: "If the same powers of the unknown occur on both sides but with different coefficients we must take like from like until we have one single expression equal to another. If there are on both sides, or on either side, terms with negative coefficients, the defects must be added on both sides, until there are the same powers on both sides with *positive* coefficients, when we must take like from like as before. We must contrive always, if possible, to reduce our equations so that they may contain one single term equated to one other. *But afterwards we will explain to you also how, when two terms are left equal to a*

---

[2] Diophantos' actual words (which I have translated freely) are: Μετὰ δὲ ταῦτα ἐὰν ἀπὸ προβλήματός τινος γένηται ὕπαρξις εἴδεσι τοῖς αὐτοῖς μὴ ὁμοπληθῆ δὲ ἀπὸ ἑκατέρων τῶν μερῶν, δεήσει ἀφαιρεῖν τὰ ὅμοια ἀπὸ τῶν ὁμοίων, ἕως ἂν ἑνὸς (!) εἶδος ἑνὶ εἴδει ἴσον γένηται· ἐὰν δέ πως ἐν ὁποτέρῳ ἐνυπάρχῃ (?), ἢ ἐν ἀμφοτέροις ἐνελλείψῃ (?) τινὰ εἴδη, δεήσει προσθεῖναι τὰ λείποντα εἴδη ἐν ἀμφοτέροις τοῖς μέρεσιν, ἕως ἂν ἑκατέρῳ τῶν μερῶν τὰ εἴδη ἐνυπάρχοντα γένηται. καὶ πάλιν ἀφελεῖν τὰ ὅμοια ἀπὸ τῶν ὁμοίων, ἕως ἂν ἑκατέρῳ τῶν μερῶν ἓν εἶδος καταλειφθῆ. πεφιλοτεχνήσθω δὲ τοῦτο ἐν ταῖς ὑποστάσεσι τῶν προτάσεων, ἐὰν ἐνδέχηται, ἕως ἂν ἓν εἶδος ἑνὶ εἴδει ἴσον καταλειφθῆ. ὕστερον δέ σοι δείξομεν καὶ πῶς δύο εἰδῶν ἴσων ἑνὶ καταλειφθέντων τὸ τοιοῦτον λύεται.

I give Bachet's text exactly, marking those places where it seems obviously wrong. καταλειφθῆ should of course be καταλειφθῇ.

It is worth observing that L. Rodet, in *Journal Asiatique*, Janvier, 1878, on "L'Algèbre d'Al-Khârizmi et les méthodes indienne et grecque," quotes this passage, not from Bachet's text, but *from the MS. which Bachet used*. His readings show the following variations:

Bachet.	L. Rodet.
γένηται	γενήσεται [?? How about the construction with ἐὰν?]
ὕπαρξις	τινὰ ἴσα
ἑνὸς εἶδος	ἓν εἶδος
ἐνελλείψῃ	ἐν λείψει.

[I doubt the latter word very much, compounded as the verb is with the prep. ἐν twice repeated.]

third, such a question is solved." That is to say, "reduce when possible the quadratic to one of the forms $x = a$, or $x^2 = b$. I will give later a method of solution of the complete equation $x^2 \pm ax = \pm b$." Now this promised solution of the complete quadratic equation is nowhere to be found in the *Arithmetics* as we have them, though in the second and following Books there are obvious cases of its employment. We have to decide, then, where it might naturally have come; and the answer is that the suitable place is between the first and second Books.

But besides the entire loss of an essential portion of Diophantos' work there is much confusion in the text even of that portion which remains. Thus clearly problems 6, 7, 18, 19 of the second Book, which contain determinate problems of the first degree, belong in reality to Book I. Again, as already remarked above, the problem enunciated in II. 19 is not solved at all, but the solution attached to it is a mere "ἄλλως" of II. 18. Moreover, problems 1—5 of Book II. recall problems already solved in I. Thus II. 1 = I. 34: II. 2 = I. 37: II. 3 is similar to I. 33: II. 4 = I. 35: II. 5 = I. 36. The problem I. 29 seems also out of place in its present position. In the second Book a new type of problem is taken up at II. 20, and examples of it are continued through the third Book. There is no sign of a marked division between Books II. and III. In fact, expressed in modern notation, the last two problems of II. and the first of III. are the solutions of the following sets of equations:

II. 35.
$$\left. \begin{array}{l} x^2 + (x + y + z) = a^2 \\ y^2 + (x + y + z) = b^2 \\ z^2 + (x + y + z) = c^2 \end{array} \right\} .$$

II. 36.
$$\left. \begin{array}{l} x^2 - (x + y + z) = a^2 \\ y^2 - (x + y + z) = b^2 \\ z^2 - (x + y + z) = c^2 \end{array} \right\} .$$

III. 1.
$$\left. \begin{array}{l} (x + y + z) - x^2 = a^2 \\ (x + y + z) - y^2 = b^2 \\ (x + y + z) - z^2 = c^2 \end{array} \right\} .$$

These follow perfectly naturally upon each other; and therefore it is quite likely that our division between the two

Books was not the original one. In fact the frequent occurrence of more definite divisions in the middle of the Books, coupled with the variation in the Vatican MS. which divides our six Books into seven, seems to show that the work may have been divided into even a larger number of Books originally. Besides the displacements of problems which have probably taken place there are many single problems which have been much corrupted, notably the fifth Book, which has, as Nesselmann expresses it[1], been "treated by Mother Time in a very stepmotherly fashion". It is probable, for instance, that between v. 21 and 22 three problems have been lost. In several other cases the solutions are confused or incomplete. How the imperfections of the text were introduced into it we can only conjecture. Nesselmann thinks they cannot be due merely to the carelessness of a copyist, but are rather due, at least in part, to the ignorance and inexpertness of one who wished to improve upon the original. The view, which was put forward by Bachet, that our six Books are a redaction or selection made from the complete thirteen by a later hand, seems certainly untenable.

The treatise on *Polygonal Numbers* is in its subject related to the *Arithmetics*, but the mode of treatment is completely different. It is not an analytical work, but a synthetic one; the author enunciates propositions and then gives their proofs; in fact the treatise is quite in the manner of Books VII.—X. of Euclid's elements, the method of representing numbers by geometrical lines being used, which Cossali has called linear Arithmetic. This method of representation is only once used in the *Arithmetics* proper, namely in the proposition v. 13, where it is used to prove that if $x + y = 1$, and x and y have to be so determined that $x + 2$, $y + 6$ are both squares, we have to divide the number 9 into two squares of which one must be > 2 and < 3. From the use of this linear method in this one case in the *Arithmetics*, and commonly in the treatise on *Polygonal Numbers*, we see that even in the time of Diophantos the geometrical representation of numbers was thought to have the advantage

[1] "Namentlich ist in dieser Hinsicht das fünfte Buch stiefmutterlich von der Mutter Zeit behandelt worden." p. 268.

of greater clearness. It need scarcely be remarked how opposed
this Greek method is to our modern ones, our tendency being
the reverse, viz., to the representation of lines by numbers. The
treatise on *Polygonal Numbers* is often, and probably rightly,
held to be one of the thirteen original Books of the *Arithmetics*.
There is absolutely no reason to doubt its genuineness; which
remark would have been unnecessary but for a statement by
Bossut to the effect: "Il avoit écrit treize livres d' arithmétiques,
les six premiers (?) sont arrivés jusqu'à nous : tous les autres
sont perdus, si, néanmoins, un septième, qu'on trouve dans
quelques (!) éditions de Diophante, n'est pas de lui"; upon which
Reimer has made a note : "This Book on *Polygonal Numbers* is
an independent work and cannot possibly belong to the Collection
of Diophantos' *Arithmetics*[1]." This statement is totally un-
founded. With respect to Bossut's own remark, we have seen
that it is almost certain that the Books we possess are not the
first six Books; again, the treatise on *Polygonal Numbers* does
not only occur in *some*, but in all of the editions of Diophantos
from Xylander to Schulz; and, lastly, Bossut is the only person
who has ever questioned its genuineness.

We mentioned above the *Porisms* of Diophantos. Our
knowledge of them is derived from his own words; in three
places in the *Arithmetics* he refers to them in the words ἔχομεν
ἐν τοῖς πορίσμασιν : the places are v. 3, 5, 19. The references
made to them are for proofs of propositions in the Theory of
Numbers, which he assumes in these problems as known. It is
probable therefore that the *Porisms* were a collection of propositions concerning the properties of certain numbers, their
divisibility into a certain number of squares, and so on ; and it
is reasonable to suppose that from them he takes also the many
other propositions which he assumes, either explicitly enunciating
them, or implicitly taking them for granted. May we not then
reasonably suppose the *Porisms* to have formed an introduction
to the indeterminate and semi-determinate analysis of the
second degree which forms the main subject of the *Arithmetics?*
And may we not assume this introduction to have formed an

[1] "Dieses Buch *de numeris multangulis* ist eine für sich bestehende Schrift
und gehört keinesweges in die Sammlung der Arithmeticorum Diophant's."

integral part, now lost, of the original thirteen books? If this
supposition is correct the *Porisms* also must have intervened between Books I. and II., where we have already said that probably
Diophantos treated of indeterminate problems of the first
degree and of the solution of the complete quadratic. The
method of the *Porisms* was probably synthetic, like the *Polygonal Numbers*, not (like the six Books of the *Arithmetics*)
analytical; this however forms no sufficient reason for refusing
to include all three treatises under the single title of thirteen
Books of *Arithmetics*. These suppositions would account easily
for the contents of the lost Books; they would also, with the
additional evidence of the division of our text of the *Arithmetics*
into seven books by the Vatican MS., show that the lost portion
probably does not bear such a large proportion to the whole as
might be imagined. This view is adopted by Colebrooke[1], and
after him by Nesselmann, who, in support of his hypothesis
that the *Arithmetics,* the *Porisms* and the treatise on *Polygonal
Numbers* formed only *one* complete work under the general
title of ἀριθμητικα, points out the very significant fact that we
never find mention of more than *one* work of Diophantos, and
that the very use of the Plural Neuter term, ἀριθμητικά, would
seem to imply that it was a collection of different treatises on
arithmetical subjects and of different content. Nesselmann, however, does not seem to have noticed an objection previously urged

---

[1] *Algebra of the Hindus*, Note M. p. LXI.

"In truth the division of manuscript books is very uncertain: and it is by
no means improbable that the remains of Diophantus, as we possess them, may
be less incomplete and constitute a larger portion of the thirteen books announced by him (Def. 11) than is commonly reckoned. His treatise on polygon
numbers, which is surmised to be one (and that the last of the thirteen), follows,
as it seems, the six (or seven) books in the exemplars of the work, as if the
preceding portion were complete. It is itself imperfect: but the manner is
essentially different from that of the foregoing books: and the solution of
problems by equations is no longer the object, but rather the demonstration
of propositions. There appears no ground, beyond bare surmise, to presume,
that the author, in the rest of the tracts relative to numbers which fulfilled
his promise of thirteen books, resumed the Algebraic manner: or in short,
that the Algebraic part of his performance is at all mutilated in the copies
extant, which are considered to be all transcripts of a single imperfect
exemplar."

against the theory that the three treatises formed only one work, by Schulz, to the effect that Diophantos expressly says that his work treats of *arithmetical problems*[1]. This statement itself does not seem to me to be quite accurate, and I cannot think that it is at all a valid objection to Nesselmann's view. The passage to which Schulz refers must evidently be the opening words of the dedication by the author to Dionysios. Diophantos begins thus: "Knowing that you are anxious to become acquainted with the solution [or 'discovery,' εὕρεσις] of problems in numbers, I set myself to systematise the method, beginning from the foundations on which the science is built, the preliminary determination of the nature and properties in numbers[2]." Now these "foundations" may surely well mean more than is given in the eleven definitions with which the treatise begins, and why should not the "properties of numbers" refer to the *Porisms* and the treatise on *Polygonal Numbers?* But there is another passage which might seem to countenance Schulz's objection, where (Def. 11) Diophantos says "let us now proceed to the propositions[3]...which we will deal with in thirteen Books[4]." The word used here is not *problem* (πρόβλημα) but *proposition* (πρότασις), although Bachet translates both words by the same Latin word "quaestio," inaccurately. Now the word πρότασις does not only apply to the analytical solution of a problem: it applies equally to the synthetic method. Thus the use of the word here might very well imply that the work was to contain

---

[1] Schulz remarks on the *Porisms* (pref. xxi.): "Es ist daher nicht unwahrscheinlich dass diese Porismen eine eigene Schrift unseres Diophantus waren, welche vorzüglich die Zusammensetzung der Zahlen aus gewissen Bestandtheilen zu ihrem Gegenstande hatte. Könnte man diese Schrift gar als eine Bestandtheil des grossen in dreizehn Büchern abgefassten arithmetischen Werkes ansehen, so wäre es sehr erklarbar, dass gerade dieser Theil, der den blossen Liebhaber weniger anzog, verloren ging. Da indess Diophantus ausdrücklich sagt, sein Werk behandele *arithmetische Probleme*, so hat wenigstens die letztere Annahme nur einen geringen Grad von Wahrscheinlichkeit."

[2] Diophantos' own words are: Τὴν εὕρεσιν τῶν ἐν τοῖς ἀριθμοῖς προβλημάτων, τιμιώτατέ μοι Διονύσιε, γινώσκων σε σπουδαίως ἔχοντα μαθεῖν, ὀργανῶσαι τὴν μέθοδον ἐπειράθην, ἀρξάμενος ἀφ' ὧν συνέστηκε τὰ πράγματα θεμελίων, ὑποστῆσαι τὴν ἐν τοῖς ἀριθμοῖς φύσιν τε καὶ δύναμιν.

[3] νῦν δὲ ἐπὶ τὰς προτάσεις χωρήσωμεν, κ. τ. λ.

[4] τῆς πραγματείας αὐτῶν ἐν τρισκαίδεκα βιβλίοις γεγενημένης.

not only problems, but propositions on numbers, i.e. might include the *Porisms* and *Polygonal Numbers* as a part of the complete *Arithmetics*. These objections which I have made to Schulz's argument are, I think, enough to show that his objection to the view adopted by Nesselmann has no weight. Schulz's own view as to the contents of the missing Books of Diophantos is that they contained new methods of solution in addition to those used in Books I. to VI., and that accordingly the lost portion came at the end of the existing six Books. In particular he thinks that Diophantos extended in the lost Books the method of solution by means of what he calls a *double-equation* (διπλῆ ἰσότης or in one word διπλοϊσότης). By means of this double-equation Diophantos shows how to find a value of the unknown, which will make two expressions containing it (linear or quadratic) simultaneously squares. Schulz accordingly thinks that he went on in the lost Books to show how to make *three* such expressions simultaneously squares, i.e. advanced to a *triple-equation*. This view, however, seems to have nothing to recommend it, inasmuch as, in the first place, we nowhere find the slightest hint in the extant Books of anything different or more advanced which is to come; and, secondly, Diophantos' system and ideas seem so self-contained, and his methods to move always in the same well-defined circle that it seems certain that we come in our six Books to the limits of his art.

There is yet another view of the probable contents of the lost Books, which must be mentioned, though we cannot believe that it is the right one. It is that of Bombelli, given by Cossali, to the effect that in the lost Books Diophantos went on to solve determinate equations of the third and fourth degree; Bombelli's reason for supposing this is that Diophantos gives so many problems the object of which is to make the sum of a square and any other number to be again a square number by finding a suitable value of the first square; these methods, argues Bombelli, of Diophantos must have been given for the reason that the author intended to use them for the solution of the equation $x^4 + px = q$[1]. Now Bombelli had occupied himself

[1] Cossali's words are (p. 75, 76): .."non tralascierò di notare l' opinione, di cui fu tentato Bombelli, che nelli sei libri cioè dal tempo, di tutto distruggitore,

much, almost during his whole life, with the then new methods of solution of equations of the third and fourth degree; and, for the solution of the latter, the usual method of his time led to the making an expression of the form $Ax^2 + Bx + C$ a square, where the coefficients involved a second unknown quantity. Nesselmann accordingly thinks it is no matter for surprise that in Diophantos' entirely independent investigations Bombelli should have seen, or fancied he saw, his own favourite idea. This solution of the equation of the fourth degree presupposes that of the cubic with the second term wanting; hence Bombelli would naturally, in accordance with his view, imagine Diophantos to have given the solution of this cubic. It is possible also that he may have been influenced by the actual occurrence in the extant Books [VI. 19] of a cubic equation, namely the equation $x^3 + x = 4x^2 + 4$, of which Diophantos at once writes down the solution $x = 4$, without explanation. It is obvious, however, that no conclusion can be drawn from this, which is a very easy particular case, and which Diophantos probably solved[1] by simply dividing out by the factor $x^2 + 1$. There are strong objections to Bombelli's view. (1) Diophantos himself states (Def. XI.) that the solution of the *problems* is the object in itself of the work. (2) If he used the method to lead up to the solution of equations of higher degrees, he certainly has not gone to work the shortest way. In support of the view it has been asked "What, on any other assumption, is the object of defining in Def. II. all powers of the unknown quantity up to the sixth?

rapitici, si avanzasse egli a sciogliere l' equazione $x^4 + px = q$, parendogli, che nei libri rimastici, con proporsi di trovar via via numeri quadrati, cammini una strada a quell' intento. Egli è di fatto procedendo su queste tracce di Diofanto, che Vieta deprime l' esposta equazione di grado quarto ad una di secondo. Siccome però ciò non si effettua che mediante una cubica mancante del secondo termine; così il pensiero sorto in animo a Bombelli importerebbe, che Diofanto nei libri perduti costituito avesse la regola di sciogliere questa sorta di equazione cubiche prima d' innoltrarsi allo scioglimento di quella equazione di quarto grado."

[1] This is certainly a simpler explanation than Bachet's, who derives the solution from the proportion $x^3 : x^2 = x : 1$.

Therefore $x^3 + x : x^2 + 1 = x : 1$.

Therefore $x^3 + x : 4x^2 + 4 = x : 4$.

    But the equation being $x^3 + x = 4x^2 + 4$, it follows that $x = 4$.

Surely Diophantos must have meant to use them." The answer to which is that he has occasion to use them in the work, but reduces all the equations which contain these higher powers by his regular and uniform method of analysis.

In conclusion, I may repeat that the most probable view is that adopted by Nesselmann, that the works which we know under the three titles formed part of one arithmetical work, which was, according to the author's own words, to consist of thirteen Books. The proportion of the lost parts to the whole is probably less than it might be supposed to be. The *Porisms* form the part, the loss of which is most to be regretted, for from the references to them it is clear that they contained propositions in the Theory of Numbers most wonderful for the time.

CHAPTER III.

§ 1. In this chapter I purpose to give a sketch of what has been done directly, and (where it is of sufficient importance) indirectly, for Diophantos, enumerating and describing briefly (so far as possible) the works which have been written on the subject. We turn first, naturally, to Diophantos' own countrymen ; and we find that, if we except the doubtful " commentary of Hypatia," spoken of above, there is only *one* Greek, who has written anything at all on Diophantos, namely the monk Maximus Planudes, to whom are attributed the scholia attached to Books I. and II. in some MSS., which are printed in Latin in Xylander's translation of Diophantos. The date of these scholia is the first half of the 14th century, and they represent all that we know to have been done for Diophantos by his own countrymen. How different his fate would have been, had he lived a little earlier, when the scientific spirit of the Greeks was still active, what an enormous impression his work would then have created, we may judge by comparing the effect which it had with that of a far less important work, that of Nikomachos. Considering then that up to the time of Maximus Planudes nothing was written about Diophantos (beyond a single quotation by Theon of Alexandria, before mentioned, and an occasional mention of the name) by any Greek, one is simply astounded at finding in Bossut's history a remark like the following : " L'auteur a eu parmi les anciens *une foule* d'interprètes (!), dont les ouvrages sont la plupart (!) perdus. Nous regrettons, dans ce nombre, le commentaire de la célèbre Hipathia (sic)." Comment is unnecessary. With respect to

the work of Maximus Planudes itself, he has only commented
upon the first two Books, the least important and most elemen-
tary, nor can his scholia be said to have any importance.
Bachet speaks contemptuously of them[1], and even the modest
Xylander has but a low opinion of their value[2].

§ 2. I have, in first mentioning Maximus Planudes, de-
parted a little from chronological order, for the greater convenience of giving first the Greek writers upon Diophantos.
But long before the time of Maximus Planudes, the work of
Diophantos had found its way to Arabia, and there met with
the respect it deserved. Unfortunately the actual works written in Arabia directly upon Diophantos are all lost, or at least
have not been discovered up to the present time. So far therefore as these are concerned we have to be contented with the
notices on the subject by Arabian historians or bibliographers.
It is therefore necessary to collect from the earliest and best
sources possible the scattered remarks about Diophantos and
his works. The earliest and therefore presumably the best and
most trustworthy authority on the subject of Diophantos in
Arabia is the *Kitāb Alfihrist* of al-Nadīm[3], the date of which
is as early as *circa* 990 A.D. The passages in this work which
refer to Diophantos are :

(*a*) p. 269, "Diophantos [the last vowel, however, being
ī = η in one codex, in the rest undetermined] the Greek of

---

[1] Bachet says: "Porro Graeci Scholiastae in duos priores libros adnota-
tiones edi non curauimus, vt quae nullius sint momenti, easque proinde
Guilielmus Xilander (!) censura sua meritò perstrinxerit, *si cui tamen oleum
operamque perdere adeò leue est, vt miras Graeculi huius ineptias peruidere
cupiat, adeat Xilandrum.*"

[2] Xylander says the Scholia are attributed to Maximus Planudes, and com-
bats the view that they might be Hypatia's thus: "Sed profecto si ea tanta
fuit, quantam Suidas et alij perhibent, istae annotationes eam autorem non
agnoscunt, de quibus quid senserim, meo more liberè dixi suis locis." *Epistola
Nuncupatoria.*

[3] This work has been edited by Flügel, 1871. The author himself dates
it 987, and Wöpcke (*Journal Asiatique*, Février-Mars, 1855, p. 256) states that
it was finished at that date. This is, however, not correct, for in his preface
Flügel shows that the work contains references to events which are certainly
later than 987, so that it seems best to say simply that the date is *circa*
990 A.D.

Alexandria. He wrote Kitāb Ṣinā'at al-jabr," i.e. "the book of the art of algebra."

(b) p. 283, Among the works of Abu'l-Wafā is mentioned "An interpretation[1] (tafsīr) of the book of Diophantos about algebra."

(c) On the same page the title of another work of Abu'l-Wafā is given as "Demonstrations of the theorems employed by Diophantos in his work, and of those employed by (Abu'l-Wafā) himself in his commentary" (the word is as before tafsīr).

(d) p. 295, On Kostā ibn Lūkā of Ba'lbek it is mentioned that one of his books is tafsīr on three-and-a-half divisions (Makālāt) of the book of Diophantos on "questions of numbers."

We have thus in the Fihrist mentions of three separate works upon Diophantos, which must accordingly have been written previously to the year 990 of our era. Concerning Abu'l-Wafā the evidence of his having studied and commented upon Diophantos is conclusive, not only because his other works which have survived show unmistakeable signs of the influence of Diophantos, but because the proximity of date of the Fihrist to that of Abu'l-Wafā makes all mistake impossible. As I have said the Fihrist was written circa 990 A.D. and the date of Abu'l-Wafā is 328—388 A.H. or 940—998 A.D. He was a native of Būzjān, a small town between Herāt and Nīshāpūr in Khorāsān, and was evidently, from what is known of his works one of the most celebrated astronomers and geometers of his time[2]. Of later notices on this subject we may mention those

---

[1] There is a little doubt as to the exact meaning of tafsīr—whether it means a translation or a commentary. The word is usually applied to the literal exegesis of the Korān; how much it means in the present case may perhaps be ascertainable from the fact that Abu'l-Wafā also wrote a tafsīr of the Algebra of Mohammed ibn Mūsā al-Khārizmī. It certainly, according to the usual sense, means a commentary not a mere translation—e.g. at p. 249 al-Nadīm clearly distinguishes translators of Aristotle from the mufassirīn or makers of tafsīr, i.e. commentators.

For this information I am indebted to the kindness of Professor Robertson Smith.

[2] Wöpcke, Journal Asiatique, Février-Mars, 1855, p. 244 foll.

Abu'l-Wafā's full name is Mohammed ibn Mohammed ibn Yahyā ibn Ismail ibn Al'abbās Abu'l-Wafā Al-Būzjāni.

in the *Ta'rīkh Hokoma* (Hajji-Khalīfa, No. 2204), by the Imām Mohammed ibn. 'Abd al-Karīm al-Shahrastāni who died A.H. 548 or A.D. 1153[1]. Of course this work is not so trustworthy an authority as the *Fihrist*, which is about 160 years earlier, and the author of the *Ta'rīkh Hokoma* stands to the *Fihrist* in the relation of a compiler to the original source. In the *Ta'rīkh Hokoma* we are told (*a*) that Abu'l-Wafā "wrote a commentary on the work of Diophantos concerning Algebra," (*b*) that "Diophantos, the Greek of Alexandria, conspicuous, perfect, famous in his time, wrote a famous work on the art of Algebra, which has gone over into Arabic," i. e. been translated. We must obviously connect these two notices. Lastly the same work mentions (*c*) another work of Abu'l-Wafā, namely "Proofs for the propositions given in his book by Diophantos."

A later writer still, the author of the *History of the Dynasties*, Abu'lfaraj, mentions, among celebrated men who lived in the time of Julian, Diophantos, with the addition that "His book[2]...on Algebra is celebrated," and again in another place he says upon Abu'l-Wafā, "He commented upon the work of Diophantos on Algebra."

The notices from al-Shahrastāni and Abu'lfaraj are, as I have

---

[1] The work *Bibliotheca arabico-hispana Escurialensis op. et studio* Mich. Casiri, Matriti, 1760, gives many important notices about mathematicians from the *Ta'rīkh Hokoma*, which Casiri denotes by the title *Bibliotheca philosophorum*.

Cossali mentions the *Ta'rīkh Hokoma* as having been written about A.D. 1198 by an anonymous person : "Il libro più antico, che ci fornisca tratti relativi all' origine dell' analisi tra gli arabi è la *Biblioteca arabica de' filosofi*, scritta circa l' anno 1198 da anonimo egiziano" (Cossali, I. p. 174). There is however now apparently no doubt that the author was al-Shahrastāni, as I have said in the text.

[2] After the word "book" in the text comes a word *Ab-kismet* which is unintelligible. Pococke, the Latin translator, simply puts A. B. for it : "cuius liber A. B. quem Algebram vocat, celebris est." The word or words are apparently a corruption of something ; Nesselmann conjectures that the original word was an Arabic translation of the Greek title, *Arithmetics*—a supposition which, if true, would give admirable sense. The passage would then mark the Arabian perception of the discrepancy (according to the accepted meaning of terms) between the title and the subject, which is obviously rather *algebra* than arithmetic in the strict sense.

said, for obvious reasons not so trustworthy as those in the *Fihrist*. They are, however, interesting as showing that Diophantos continued to be known and recognised for a considerable period after his work found its way to Arabia, and was commented upon, though they add nothing to our information as to what was done for Diophantos in Arabia. It is clear that the work of Abu'l-Wafā was the most considerable that was written in Arabia upon Diophantos *directly*; about the obligations to Diophantos of other Arabian writers, as *indirectly* shown by similarity of matter or method, without direct reference, I shall have to speak later.

§ 3. I now pass to the writers on Diophantos in Europe. From the time of Maximus Planudes to a period as late as about 1570 Diophantos remained practically a sealed book, and had to be rediscovered even after attention had been invited to it by Regiomontanus, who, as was said above, was the first European to mention it as extant. We have seen (pp. 21, 22) that Regiomontanus referred to Diophantos in the *Oration* at Padua, about 1462, and how in a very interesting letter to Joannes de Blanchinis he speaks of finding a MS. of Diophantos at Venice, of the pleasure he would have in translating it if he could only find a copy containing the whole of the thirteen books, and his readiness to translate even the incomplete work in six books, in case it were desired. But it does not appear that he ever began the work; it seems, however, very extraordinary that the interest which Regiomontanus took in Diophantos and tried to arouse in others should not have incited some of his German countrymen to follow his leading, at least as early as 1537, when we know that his *Oration* at Padua was published. Hard to account for as the fact may appear, it was left for an Italian, Bombelli, to rediscover Diophantos about 1570; though the mentions by Regiomontanus may be said at last to have borne their fruit, in that about the same time Xylander was encouraged by them to persevere in his intention of investigating Diophantos. Nevertheless between the time of Regiomontanus and that of Rafael Bombelli Diophantos was once more forgotten, or rather unknown, for in the interval we find two mentions of the name, (*a*) by Joachim Camerarius in a letter published 1556[1], in which he mentions that there is a MS. of Diophantos in the Vatican, which he is anxious to see, (b) by James Peletarius[2] who merely mentions the name. Of the important mathematicians who preceded Bombelli, Fra Luca Pacioli towards the end of the 15th century, Cardan and Tartaglia in the 16th, not one so much as mentions Diophantos[3]. The first Italian to whom Diophantos seems to have been known, and who was the first to discover a MS. in the Vatican Library, and to conceive the idea of publishing the work, was Rafael Bombelli. Bachet falls into an anachronism when he says that Bombelli began his work upon Diophantos after the appearance of Xylander's translation[4], which was published in 1575. The Algebra of Bombelli appeared in 1572, and in the

[1] *De Graecis Latinisque numerorum notis et praeterea Saracenis seu Indicis,* etc. etc., *studio* Joachimi Camerarii, Papeberg, 1556.

In a letter to Zasius : "Venit mihi in mentem eorum quae et de hac et aliis liberalibus artibus dicta fuere, in eo convivio cujus in tuis aedibus me et Peucerum nostrum participes esse, suavissima tua invitatio voluit. Cum autem de autoribus Logistices verba fierent, et a me *Diophantus* Graecus nominaretur, qui extaret in Bibliotheca Vaticana, ostendebatur tum spes quaedam, posse nobis copiam libri illius. Ibi ego cupiditate videndi incensus, fortasse audacius non tamen infeliciter, te quasi procuratorem constitui negotii gerendi, mandato voluntario, cum quidem et tu libenter susciperes quod imponebatur, et fides solenni festivitate firmaretur, de illo tuo et poculo elegante et vino optimo. Neque tu igitur obliviosceris ejus rei, cujus explicationem tua benignitas tibi commisit, neque ego non meminisse potero, non modo excellentis virtutis et sapientiae, sed singularis comitatis et incredibilis suavitatis tuae."

[2] *Arithmeticae practicae methodus facilis, per Gemmam Frisium, etc. Huc accedunt Jacobi Peletarii annotationes,* Coloniae, 1571. (But pref. of Peletarius bears date 1558.) P. 72, *Nota Peletarii :* "Algebra autem dicta videtur a Gebro Arabe ut vox ipsa sonat; hujus artis si non inventore, saltem excultore. Alii tribuunt Diophanto cuidam Graeco."

[3] Cossali I. p. 59, "Cosa pero, che reca la somma maraviglia si è, che largo in Italia non si spandesse la cognizione del codice di Diofanto : che in fiore essendovi lo studio della greca lingua, non venisse da qualche dotto a comun vantaggio tradotta; che per l' opposto niuna menzione ne faccia Fra Luca verso il fine del secolo xv, e niuna Cardano, e Tartaglia intorno la metà del secolo xvi ; che nelle biblioteche rimanesse sepolto, ed andasse dimenticato per modo, che poco prima degli anni 70 del secolo xvi si riguardasse per una scoperta l' averlo rinvenuto nella Vaticana Biblioteca."

[4] "Non longo post Xilandrum interuallo Raphaël Bombellius Bononiensis, Graecum e Vaticana Bibliotheca Diophanti codicem nactus, omnes priorum quattuor librorum quaestiones, et è libro quinto nonnullas, problematibus suis inseruit, in Algebra sua quam Italico sermone conscripsit."

preface to this work [1] the author tells us that he had recently discovered a Greek book on Algebra in the Vatican Library, written by a certain Diofantes, an Alexandrine Greek author who lived in the time of Antoninus Pius; that, thinking highly of the contents of this work, he and Antonio Maria Pazzi determined to translate it; that they actually translated five books out of the seven into which the MS. was divided; but that, before the whole was finished, they were called away from it by other labours. The date of these occurrences must be a few years before 1572. Though Bombelli did not carry out his plan of publishing Diophantos in a translation, he has nevertheless taken all the problems of Diophantos' first four Books and some of those of the fifth, and embodied them in his Algebra, interspersing them with his own problems. Though he has taken no pains to distinguish Diophantos' problems from his own, he has in the case of Diophantos' work adhered pretty closely to the original, so that Bachet admits his obligations to Bombelli, whose reproduction of the problems of Diophantos he maintains that he found in many points better than Xylander's translation[2]. It may be interesting to mention a few points of

[1] This book Nesselmann tells us that he has never seen, but takes his information about it from Cossali. I was fortunate enough to find a copy of it published in 1579 (not the original edition) in the British Museum, the title being *L'Algebra, opera di Rafael Bombelli da Bologna diuisa in tre Libri......In Bologna, Per Giovanni Rossi. MDLXXIX.* I have thus been able to verify the quotations from the preface. The whole passage is :

"Questi anni passati, essendosi ritrouato una opera greca di questa disciplina nella libraria di Nostro Signore in Vaticano, composta da un certo Diofante Alessandrino Autor Greco, il quale fù à tempo di Antonin Pio, e havendo mela fatta vedere Messer Antonio Maria Pazzi Reggiano publico lettore delle Matematiche in Roma, e giu dicatolo con lui Autore assai intelligente de numeri (ancorche non tratti de numeri irrationali, ma solo in lui si vede vn perfetto ordine di operare) egli, ed io, per arrichire il mondo di cosi fatta opera, ci dessimo à tradurlo, e cinque libri (delli sette che sono) tradutti ne habbiamo ; lo restante non hauendo potuto finire per gli trauagli auenuti all' uno, e all' altro, e in detta opera habbiamo ritrouato, ch' egli assai volte cita gli Autori Indiani, col che mi ha fatto conoscere, che questa disciplina appo gl' indiani prima fù, che a gli Arabi."

The parts of this quotation which refer to the personality of Diophantos, the form Diofante, &c., have already been commented upon ; the last clauses we shall have occasion to mention again.

[2] Continuation of quotation in note 4, p. 43 :

"Sed suas Diophanteis quaestionibus ita immiscuit, ut has ab illis distin-

notation in this work of Bombelli. At beginning of Book II he explains that he uses the word "tanto" to denote the unknown quantity, not "cosa" like his predecessors; and his symbol for it is $\overset{1}{\smile}$, the square of the unknown (x^2) is $\overset{2}{\smile}$, the cube $\overset{3}{\smile}$; and so on. For *plus* and *minus* (*più* and *meno*) he uses the initial letters *p.* and *m.* Thus corresponding to $x + 6$ we should find in Bombelli $1\overset{1}{\smile}\ p.\ 6$, and for $x^2 + 5x - 4$, $1\overset{2}{\smile}\ p.\ 5\overset{1}{\smile}\ m.\ 4$. This notation shows, as will be seen later, some advance upon that of Diophantos in one important respect.

The next writer upon Diophantos was Wilhelm Holzmann who published, under the Graecised form of his name *Xylander* by which he is generally known, a work bearing the title: *Diophanti Alexandrini Rerum Arithmeticarum Libri sex, quorum primi duo adiecta habent Scholia Maximi (ut coniectura est) Planudis. Item Liber de Numeris Polygonis seu Multangulis. Opus incomparabile, uerae Arithmeticae Logisticae perfectionem continens, paucis adhuc uisum. A Guil. Xylandro Augustano incredibili labore Latinè redditum, et Commentariis explanatum, inque lucem editum ad Illustriss. Principem Ludovicum Vuirtembergensem Basileae per Eusebium Episcopium, et Nicolai Fr. haeredes.* MDLXXV. Xylander was according to his own statement a "public teacher of Aristotelian philosophy in the school at Heidelberg[1]." He was a man of almost universal culture[2], and was so thoroughly imbued with the classical literature, that the extraordinary aptness of his quotations and his wealth of expression give exceptional charm to his writing whenever he is free from the shackles of mathematical formulae and technicalities. The *Epistola Nuncupatoria* is addressed to the Prince Ludwig, and Xylander neatly introduces it by the line "Offerimus numeros, numeri sunt principe digni." This preface is very quaint and interesting. He tells us how he first saw the name of Diophantos mentioned in Suidas, and

guere non sit in promptu, neque vero se fidum satis interpretem praebuit, cum passim verba Diophanti immutet, hisque pleraque addat, pleraque pro arbitrio detrahat. In multis nihilominus interpretationem Bombellii, Xilandriana praestare, et ad hanc emendandam me adjuvisse ingenue fateor." *Ad lectorem.*

[1] "Publicus philosophiae Aristoteleae in schola Heidelbergensi doctor."

[2] Even Bachet, who, as we shall see, was no favourable critic, calls him "Vir omnibus disciplinis excultus."

46 DIOPHANTOS OF ALEXANDRIA.

then found that mention had been made of his work by Regiomontanus as being extant in an Italian Library and having
been seen by him. But, as the book had not been edited, he
tried to reconcile himself to the want of it by making himself
acquainted with the works on Arithmetic which were actually
known and in use, and he apologises for what he considers to
have been a disgrace to him[1]. With the help of books only he
studied the subject of Algebra, so far as was possible from what
men like Cardan had written and by his own reflection, with
such success that not only did he fall into what Herakleitos
called οἴησιν, ἱερὰν νόσον, or the conceit of " being somebody " in
the field of Arithmetic and " Logistic," but others too who were
themselves learned men thought him (as he modestly tells us)
an arithmetician of exceptional merit. But when he first
became acquainted with the problems of Diophantos (he con-
tinues) his pride had a fall so sudden and so humiliating that he
might reasonably doubt whether he ought previously to have

[1] I cannot refrain from quoting the whole of this passage:
"Sed cùm ederet nemo : cepi desiderium hoc paulatim in animo consopire, et
eorum quos consequi poteram Arithmeticorum librorum cognitione, et medita-
tionibus nostris sepelire. Veritatis porrò apud me est autoritas, ut ei con-
iunctum etiam cum dedecore meo testimonium lubentissimè perhibeam. Quod
Cossica seu Algebrica (cum his enim reliqua comparata, id sunt quod umbrae
Homericè in Necya ad animam Tiresiae) ea ergo quòd non assequebar modò,
quanquam mutis duntaxat usus preceptoribus caetera αὐτοδίδακτος, sed et augere,
uariare, adeoque corrigere in loco didicissem, quae summi et fidelissimi in
docendo uiri Christifer Rodolphus Silesius, Micaelus, Stifelius, Cardanus, No-
nius, aliique litteris mandauerant : incidi in οἴησιν, ἱερὰν νόσον, ut scitè appel-
lauit Heraclitus sapientior multis aliis philosophis, hoc est, in Arithmetica, et
uera Logistica, putaui me esse aliquid : itaque de me passim etiam a multis,
iisque doctis uiris iudicatum fuit, me non de grege Arithmeticum esse. Verum
ubi primùm in Diophantea incidi : ita me recta ratio circumegit, ut flendúsne
mihi ipsi anteà, an uerò ridendus fuissem, haud iniuria dubitauerim. Operae
precium hoc loco et meam inscitiam inuulgare, et Diophantei operis,
quod mihi nebulosam istam caliginem ab oculis detersit, immò eos in coenum
barbaricum defossos eleuauit et repurgauit, gustum aliquem exhibere. Surdorum
ego numerorum tractationem ita tenebam, ut etiam addere aliorum inuentis
aliquid non poenitendum auderem, atque id quidem in rebus arithmeticis mag-
num habetur, et difficultas istarum rerum multos a mathematibus deterret.
Quanto autem hoc est praeclarius, in iis problematis, quae surdis etiam numeris
uix posse uidentur explicari, rem eo deducere, ut quasi solum arithmeticum
uertere iussi obsurdescant illi planè, et ne mentio quidem eorum in tractatione
ingeniosissimarum quaestionum admittatur."

bewailed, or laughed at himself. He considers it therefore worth while to confess publicly in how disgraceful a condition of ignorance he had previously been content to live, and to do something to make known the work of Diophantos, which had so opened his eyes. Before this critical time he was so familiar with methods of dealing with surds that he actually had ventured to add something to the discoveries of others relating to them; these were considered to be of great importance in questions of Arithmetic, and their difficulty was of itself sufficient to deter many from the study of Mathematics. "But how much more splendid" (says Xylander) "the methods which reduce the problems which seem to be hardly capable of solution even with the help of surds in such a way that, while the surds, when bidden (so to speak) to plough the arithmetic soil, become true to their name and deaf to entreaty, they are not so much as mentioned in these most ingenious solutions!" He then describes the enormous difficulties which beset his work owing to the corruptions in his text. In dealing, however, with the mistakes and carelessness of copyists he was, as he says, no novice; for proof of which he appeals to his editions of Plutarch, Stephanus and Strabo. This passage, which is delightful reading, but too long to reproduce here, I give in full in the note [1].

---

[1] "Id uerò mihi accidit durum et uix superabile incommodum, quòd mirificè deprauata omnia inueni, cùm neque problematum expositio interdum integra esset, ac passim numeri (in quibus sita omnia esse in hoc argumento, quis ignorat?) tam problematum quàm solutionum siue explicationum corruptissimi. Non pudebit me ingenuè fateri, qualem me heic gesserim. Audacter, et summo cum feruore potius quàm alacritate animi opus ipsum initio sum aggressus, laborque mihi omnis uoluptati fuit, tantus est meus rerum arithmeticarum amor. quin et gratiam magnam me apud omnes liberalium scientiarum amatores ac patronos initurum, et praeclare de rep. litteraria meriturum intelligebam, eamque rem mihi laudi (quam à bonis profectam nemo prudens aspernatur) gloriaeque fortasse etiam emolumento fore sperabam. Progressus aliquantulum, in salebras incidi: quae tantum abest ut alacritatem meam retuderint, ut etiam animos mihi addiderint, neque enim mihi nouum aut insolens est aduersus librariorum incuriam certamen, et hac in re militaui, (ut Horatii nostri uerbis utar) non sine gloria. quod me non arroganter dicere, Dio, Plutarchus, Strabo, Stephanusque nostri testantur. Sed cum mox in ipsum pelagus monstris scatens me cursus abripuit: non despondi equidem animum, neque manus dedi, sed tamen saepius ad oram unde soluissem respexi, quàm portum in quem esset euadendum cogitando prospicerem, depraehendique non minus uerè quàm ele-

Next Xylander tells us how he came to get possession of a manuscript of Diophantos. In October of the year 1571 he made a journey to Wittenberg; while there he had conversations on mathematical subjects with two professors, Sebastian Theodoric and Wolfgang Schuler by name, who showed him a few pages of a Greek manuscript of Diophantos and informed him that it belonged to Andreas Dudicius whom Xylander describes as "Andreas Dudicius Sbardellatus, hoc tempore Imperatoris Romanorum apud Polonos orator." On his departure from Wittenberg Xylander wrote out and took with him the solution of a single problem of Diophantos, to amuse himself with on his journey. This he showed at Leipzig to Simon Simonius Lucensis, a professor at that place, who wrote to Dudicius on his behalf. A few months afterwards Dudicius sent the MS. to Xylander and encouraged him to persevere in his undertaking to translate the *Arithmetics* into Latin. Accordingly Xylander insists that the glory of the whole achievement belongs in no less but rather in a greater degree to Dudicius than to himself. Finally he commends the work to the favour of the Prince Ludwig, extolling the pursuit of arithmetical and algebraical science and dwelling in enthusiastic anticipation on the influence which the Prince's patronage would have in helping and advancing the study of Arithmetic[1]. This *Epistola*

ganter ea cecinisse Alcaeum, quae (si possum) Latinè in hac quasi uotiua mea tabula scribam.

> Qui uela uentis uult dare, dum licet,
> Cautus futuri praeuideat modum
> Cursus. mare ingressus, marino
> Nauiget arbitrio necesse est.

Sanè quod de Echeneide pisce fertur, eum nauim cui se adplicet remorari, poenè credibile fecit mihi mea cymba tot mendorum remoris retardata. Expediui tamen me ita, ut facilè omnes mediocri de his rebus iudicio praediti, intellecturi sint incredibilem me laborem et aerumnas difficilimas superasse : pudore etiam stimulatum oneris quod ultro mihi imposuissem, non perferendi. Paucula quaedam non planè explicata, studio et certis de causis in alium locum reiecimus. Opus quidem ipsum ita absoluimus ut neque eius nos pudere debeat, et Arithmeticae Logisticesque studiosi nobis se plurimum debere sint haud dubie professuri."

[1] "Hoc non modò tibi Princeps Illustrissime, honorificum erit, atque gloriosum; sed te labores nostros approbante, arithmeticae studium cùm alibi, tum in tua Academia et Gymnasiis, excitabitur, confirmabitur, prouehetur, et ad

Nuncupatoria bears the date 14th August, 1574[1]. Xylander died on the 10th of February in the year following that of the publication, 1576. Some have stated that Xylander published the Greek text of Diophantos as well as the Latin translation. There appears to be no foundation for the statement, which probably rests on a misunderstanding of certain passages in which Xylander refers to the Greek text. It is possible that he intended to publish the Greek original but was prevented by his death which so soon followed the appearance of his translation. It is a sufficient proof, however, that if such was his purpose it was never carried out, that Bachet asserts that he himself had never seen or found any one who had ever seen such an edition of the Greek text[2].

Concerning the merits of Xylander and his translation of Diophantos much has been written, and chiefly by authors who were not well acquainted with the subject, but whose very ignorance seems to have been their chief incitement to startling statements. Indeed very few persons at all seem to have studied the book itself: a fact which may be partly accounted for by its rarity. Nesselmann, whose book appeared in 1842, tells us honestly that he has never been able to find a copy, but has been obliged to take all information on the subject at second hand from Cossali and Bachet[3]. Even Cossali, so far as he gives any opinion at all upon the merits of the book, seems to do no more than reproduce what Bachet had said before him. Nor does Schulz seem to have studied Xylander's work : at least all his statements about it are vague and may very well have been gathered at second hand. Both he and

perfectam eius scientiam multi tuis auspiciis, nostro labore perducti, magnam hac re tuis in remp. beneficiis accessionem factam esse gratissima commemoratione praedicabunt."

[1] "Heidelberga. postrid. Eidus Sextiles cɪɔ ɪɔ lxxiv."

[2] "An vero et Graecè a Xilandro editus sit Diophantus, nondum certè comperire potui. Videtur sanè in multis suorum Commentariorum locis, de Graeco Diophanto tanquam a se edito, vel mox edendo, verba facere. Sed hanc editionem, neque mihi vidisse, neque aliquem qui viderit hactenus audivisse contigit." Bachet, *Epist. ad Lect.*

[3] There is not, I believe, a copy even in the British Museum, but I had the rare good fortune to find the book in the Library of Trinity College, Cambridge.

Nesselmann confine themselves to saying that it was not so worthless as many writers had stated it to be (Nesselmann on his part confessing his inability to form an opinion for the reason that he had never seen the book), and that it was well received among *savants* of the period, while its effect on the growth of the study of Algebra was remarkable[1]. On the other hand, the great majority of writers on the subject may be said to shout in chorus a very different cry. One instance will suffice to show the quality of the statements that have been generally made : to enumerate more would be waste of space. Dr Heinrich Suter in a *History of Mathematical Sciences* (Zürich 1873) says[2] "This translation is very poor, as Xylander was very little versed in Mathematics." If Dr Heinrich Suter had taken the trouble to read a few words of Xylander's preface, he could hardly have made so astounding a statement as that contained in the second clause of this sentence. This is only a specimen of the kind of statements which have been made about Xylander's book ; indeed I have been able to find no one who seems to have adequately studied Xylander except Bachet ; and Bachet's statements about the work of his predecessor and his own obligations to the same have been unhesitatingly accepted by the great majority of later writers. The result has been that Bachet has been universally considered the only writer who has done anything considerable for Diophantos, while the labours of his predecessor have been ignored or despised. This view of the relative merits of the two authors is, in my view, completely erroneous. From a careful study and comparison of the two editions I have come to the conclusion that honour has not been paid where honour was due. It would be tedious to give here in

---

[1] Schulz. "Wie unvollkommen Xylanders Arbeit auch ausfiel, wie oft er auch den rechten Sinn verfehlte, und wie oft auch seine Anmerkungen den Leser, der sich Rathes erholen will, im Stiche lassen, so gut war doch die Aufnahme, welche sein Buch bei den Gelehrten damaliger Zeit fand; denn in der That ging den Mathematikern durch die Erscheinung dieses Werkes ein neues Licht auf, und es ist mir sehr wahrscheinlich, dass er viel dazu beigetragen hat, die allgemeine Arithmetik zu ihrer nachmaligen Höhe zu erheben."

[2] "Diese Uebersetzung aber ist sehr schwach, da Xylander in Mathematik sehr wenig bewandert war."

detail the particular facts which led me to this conclusion. I will only say in this place that my suspicions were first aroused by reading Bachet's work alone, before I had seen the earlier one. From perusing Bachet I received the impression that his repeated emphatic and almost violent repudiation of obligation to Xylander, and his disparagement of that author suggested the very thing which he disclaimed, that he was under too great obligation to his predecessor to acknowledge it duly.

I must now pass to Bachet's work itself. It was the first edition published which contained the Greek text, and appeared in 1621 bearing the title: *Diophanti Alexandrini Arithmeticorum libri sex, et de numeris multangulis liber unus. Nunc primùm Graecè et Latinè editi, atque absolutissimis Commentariis illustrati. Auctore Claudio Gaspare Bacheto Meziriaco Sebusiano, V.C. Lutetiae Parisiorum, Sumptibus Hieronymi Drovart[1], via Jacobaea, sub Scuto Solari. MDCXXI.* (I should perhaps mention that we have a statement[2] that in Carl von Montchall's Library there was a translation of Diophantos which the mathematician "Joseph Auria of Neapolis" made, but did not apparently publish, and which was entitled "Diophanti libri sex, cum scholiis graecis Maximi Planudae, atque liber de numeris polygonis, collati cum Vaticanis codicibus, et latine versi a Josepho Auria." Of this work we know nothing; neither Bachet nor Cossali mentions it. The date would presumably be about the same as that of Xylander's translation, or a little later.) Bachet's Greek text is based, as he tells us, upon a MS. which he calls "codex Regius", now in the Bibliothèque Nationale at Paris; this MS. is his sole authority, except that Jacobus Sirmondus had part of a Vatican MS. transcribed for him. He professes to have produced a good Greek text, having spent incalculable labour upon its emendation, to have inserted

[1] For "sumptibus Hieronymi Drovart" Nesselmann has "sumptibus Sebastiani Cramoisy, 1621" which is found in some copies. The former (as given above) is taken from the title-page of the copy which I have used (from the Library of Trinity College, Cambridge).
[2] Schulz, Vorr. XLIII.: "Noch erwähnen die Litteratoren, dass sich in der Bibliothek eines Carl von Montchall eine Bearbeitung des Diophantus von dem berühmten *Joseph Auria* von Neapel (vermuthlich doch nur handschriftlich) befunden habe, welche den Titel fuhrte u. s. w." (see Text).

in brackets all additions which he made to it and to have
given notice of all corrections, except those of an obvious or
trifling nature; a few passages he has left asterisked, in cases
where correction could not be safely ventured upon. In spite
however of Bachet's assurance I cannot help doubting the
quality of his text in many places, though I have not seen
the MS. which he used. He is careful to tell us what previous works relating to the subject he had been able to consult. First he mentions Xylander (whom he invariably quotes
as Xilander), who had translated the whole of Diophantos, and
commented upon him throughout, "except that he scarcely
touched a considerable part of the fifth book, the whole of the
sixth and the treatise on multangular numbers, and even the
rest of his work was not very successful, as he himself admits
that he did not thoroughly understand a number of points."
Then he speaks of Bombelli (already mentioned) and the
Zetetica of Vieta (in which the author treats in his own way a
large number of Diophantos' problems : Bachet thinks that he
so treated them because he despaired of restoring the book
completely). Neither Bombelli nor Vieta (says Bachet) made
any attempt to demonstrate the difficult porisms and abstruse
theorems in numbers which Diophantos assumes as known in
many places, or sufficiently explained the causes of his operations and artifices. All these omissions on the part of his
predecessors he thinks he has supplied in his notes to the
various problems and in the three Books of "Porisms" which he
prefixed to the work[1]. As regards his Latin translation, he
says that he gives us Diophantos in Latin from the version of
Xylander most carefully corrected, in which he would have us
know that he has done two things in particular, first, corrected

---

[1] On the nature of some of Bachet's proofs Nicholas Saunderson (formerly
Lucasian Professor) remarks in *Elements of Algebra*, 1740, apropos of Dioph.
III. 17. "M. Bachet indeed in the 16th and 17th props. of his second book of
Porisms has given us demonstrations, such as they are, of the theorems in the
problem: but in the first place he demonstrates but one single case of those
theorems, and in the next place the demonstrations he gives are only synthetical,
and so abominably perplexed withal, that in each demonstration he makes use
of all the letters in the alphabet except I and O, singly to represent the quantities
he has there occasion for."

what was wrong and supplied the numerous lacunae, secondly, explained more clearly what Xylander had given in obscure or ambiguous language: "I confess however", he says "that this made so much change necessary, that it is almost more fair to attribute the translation to me than to Xilander. But if anyone prefers to consider it as his, because I have held fast, tooth and nail, to his words when they do not misrepresent Diophantus, I do not care"[1]. Such sentences as these, which are no rarity in Bachet's book, are certainly not calculated to increase our respect for the author. According to Montucla[2], "the historian of the French Academy tells us" that Bachet worked at this edition during the course of a quartan fever, and that he himself said that, disheartened as he was by the difficulty of the work, he would never have completed it, had it not been for the stubbornness which his malady generated in him.

As the first and only edition of the Greek text of Diophantos, this work, in spite of any imperfections we may find in it, does its author all honour.

The same edition was reprinted and published with the addition of Fermat's notes in 1670. *Diophanti Alexandrini Arithmeticorum libri sex, et de numeris multangulis liber unus. Cum commentariis C. G. Bacheti V. C. et obseruationibus D. P. de Fermat Senatoris Tolosani. Accessit Doctrinae Analyticae inuentum nouum, collectum ex variis eiusdem D. de Fermat Epistolis. Tolosae, Excudebat Bernardus Bosc, è Regione Collegii Societatis Jesu. MDCLXX.* This edition was not published by Fermat himself, as certain writers imply[3], but by his son

---

[1] "Deinde Latinum damus tibi Diophantum ex Xilandri versione accuratissimè castigata, in qua duo potissimum nos praestitisse scias velim, nam et deprauata correximus, hiantesque passim lacunas repleuimus: et quae subobscurè, vel ambiguè fuerat interpretatus Xilander, dilucidius exposuimus; fateor tamen, inde tantam inductam esse mutationem, vt propemodum aequius sit versionem istam nobis quàm Xilandro tribuere. Si quis autem potius ad eum pertinere contendat, quòd eius verba, quatenus Diophanto fraudi non erant, mordicus retinuimus, per me licet."

[2] I. 323.

[3] So Dr Heinrich Suter: "*Diese Ausgabe wurde* 1670 *durch Fermat erneuert, der sie mit seinen eigenen algebraischen Untersuchungen und Erfindungen ausstattete.*"

after his death. S. Fermat tells us in the preface that this
publication of Fermat's notes to Diophantos was part of an
attempt to collect together from his letters and elsewhere his
contributions to mathematics. The "Doctrinae Analyticae Inuentum nouum" is a collection made by Jacobus de Billy from
various letters which Fermat sent to him at different times.
The notes upon Diophantos' problems, which his son hopes will
prove of value very much more than commensurate with their
bulk, were (he says) collected from the margin of his copy of
Diophantos. From their brevity they were obviously intended
for the benefit of experts[1], or even perhaps solely for Fermat's
own, he being a man who preferred the pleasure which he had
in the work itself to all considerations of the fame which might
follow therefrom. Fermat never cared to publish his investigations, but was always perfectly ready, as we see from his letters,
to acquaint his friends and contemporaries with his results. Of
the notes themselves this is not the place to speak in detail.
This edition of Diophantos is rendered valuable only by the
additions in it due to Fermat; for the rest it is a mere reprint
of that of 1621. So far as the Greek text is concerned it is
very much inferior to the first edition. There is a far greater
number of misprints, omissions of words, confusions of numerals;
and, most serious of all, the brackets which Bachet inserted in
the edition of 1621 to mark the insertion of words in the text
are in this later edition altogether omitted. These imperfections have been already noticed by Nesselmann[2]. Thus the
reprinted edition of 1670 is untrustworthy as regards the text.

[1] *Lectori Beneuolo*, p. iii.: "Doctis quibus tantum pauca sufficiunt, harum
obseruationum auctor scribebat, vel potius ipse sibi scribens, his studiis exerceri
malebat quam gloriari; adeo autem ille ab omni ostentatione alienus erat, vt nec
lucubrationes suas typis mandari curauerit, et suorum quandoque responsorum
autographa nullo seruato exemplari petentibus vltro miserit; norunt scilicet ple-
rique celeberrimorum huius saeculo Geometrarum, quam libenter ille et quantâ
humanitate, sua iis inuenta patefecerit."

[2] "Was dieser Abdruck an äusserer Eleganz gewonnen hat (denn die Bachet'sche Ausgabe ist mit äusserst unangenehmen, namentlich Griechischen
Lettern gedruckt), das hat sie an innerm Werthe in Bezug auf den Text verloren. Sie ist nicht bloss voller Druckfehler in einzelnen Worten und Zeichen
(z. B. durchgehends π statt ϡ, 900) sondern auch ganze Zeilen sind ausgelassen
oder doppelt gedruckt, (z. B, III. 12 eine Zeile doppelt, IV. 25 eine doppelt und

I omit here all mention of works which are not directly upon Diophantos (e.g. the so called "Translation" by Stevin and Alb. Girard). We have accordingly to pass from 1670 to 1810 before we find another extant work directly upon Diophantos. In 1810 was published an excellent translation (with additions) of the fragment upon *Polygonal Numbers* by Poselger : *Diophantus von Alexandrien über die Polygonal-Zahlen. Uebersetzt mit Zusätzen von F. Th. Poselger. Leipzig*, 1810.

Lastly, in 1822 Otto Schulz, professor in Berlin, published a very meritorious German translation with notes : *Diophantus von Alexandria arithmetische Aufgaben nebst dessen Schrift über die Polygon-Zahlen. Aus dem Griechischen übersetzt und mit Anmerkungen begleitet von Otto Schulz, Professor am Berlinisch-Cölnischen Gymnasium zum grauen Kloster. Berlin*, 1822. *In der Schlesingerschen Buch- und Musikhandlung.* The former work of Poselger is with the consent of its author incorporated in Schulz's edition along with his own translation and notes upon the larger treatise, the *Arithmetics.* According to Nesselmann Schulz was not a mathematician by profession : he produced, however, a most excellent and painstaking edition, with notes chiefly upon the matter of Diophantos and not on the text (with the exception of a very few emendations) : notes which, almost invariably correct, help much to understand the author. Schulz's translation is based upon the edition of Bachet's text published in 1670; so that nothing has been done for the Greek text since the original edition of Bachet (1621).

I have now mentioned all the extant books which have been written directly upon Diophantos. Of books here omitted which are concerned with Diophantos *indirectly*, i.e. those which reproduce the substance of his solutions or solve his

gleich hinterher eine ausgelassen, iv. 52 eine doppelt, v. 11 eine ausgelassen, desgleichen v. 14, 25, 33, vi. 8, 13 und so weiter), die Zahlen verstümmelt, was aber das Aergste ist, die Bachet'schen kritischen Zeichen sind fast überall, die Klammer durchgängig weggefallen, so dass diese Ausgabe als Text des Diophant völlig unbrauchbar geworden ist," p. 283.

Accordingly Cantor errs when he says "Die beste *Textausgabe* ist die von Bachet de Meziriac mit Anmerkungen von Fermat. Toulouse, 1670." (*Gesch.* p. 396.)

problems or the like of them by different methods a list has been given at the outset. As I have already mentioned a statement that Joseph Auria of Naples wrote *circa* 1580 a translation of Diophantos which was found (presumably in MS. form) in the library of one Carl von Montchall, it is necessary here to give the indications we have of lost works upon Diophantos. First, we find it asserted by Vossius (as some have understood him) that the Englishman John Pell wrote an unpublished Commentary upon Diophantos. John Pell was at one time a professor of mathematics at Amsterdam and gave lectures there on Diophantos, but what Vossius says about his commentary may well be only a recommendation to undertake a commentary, rather than a historical assertion of its completion. Secondly, Schulz states in his preface that he had lately found a note in Schmeisser's *Orthodidaktik der Mathematik* that Hofrath Kausler by command of the Russian Academy prepared an edition of Diophantos[1]. Of this nothing whatever is known; if ever written, this edition must have been only for private use at St Petersburg.

I find a statement in the *New American Cyclopaedia* (New York, D. Appleton and Company), vol. VI. that "a complete translation of his (Diophantos') works into English was made by the late Miss Abigail Lousada, but has not been published."

---

[1] The whole passage of Schmeisser is: "Die mechanische, geistlose Behandlung der Algebra ist ins besondere von Herrn Hofrath Kausler stark gerügt worden. In der Vorrede zu seiner Ausgabe des *Uflakerschen Exempelbuchs* beginnt er so: 'Seit mehreren Jahren arbeitete ich für die Russisch-Kaiserliche Akademie der Wissenschaften Diophants unsterbliches Werk über die Arithmetik aus, und fand darin einen solchen Schatz von den feinsten, scharfsinnigsten algebraischen Auflösungen, dass mir die mechanische, geistlose Methode der neuen Algebra mit jedem Tage mehr ekelte u. s. w.'" (p. 33.)

CHAPTER IV.

§ 1. As it is my intention, for the sake of brevity and perspicuity, to make use of the modern algebraical notation in giving my account of Diophantos' problems and general methods, it will be necessary to describe once for all the machinery which our author uses for working out the solutions of his problems, or the notation by which he expresses the relations which would be represented in our time by algebraical equations, the extent to which he is able to manipulate unknown quantities, and so on. Apart, however, from the necessity of such a description for the proper and adequate comprehension of Diophantos, the general question of the historical development of algebraical notation possesses great intrinsic interest. Into the general history of this subject I cannot enter in this essay, my object being the elucidation of Diophantos; I shall accordingly in general confine myself to an account of his notation solely, except in so far as it is interesting to compare it with the corresponding notation of his editors and (in certain cases) that of other writers, as for example certain of the early Arabian algebraists.

§ 2. First, as to the representation of an unknown quantity. The unknown quantity, which Diophantos calls πλῆθος μονάδων ἄλογον i.e. "a number of units of which no account is given, or undefined" is denoted throughout (def. 2) by what is universally printed in the editions as the Greek letter ς with an accent, thus ς', or in the form ςᵒ. This symbol in verbal description he calls ὁ ἀριθμός, "the number" i.e. by implication, the number *par excellence* of the problem in question. In the cases where the symbol is used to denote inflected forms, e.g. accusative singular or dative plural, the terminations which would have been added to the stem of the full word ἀριθμός are printed above the symbol ς in the manner of an exponent, thus ς" (for ἀριθμόν, as τ" for τόν), ςⁿᵘ, the symbol being in addition doubled in the plural cases, thus ςςᵒⁱ, ςςⁿᵘˢ, ςςⁿⁿ ςςᵒⁱˢ for ἀριθμοί κ.τ.λ. When the symbol is used in practice, the coefficient is expressed by putting the required Greek numeral immediately after it, thus ςςᵒⁱ $\overline{ια}$ corresponds to $11x$, ς'$\bar{α}$ to x and so on.

Respecting the symbol ς as printed in the editions it is clear that, if ς' represents ἀριθμός, this sign must be different in kind from all the others described in the same definition, for they are clearly mere contractions of the corresponding names[1]. The opinion which seems to have been universally held as to the nature of the symbol of the text by the best writers on Diophantos is that of Nesselmann and Cantor[2]. Both authors tell us that the final sigma is used to denote the unknown quantity representing ἀριθμός, the complete word for it; and they imply in the passages referred to that this final sigma corresponds exactly to the x of modern equations, and that we have here the beginning of algebraical notation in the strict sense of the term, notation, that is, which is purely conventional and shows in itself no necessary connection between the symbol and the thing denoted by it. I must observe, however, that Nesselmann has in another place[3] corrected the impression which the reader might have got from the first passage referred to, that he regarded the use of the sign for ἀριθμός as a step towards genuine algebraical notation. He makes the acute observation that, as the symbol occurs in many places where it represents ἀριθμός used in the ordinary untechnical sense, and is therefore not exclusively used to designate the unknown quantity, the technical ἀριθμός, it must after all be more of the nature of an abbreviation than

[1] *Vide infra* δ̄ᵘ, κ̄ᵘ, δδ̄ᵘ, &c. contractions for δύναμις, κύβος, δυναμοδύναμις, &c.

[2] Nesselmann, pp. 290, 291. Cantor, p. 400.

[3] pp. 300, 301.

an algebraical symbol. This view is, I think, undoubtedly correct; but the question now arises: how can the final sigma of the Greek alphabet be an abbreviation for ἀριθμός? The difficulty of answering this question suggests a doubt which, so far as I am aware, has been expressed by no writer upon Diophantos up to the present time. Is the sign, which Bachet's text gives as a final sigma, really the final sigma at all? Nesselmann and Cantor seem never to have doubted it, for they both assign a reason why the final ς was appropriated for the designation of the unknown quantity, namely that it was the only letter of the Greek alphabet which was not already in use as a numeral. The question was suggested to me principally by the doubt whether the final sigma, ς, was developed as distinct from the form σ as early as the date of the MS. of Diophantos which Bachet used, or rather as early as the first copy of Diophantos, for the explanation of the sign is given by the author himself in the text of the second definition. This being extremely doubtful, if not absolutely impossible, in what way is its representation as a final sigma in Bachet's text to be accounted for? The MS. from which Bachet edited his Greek text is in the Bibliothèque Nationale, Paris, and I have not yet been able to consult it: but, fortunately, in a paper by M. Rodet in the *Journal Asiatique* (Janvier 1878), I found certain passages quoted by the author from Diophantos for the purpose of comparison with the algebra of Mohammed ibn Mūsā Al-Khārizmi. These passages M. Rodet tells us that he copied accurately from the identical MS. which Bachet used. On examination of these passages I found that in all but two cases of the occurrence of the sign for ἀριθμός it was given as the final sigma. In one of the other cases he writes for ὁ ἀριθμός (in this instance untechnical) the abbreviation ὁ ᾱˢ, and in the other case we find $\overline{qq}^{οι}$ for ἀριθμοί. In this last place Bachet reads $\overline{ςς}^{οι}$. But the same symbol $qq^{οι}$ which M. Rodet gives is actually found in three places in Bachet's own edition. (1) In his note to IV. 3 he gives a reading from his MS. which he has corrected in his own text and in which the signs $q\bar{a}$ and $qq\bar{η}$ occur. They must here necessarily signify ἀριθμός ᾱ and ἀριθμοί ῆ respectively because, although the sense requires

the notation corresponding to $\frac{1}{x}$, $\frac{8}{x}$, not x, $8x$, we know, not
only from Bachet's direct statement but also from the trans-
lation of certain passages by Xylander, that the sign for ἀριθμός
is in the MSS. very often carelessly written for ἀριθμοστόν and
its sign. (2) In the text of IV. 14 there is a sentence (marked
by Bachet as interpolated) which has the expression ꞯꞯϛ̄ where
again the context shows that ꞯꞯ is for ἀριθμοί. (3) At the
beginning of V. 12 there is a difficulty in the text; and Bachet
notes that his MS. has ὁ διπλασίων αὐτοῦ ꞯ...where a Vatican
MS. reads ὁ διπλασίων αὐτοῦ ἀριθμὸν... Xylander also notes
that his MS. had μήτε ὁ διπλασίων αὐτοῦ ᾱρ.... It is thus clear
that the MS. which Bachet used sometimes has the sign for
ἀριθμός in a form which is at least sufficiently like ꞯ to
be taken for it. This last very remarkable variation as compared with ϛ̄ᵒⁱ seemed at first sight inexplicable; but on reference to Gardthausen, *Griechische Palaeographie*, I found under
the head " hieroglyphisch-conventionell " an abbreviation ζ, $\zeta\!\zeta$
for ἀριθμός, ἀριθμοί, which the author gives as occurring in
the Bodleian MS. of Euclid[1]. The same statement is made
by Lehmann[2] (*Die tachygraphischen Abkürzungen der griechischen Handschriften*, 1880) who names as a sign for ἀριθμός,
found in the Oxford MS. of Euclid, a curved line similar to
that used as an abbreviation for καί. He adds that the ending
is placed above it, and the simple sign is doubled for the
plural. Lehmann's facsimile of the sign is like the form given
by Gardthausen, except that the angle in the latter is a little
more rounded by Lehmann. The form ꞯꞯᵒⁱ above mentioned
as given by M. Rodet and Bachet is also given by Lehmann
with a remark that it seems to be only a modification of the
other. If we take the form as given by Gardthausen, the change
necessary is the very slightest possible. Thus by assuming
this conventional abbreviation for ἀριθμός it is easy to see

---

[1] D'Orville MSS. x. 1 inf. 2, 30.

[2] p. 107: "Von Sigeln, welchen ich auch anderwärts begegnet bin, sind zu
nennen ἀριθμός, das in der Oxforder Euclidhandschrift mit einer der Note
καί ähnlichen Schlangenlinie bezeichnet wird. Die Endung wird darüber
gesetzt, zur Bezeichnung des Plurals wird das einfache Zeichen verdoppelt."

how it was thought by Bachet to be a final sigma and how
also it might be taken for the isolated form given by M. Rodet.

As I have already implied, I cannot think that the symbol
used by Diophantos is really a final sigma, ς. That the conventional abbreviation in the Euclid MS. and the sign in
Diophantos are identical is, I think, certain; and that neither
of the two is a final sigma must be clear if it can be proved
that one of them is not. Having consulted the MS. of the first
ten problems of Diophantos in the Bodleian Library, I conclude
that the symbol in this work cannot be a final sigma for the
following reasons. (1) The sign in the Bodleian MS. is written
thus, 'ᴄͦ͞ for ἀριθμός; and though the final sigma is used universally in this MS. at the end of words there is, besides
a slight difference in shape between the two, a very distinct
difference in size, the sign for ἀριθμός being always very much
larger. There are some cases in which the two come close
together, e.g. in the expression εἰς 'ᴄͦ͞ κ͞ε, and the difference is
very strongly marked. (2) As I have shown, the breathing is
prefixed before the sign. This, I think, shows clearly that the
symbol was regarded as an abbreviation of certain letters beginning with α the first letter of ἀριθμός. It is interesting also
to observe that in the Bodleian MS. there are certain cases in
which ἀριθμός in its untechnical, and ἀριθμός in its technical
sense follow each other as in ἔταξα τὸ τοῦ δευτέρου 'ᴄ͡ ἀριθμοῦ
ἑνός, where (contrary to what might be expected) the sign is
used for the untechnical ἀριθμός and the other is written in
full. This is a very remarkable piece of evidence to show that
the sign is an abbreviation and in no sense an algebraical
symbol. More remarkable still as evidence of this view is the
fact that in the same MS. the *word* ἀριθμός in the definition
ὁ δὲ μηδὲν τούτων τῶν ἰδιωμάτων κτησάμενος...ἔχων δὲ...
ἀριθμὸς καλεῖται is itself denoted by the symbol, so that in
the MS. there is absolutely no difference between the full name
and the symbol.

My conclusion therefore being (1) that the sign given as ς
in Bachet's text of Diophantos is not really the final sigma,
(2) that it is an abbreviation of some kind for ἀριθμός, the
question arises, How was this abbreviation arrived at? If it is

not a hieroglyph (and I have not yet found any evidence of its hieroglyphic origin), I would suggest that *it might very well be a corruption, after combination, of the two first letters of the word, Alpha and Rho.*

Before I go on to state when and how I conceive this contraction may have come about, I may observe that, given its possibility, my supposition has, it seems to me, everything in its favour. (1) It would explain, and is countenanced by, the solitary occurrence in M. Rodet's transcription of the contraction $\bar{a}^s$. (2) It would also explain the remarkable variation in the few words quoted from Xylander's note on v. 12, μήτε ὁ διπλασίων αὐτοῦ αρ̄ μο̄ ᾱ... These words are important because in no other sentence which he quotes in the Greek does any abbreviation of ἀριθμός occur. As his work is a Latin translation he rarely quotes the original Greek at all: hence we might have doubted whether the sign for ἀριθμός occurred in his MS. in the same form as in Bachet's. That it did occur in the same form is, however, clear from the note to III. 12[1]. That is to say, both αρ̄ and ⌐ are used in one and the same MS. to signify ἀριθμός. This circumstance is easily explained on my hypothesis; and I do not see how it can be explained on any other. But (3) the most important advantage that my theory would have is that it would establish uniformity between the different abbreviations used by Diophantos. It would show him to have proceeded on one invariable principle in fixing those abbreviations which we should naturally have expected to be parallel. Diophantos, in fact, appears to have proceeded thus. He took in all cases the first letter of the corresponding words *i.e. a, δ, κ, μ.* Then, as these could not be used alone for the reason that they all represented numbers, he added another letter to each. Now, as it happened, the second letter in each of the four words named occurred later in the

---

[1] In this problem it evidently occurred wrongly instead of the sign for the fraction ἀριθμοστόν (as was commonly the case in the MSS.), for after stating that the context showed the reading ἀριθμός to be wrong Xylander says: "Est sane in Graeco nota senarii ς. Sed locum habere non potest." Now s and ς are so much alike that what was taken for one might easily be taken for the other.

alphabet than the respective first letters. Thus a with ρ added, δ with v added, κ with v added, and μ with o added gave abbreviations *which could not be confounded with particular numbers.* No doubt, if the two letters in each case were not written in the same line by Diophantos, but the second raised above the other, the signs might, unless they or the separate letters were distinguished by some special marks, have been confused with numerical fractions. There would however be little danger of this; such confusion would be very unlikely to arise, for (a) the context would nearly always render it impossible, as also would (b) the constant recurrence of the same sign for a constantly recurring term, coupled with the fact that, if on any particular occasion it denoted a numerical fraction, it could and would naturally be expressed in lower terms. Thus, if δ^v, κ^v, μ^o were numerical fractions, they would be as unlikely to be written thus as we should be unlikely to write $\frac{4}{400}$, $\frac{20}{400}$, $\frac{40}{70}$. Indeed the only sign of the four which, written with the second letter placed as an *exponent* to the second, could reasonably be supposed to represent a numerical fraction is a^ρ, which might mean $\frac{1}{100}$. But, by a curious coincidence, confusion is avoided in this case; and the contraction, which I suppose to have taken place, might very well be an expedient adopted .for the purpose: thus we may have here an explanation why only *one* of the four signs $a\rho$, δv, κv, μo is contracted. (4) Again, if we assume ς to be a contraction of $a\rho$, we can explain the addition of terminations to mark cases and number in the place where the second letter of the other abbreviations is written. The sign $'\varsigma$ having no letter superposed originally, this addition of terminations was rendered practicable without resulting in any confusion. On its convenience it is unnecessary to enlarge, because it is clear that the symbol could then be used instead of the full word far more frequently than the others. Thus oblique cases of $\delta\acute{v}\nu\alpha\mu\iota\varsigma$ are written in full where oblique cases of $\dot{a}\rho\iota\theta\mu\acute{o}\varsigma$ would be abbreviated. For $\delta^{\tilde{v}}$, $\kappa^{\tilde{v}}$, $\mu^{\hat{o}}$ did not admit of the addition of terminations without possible confusion and certain clumsiness.

A few words will suffice to explain my views concerning the evolution of the sign for $\dot{a}\rho\iota\theta\mu\acute{o}\varsigma$. There are two alternatives possible. (1) Diophantos may not himself have made the contraction at all; he may have written the two letters in full. In that case I suppose the sign to be a cursive contraction used by scribes. I conceive it would then have come about through a tolerably obvious intermediate form, ς. The change from this to either of the two forms of the symbol used in MSS. for ἀριθμός is very slight, in one case being the loss of a stroke, in the other the loss of the loop of the ρ. (2) Diophantos may have used a sign approximately, if not exactly, like the form which we now find in the MSS. Now Gardthausen divides cursive writing into two kinds, which he calls "Majuskelcursive" and "Minuskelcursive." One or other of these terms would be applied to a type of writing according as the uncial or cursive element predominates. That in which the uncial element predominates is the "Majuskelcursive," which is intermediate between the uncial and the *cursive* as commonly understood. Gardthausen gives examples of MSS. which show the gradations through which writing passed from one to the other. Among the specimens of the "Majuskelcursive" writing he mentions a Greek papyrus, the date of which is 154 A.D., *i.e.* earlier than the time of Diophantos. From this MS. he quotes a contraction for the two letters *a* and *ρ*, namely *ᴄρ*. This may very well be the way in which Diophantos wrote the symbol; and, after being copied by a number of scribes successively, it might very easily come into the MSS. which we know in the slightly simplified form in which we find it[1].

---

[1] Much of what I have written above concerning the symbol for ἀριθμός appeared in an article "On a point of notation in the *Arithmetics* of Diophantos," which I contributed to the *Journal of Philology* (Vol. XIII. No. 25, pp. 107—113). Since that was written I have considered the subject more thoroughly, and I have been able to profit by a short criticism of my theory, as propounded in the article alluded to, by Mr James Gow in his recent *History of Greek Mathematics* (Camb. Univ. Press, 1884). In the Addenda thereto Mr Gow states that he does not think my suggestion that the supposed final sigma is a contraction of the first two letters of ἀριθμός is true, for three reasons. It is right that I should answer these objections in this place. I will take them in order.

1. Mr Gow argues:—"The contraction must be supposed to be as old as the time of Diophantus, for he describes the symbol as τὸ ς instead of τὰ or τῶ ἀρ. Yet Diophantus can hardly (as Mr Heath admits) have used cursive characters." Upon this objection I will remark that I do not think the descrip-

In the following pages, as it is impossible to say for certain what this sign really is, I shall not hesitate, where it is neces-

tion of the symbol as τὸ ς proves that the supposed contraction must be as old as the time of Diophantos himself. I see no reason, even, why Diophantos himself should not have written καὶ ἔστιν αὐτοῦ σημεῖον τὸ ἀρ. For (a) it seems to me most natural that the article should be in the same number as σημεῖον. Mr Gow might, I think, argue with equal force that the Greek should run, καὶ ἔστιν αὐτοῦ σημεῖα τὰ ἀρ. And yet σημεῖον is not disputed. Supposing, then, that we have assumed on other grounds that Diophantos used the first two letters, contracted or uncontracted, of ἀριθμός as his symbol for it, I do not see that the use of the article in the singular constitutes any objection to our assumption. (b) Besides the consideration that τὸ ἀρ is perfectly possible grammatically, we have yet other evidence for its possibility in expressions which we actually find in the text. The symbol for the fifth power of the unknown, or for δυναμόκυβος, is described thus: καὶ ἔστιν αὐτοῦ σημεῖον τὸ δκ̄ ἐπίσημον ἔχοντα υ, δκ^υ. In this case much more than in the supposed case of ἀρ should we have expected the plural article with δκ instead of the singular; but δκ̄ ἐπίσημον ἔχοντα υ is in apposition with δκ^υ and is looked upon as a single expression, and therefore preceded by the singular article τό. If we give full weight to these considerations, it must, I think, be admitted that Mr Gow's conclusion that the contraction must be as old as the time of Diophantos, whether true or not, is certainly not established by his argument from the description of the symbol as τὸ ς. Hence, as one link in the reasoning em- bodied in Mr Gow's first objection fails, the objection itself breaks down. Mr Gow appears to have misunderstood me when he attributes to me the inconsistency of supposing Diophantos to have used cursive characters, while in another place I had disclaimed such a supposition. It will be sufficiently clear from the explanation which I have given of the origin of the contraction that I am very far from assuming that Diophantos used cursive characters such as we now use in writing Greek. At the same time it is possible that Mr Gow's apparent mistake as to my meaning may be due to my own inadvertence in saying (in the article above-mentioned) "If it [the symbol] is not a hiero- glyph (and I have not found any evidence of its hieroglyphic origin), I would suggest that it might very well be a corruption of the two letters ἀρ" (printed thus), where, however, I did not mean the *cursive* letters any more than *uncials*.

2. I now pass to Mr Gow's second objection to my theory.

"The abbreviation s^ο for ἀριθμός in its ordinary sense is very rare indeed. It is not found in the MSS. of Nicomachus or Pappus, where it might most readily be expected. It may therefore be due only to a scribe who had some reminiscence of Diophantus." The meaning of this last sentence does not seem quite clear. I presume Mr Gow to mean "*In the rare cases where it does occur*, it may be due, &c." I do not know that I am concerned to prove that ς^ο for ἀριθμός is of very frequent occurrence in MSS. other than those of Diophantos. Still the form ς, which I have no hesitation in stating to be the same as ς̄, occurs often enough in the Oxford MS. of Euclid to make Gardthausen and

sary to designate it, to call it the final sigma for convenience'

Lehmann notice it. And, even if its use in that MS. is due to a scribe who had some reminiscence of Diophantos, I do not see that this consideration affects my theory in the least. In fact, it is not essential for my theory that this sign should occur in a single instance elsewhere than in Diophantos. It is really quite sufficient for my purpose that $\backsim^{\bar{o}}$ occurs in *Diophantos* for ἀριθμός *in its ordinary sense*, which I hold that I have proved.

3. Mr Gow's third objection is stated thus: "If *s* is *for* ἀρ. then, by analogy, the full symbol should be $s^{\bar{\iota}}$ (like $\delta^{\bar{\nu}}$, $\kappa^{\bar{\nu}}$) and not $s^{\bar{o}}$." (*a*) I must first remark that I consider that arguments from analogy are inapplicable in this case. The fact is that there are some points in which all the five signs of which I have been speaking are undoubtedly analogous, and others in which some are not; therefore to argue from analogy here is futile, because it would be equally easy to establish by that means either of two opposite conclusions. I might, with the same justice as Mr Gow, argue backwards that, since there is undoubtedly one point in which $s^{\bar{o}}$ and $\delta^{\bar{\nu}}$ are not analogous, namely the superposition in one case of terminations, in the other case of the second letter of the word, *therefore* the signs must be differently explained: a result which, so far as it goes, would favour my view. (*b*) Besides, even if we admit the force of Mr Gow's argument by analogy, is it true that $s^{\bar{\iota}}$ (on the supposition that *s* is for ἀρ) is analogous to $\delta^{\bar{\nu}}$ at all? I think not; for *s* does not correspond to δ, but (on my supposition) to δυ, and $\bar{\iota}$ only partially corresponds to ῡ, inasmuch as ι is the *third* letter of the complete word in one case, in the other υ is the *second* letter. (*c*) As a matter of fact, however, I maintain that my suggestion does satisfy analogy in one, and (I think) the most important respect, namely that (as I have above explained) Diophantos proceeded on one and the same system in making his abbreviations, taking in each case the two first letters of the word, the only difference being that in one case only are the two letters contracted into one sign.

Let us now enquire whether my theory will remove the difficulties stated by Mr Gow on p. 108 of his work. As reasons for doubting whether the symbol for ἀριθμός is really a final sigma, he states the following. "It must be remembered: (1) that it is only *cursive* Greek which has a final *sigma*, and that the cursive form did not come into use till the 8th or 9th century: (2) that inflexions are *appended* to Diophantus' symbol s′ (e.g. $s^{o\bar{\nu}}$, $ss^{o\bar{\iota}}$, etc.), and that his other symbols (except ϡ) are initial letters or syllables. The objection (1) might be disposed of by the fact that the Greeks had two *uncial* sigmas C and Σ, one of which might have been used by Diophantus, but I do not see my way to dismissing objection (2)." *First*, with regard to objection (1) Mr Gow rightly says that, supposing the sign were really s, it would be possible to dismiss this objection. On my theory, however, it is not necessary even to dismiss it: it does not exist. *Secondly*, my theory will dismiss objection (2). "Diophantus' other symbols (except ϡ) are *initial* letters or syllables." I answer "So is $\backsim$." "Inflexions are *appended* to Diophantus' symbol s′." I answer "True; but the nature of the sign itself made this convenient," as I have above explained.

sake, subject to the remarks which I have here made on the subject.

§ 3.   Next, as regards the notation which Diophantos used to express the different powers of the unknown quantity, i.e. corresponding to x^2, x^3 and so on. The square of the unknown is called by Diophantos δύναμις and denoted by the abbreviation[1] $δ^ῦ$. Now the word δύναμις ("power") is commonly used in Greek to express a square number. The first occurrence of the word in its technical sense is probably as early as the second half of the fifth century B.C. Eudemos uses it in quoting from Hippokrates (no doubt word for word) who lived about that time. The difference in use between the words δύναμις and τετράγωνος corresponds, in Cantor's view[2], to the difference between our terms "second power" and "square" respectively, the first having an arithmetical signification as referring to a number, the second a geometrical reference to a plane surface-area. The difference which Diophantos makes in their use is, however, not of this kind, and δύναμις in a geometrical sense, is not at all uncommon; hence the correctness of Cantor's suggestion is not at all certain. Both terms are used by Diophantos, but in very different senses. δύναμις, as we have said, or the contraction $δ^ῦ$ stands for the second power *of the unknown quantity*. It is the square of the unknown, ἀριθμός or $'ς^ο$, *only* and is never used to express the square of any other, i.e. any known number. For the square of any known number Diophantos uses τετράγωνος. The higher powers of the unknown quantity which Diophantos makes use of he calls κύβος, δυναμοδύναμις, δυναμόκυβος, κυβόκυβος, corresponding respectively to x^3, x^4, x^5, x^6. Beyond the sixth power he does not go, having no occasion for higher powers in the solutions of his

---

[1] I should observe with respect to the mark over the υ that it is given in the Greek text of Bachet as a circumflex accent printed in the form ~. By writers on Diophantos later than Bachet the sign has been variously printed as $δ^ῦ$, $δ^ῡ$ or $δ^ῠ$. I have generally denoted it by $δ^ῦ$, except in a few special cases, when quoting or referring to writers who use either of the other forms. The same remark applies to $μ^ο$, the abbreviation for μονάδες, as well as to the circumflex written above the denominators of Greek numerical fractions given in this chapter as examples from the text of Diophantos.

[2] *Geschichte der Mathematik*, p. 178.

problems. For these powers he uses the abbreviations $\kappa^{\bar{\nu}}$, $\delta\delta^{\bar{\nu}}$, $\delta\kappa^{\bar{\nu}}$, $\kappa\kappa^{\bar{\nu}}$ respectively. There is a difference between Diophantos' use of the complete words for the third and higher powers and that of δύναμις, namely that they are not always restricted like δύναμις to powers of the *unknown*, but may denote powers of ordinary known numbers as well. This is probably owing to the fact that, while there are two words δύναμις and τετράγωνος which both signify "square", there is only one word for a third power, namely κύβος. It is important, however, to observe that the abbreviations $\kappa^{\bar{\nu}}$, $\delta\delta^{\bar{\nu}}$, $\delta\kappa^{\bar{\nu}}$, $\kappa\kappa^{\bar{\nu}}$ are, like δύναμις and $\delta^{\bar{\nu}}$, *only* used to denote powers of the unknown. It is therefore obviously inaccurate to say that Diophantos "denotes the square of a number (δύναμις) by $\delta^{\bar{\nu}}$, the cube by $\kappa^{\bar{\nu}}$, and so on", the only number of which this could be said being the ς' (ἀριθμός) of the particular problem. The coefficients which the different powers of the unknown have are expressed by the addition of the Greek letters denoting numerals (as in the case of ἀριθμός itself), thus $\delta\kappa^{\bar{\nu}}$ $\overline{\kappa\varsigma}$ corresponds to $26x^5$. Thus in Diophantos' system of notation the signs $\delta^{\bar{\nu}}$ and the rest represent not merely the exponent of a power like the 2 in x^2, but the whole expression, x^2. There is no obvious connection between the symbol $\delta^{\bar{\nu}}$ and the symbol ς' of which it is the square, as there is between x^2 and x, and in this lies the great inconvenience of the notation. But upon this notation no advance was made by Xylander, or even by Bachet and Fermat. They wrote N (abbreviation of *Numerus*) for ς' of Diophantos, Q (*Quadratus*) for $\delta^{\bar{\nu}}$, C for $\kappa^{\bar{\nu}}$ (cubus) so that we find, for example, $1Q + 5N = 24$, corresponding to $x^2 + 5x = 24$. Thus these writers do in fact no more than copy Diophantos. We do, however, find other symbols used even before the publication of Xylander's Diophantos, e g. in 1572, the date of Bombelli's Algebra. Bombelli denotes the unknown and its powers by the symbols $\underset{\sim}{1}$, $\underset{\sim}{2}$, $\underset{\sim}{3}$, and so on. But it is certain that up to this time the common symbols had been *R* (*Radix* or *Res*), *Z* (*Zensus* i.e. square), *C* (*Cubus*). Apparently the first important step towards x^2, x^3 &c. was taken by Vieta, who wrote *Aq*, *Ac*, *Aqq*, &c. (abbreviated for *A quadratus* and so on) for the powers of *A*. This system, besides showing in itself the connection between the different

NOTATION AND DEFINITIONS OF DIOPHANTOS.

powers, has the infinite advantage that by means of it we can use in one and the same solution any number of unknown quantities. This is absolutely impossible with the notation used by Diophantos and the earlier algebraists. Diophantos does in fact never use more than one unknown quantity in the solution of a problem, namely the $\dot{a}\rho\iota\theta\mu\acute{o}s$ or ς'.

§ 4. Diophantos has no symbol for the operation of multi-plication: it is rendered unnecessary by the fact that his coefficients are all definite numerals, and the results are simply put down without any preliminary step which would make a symbol essential. On the ground that Diophantos uses only numerical expressions for coefficients instead of general symbols, it would occur to a superficial observer that there must be a great want of generality in his methods, and consequently that these, being (as might appear) only applicable to the particular numbers which the author uses, are necessarily interesting only as clever puzzles, but not general enough to be valuable to the serious student. To this objection I reply that, in the first place, it was absolutely impossible that Diophantos should have used any other than numerical coefficients for the reason that the available symbols of notation were already employed, the letters of the Greek alphabet always doing duty as numerals, with the exception of the final ς, which Diophantos was supposed to have used to represent the unknown quantity. In the second place I do not admit that the use of numerical coefficients only makes his solutions any the less general. This will be clearly seen when I come to give an account of his problems and methods. Next as to Diophantos' symbols for the operations of Addition and Subtraction. For the former no symbol at all is used: it is expressed by mere juxta-position, thus $\kappa^\upsilon\ \bar{a}\ \delta^\upsilon\ \overline{\iota\gamma}\ \overline{\varsigma\varsigma}\ \bar{\epsilon}$ corresponds to $x^3 + 13x^2 + 5x$. In this expression, however, there is no absolute term, and the addition of a simple numeral, as for instance $\bar{\beta}$, directly after $\bar{\epsilon}$, the coefficient of $\overline{\varsigma\varsigma}$, would cause confusion. This fact makes it necessary to have some term to indicate an absolute term in contradistinction to the variable terms. For this purpose Diophantos uses the word $\mu o\nu\acute{a}\delta\epsilon s$, or units, and denotes them after his usual manner by the abbreviation μ^δ. The *number* of monads is expressed as a coefficient.

Thus corresponding to the above expression $x^3 + 13x^2 + 5x + 2$ we should find in Diophantos $\kappa^{\hat{v}}\ \bar{a}\ \delta^{\hat{v}}\ \overline{\iota\gamma}\ \overline{\varsigma\varsigma}\ \bar{\epsilon}\ \mu^{\hat{o}}\ \bar{\beta}$. As Bachet uses the sign + for addition, he has no occasion for a distinct symbol to mark an absolute term. He would accordingly write $1\,C + 13\,Q + 5\,N + 2$. It is worth observing, however, that the Italians do use a symbol in this case, namely N (*Numero*), the first power of the unknown being with them R (*Radice*). Cossali[1] makes an interesting comparison between the terms used by Diophantos for the successive powers of the unknown and those employed by the Italians after their instructors, the Arabians. He observes that Fra Luca, Tartaglia, and Cardan begin their scale of powers from the power **0**, not from the power **1**, as does Diophantos, and compares the scales thus:

Scala Diofantea.			*Scala Araba.*	
	... ...		1.	Numero...il Noto.
x	1.	Numero...l'Ignoto.	2.	Cosa, Radice, Lato.
x^2	2.	Podestà.	3.	Censo.
x^3	3.	Cubo.	4.	Cubo.
x^4	4.	Podestà-Podestà.	5.	Censo di Censo.
x^5	5.	Podestà-Cubo.	6.	Relato 1^0.
x^6	6.	Cubo-Cubo.	7.	Censo di Cubo, o Cubo di Censo.
x^7	7.	. . ..	8.	Relato 2^0.
x^8	8.	. .. .	9.	Censo di Censo di Censo.
x^9	9.	. ...	10.	Cubo di Cubo.

and so on. So far, however, as this is meant to be a comparison between Diophantos and the early Arabian algebraists themselves (as the title Scala *Araba* would seem to imply), there appears to be no reason why Cossali should not have placed some term to express Diophantos' $\mu o \nu \acute{a} \delta \epsilon \varsigma$ in the same line with *Numero* in the other scale, and moved the numbers 1, 2, 3, &c. one place upwards in the first scale, or downwards

---

[1] Upon Wallis' comparison of the Diophantine with the Arabian scale Cossali remarks: "ma egli non ha riflettuto a due altre differenze tra le scale medesime. La prima si è, che laddove Diofanto denomina con singolarità *Numero* il numero ignoto, denominando *Monade* il numero dato di comparazione: gli antichi italiani degli arabi seguaci denominano questo il *Numero*; e *Radice*, o *Lato*, o *Cosa* il numero sconosciuto. La seconda è, che Diofanto comincia la scala dal numero ignoto; e Fra Luca, Tartaglia, Cardano la incominciano dal numero noto. Ecco le due scale di rincontro, onde meglio risaltino all' occhio le differenze loro." I. p. 195.

in the second.   As Diophantos does not go beyond the sixth power, the last three places in the first scale are left blank. An examination of these two scales will show also that the generation of the successive powers differs in the two systems. The Diophantine terms for them are based on the *addition* of exponents, the Arabic on their *multiplication*[1].   Thus the "cube-cube" means in Diophantos x^6, in the Italian and Arabic system x^9.   The first method of generation may (says Cossali) be described as the method by which each power is represented by the product of the two lesser powers which are nearest to it, *the method of multiplication;* the second the *method of elevation,* i.e. the method which forms by raising to the second or third power all powers which can be so formed, or the 4th, 6th, 8th, 9th, &c.   The intermediate powers which cannot be so formed are called in Italian *Relati.*   Thus the fifth power is Relato 1^0, x^7 is Relato 2^0, x^{10} is Censo di Relato 1^0, x^{11} is Relato 3^0, and so on.   Wallis calls these powers *supersolida,* reproduced by Montucla as *sursolides.*

For Subtraction Diophantos uses a symbol.   His full term for *Negation* is λεῖψ.ς, corresponding to ὕπαρξις, which denotes the opposite.   Thus λείψει (i.e. with the want of) stands for *minus,* and the symbol used to denote it in the MSS. is an inverted ψ or ⋏ (Def. 9 καὶ τῆς λείψεως σημεῖον ψ ἐλλιπὲς κάτω νεῦον ⋏) with the top shortened.   As Diophantos uses no distinct sign for +, it is clearly necessary, to avoid confusion, that all the negative terms in an expression should be placed together after all the positive terms.   And so in fact he does place them[2].   Thus corresponding to $x^3 - 5x^2 + 8x - 1$,

---

[1] This statement of Cossali's needs qualification however. There is at least one Arabian algebraist, Alkarkhī, the author of the *Fakhrī* referred to above (pp. 24, 25), who uses the Diophantine system of powers of the unknown depending on the *addition* of exponents. Alkarkhī, namely, expresses all powers of the unknown above the third by means of *māl,* his term for the square, and *ka'b,* his term for the cube of the unknown, as follows. The fourth power is with him *māl māl,* the fifth *māl ka'b,* the sixth *ka'b ka'b,* the seventh *māl māl ka'b,* the eighth *māl ka'b ka'b,* the ninth *ka'b ka'b ka'b,* and so on.

[2] Dr Heinrich Suter however has the erroneous statement that Diophantos would express $x^3 - 5x^2 + 8x - 1$ by $\kappa^{\bar{v}}$ $\bar{a}$ ⋏ $\delta^{\bar{v}}\epsilon$ s.$\bar{\eta}$ ⋏ $\mu^{\overset{o}{}}$ $\bar{a}$, which is exactly what he would *not* do.

Diophantos would write $\kappa^{\bar{v}}$ $\bar{a}$ ς^{oi} $\bar{\eta}$ ⅄ $\delta^{\bar{v}}$ $\bar{\epsilon}$ $\mu^{\bar{o}}$ $\bar{a}$. With respect
to this curious sign, given in the MSS. as ⅄ and described as an
inverted truncated ψ, I must here observe that I do not believe
it to be what it is represented as being. I do not believe that
Diophantos used so fantastic a sign for *minus* as an inverted
truncated ψ. In the first place, an inverted ψ seems too
curious a sign, and too far-fetched. To one who was looking
for a symbol to express *minus* many others more natural
and less fantastic than ⅄ must have suggested themselves.
Secondly, given that Diophantos used an inverted ψ, why
should he truncate it? Surely that must have been unnecessary; we could hardly have expected it unless, without it,
confusion was likely to arise; but ⅄ could hardly have been
confused with anything. It seems to me that this very trunca-
tion throws doubt on the symbol as we find it in the MS.
Hence I believe that the conception of this symbol as an
inverted truncated ψ is a mistake, and that the description of
it as such is not Diophantos' description; it appears to me to be
an explanation by a scribe of a symbol which he did not understand[1]. It seems to me probable that the true explanation is
the following: Diophantos proceeded in this case as in the others
which we have discussed (the signs for $\dot{a}\rho\iota\theta\mu\dot{o}s$, $\delta\dot{v}\nu\alpha\mu\iota s$, etc.).
As in those cases he took for his abbreviation the first letter of
the word with such an addition as would make confusion with
numbers impossible (namely the second letter of the word,
which in all happens to come later in the alphabet than the
corresponding first letter), so, in seeking an abbreviation for
$\lambda\epsilon\hat{\iota}\psi\iota s$ and cognate inflected forms developed from $\lambda\iota\pi$, he
first took the initial letter of the word. The uncial[2] form is
Λ. Clearly Λ by itself would not serve his purpose, since it
denotes a number. Therefore an addition is necessary. The
second letter is E, but ΛE is equally a number. The second

---

[1] I am not even sure that the description can be made to mean all that it is
intended to mean. $\dot{\epsilon}\lambda\lambda\iota\pi\dot{\epsilon}s$ scarcely seems to be sufficiently precise. Might it
not be applied to ⅄ with *any* part cut off, and not only shortened at the top?

[2] I adhere to the uncial form above for clearness' sake. If Diophantos used
the "Majuskelcursive" form, the explanation will equally apply, the difference
of form being for our purpose negligible.

letter of the stem λιπ is Ι, but ΛΙ is open to objection when so written. Hence Diophantos placed the Ι *inside* the Λ, thus, Λ. Of the possibility of this I entertain no doubt, because there are indubitable cases of combination, even in uncial writing, of two letters into one sign. I would refer in particular to Ⲧ, which is an uncial abbreviation for· ΤΑΛΑΝΤΟΝ. Now this sign, Λ, is an inverted and truncated ψ (written in the uncial form, Ⲩ); and we can, on this assumption, easily account for the explanation of the sign for *minus* which is given in the text.

For Division it often happens that no symbol is necessary, i.e. in the cases where one number is to be divided by another which will divide it without a remainder. In other cases the division has to be expressed by a fraction, whether the divisor be an absolute number or contain the variable. Thus the case of Division comes under that of Fractions. To express numerical fractions Diophantos adopts a uniform system, which is also seen in other writers. The numerator he writes in the ordinary line like a number; then he places the denominator above the line to the right of the numerator, in the same place as we should write an exponent, usually placing a circumflex accent over the end of it. Thus $\frac{17}{12}$ is represented by $ιζ^{\iota\hat{β}}$, $\frac{1}{100}$ is $\bar{α}^{\bar{ρ}}$, $\frac{5358}{10201}$ is (v. 12) ‚ετι $\bar{η}^{α.σ\hat{α}}$, $\frac{36621}{2704}$ is (IV. 17) γ.ϛχκ$\bar{α}^{β\psi\hat{δ}}$. Diophantos, however, often expresses fractions by simply putting ἐν μορίῳ or μορίου between the numerator and the denominator, i.e. one number divided by another. Cf. IV. 29 ρ$\bar{ν}$.‚ζ ᒧπδ μορίου κϛ.‚βρμδ, i.e. $\frac{1507984}{262144}$, and v. 25 β.‚εχ ἐν μορίῳ ρκβ.‚ακε, i.e. $\frac{25600}{1221025}$. There is a peculiarity in the way in which Diophantos expresses such complex fractions as $\dfrac{1834\frac{1}{2}}{121}$. It will be best understood by giving a typical case. This particular fraction Diophantos writes thus, ‚αωλδ$^{ρκ\hat{α}}$.$\bar{α}^{\hat{β}}$, that is, it is as if he had written with our notation $\frac{1834}{121}\frac{1}{2}$. Instances of this notation occur *passim*, cf. v. 2 τπθ$^{ρν\hat{β}}$.$\bar{α}^{\hat{β}}$ is equivalent to $\dfrac{389\frac{1}{2}}{152}$.

Bachet reproduces Diophantos' notation by writing in these cases $\frac{1834}{121}\frac{1}{2}$ and $\frac{389}{152}\frac{1}{2}$ respectively.

But there is another kind of fraction, besides the purely numerical one, which is continually occurring in the *Arithmetics*, such fractions namely as involve the unknown quantity in some form or other in their denominators. The simplest case is that in which the denominator is simply a power of the unknown, ς'. Concerning fractions of this kind Diophantos says (Def. 3) "As fractions named after numbers have similar names to those of the numbers themselves (thus a third is named from three, a fourth from four), so the fractions homonymous with what are called ἀριθμοί, or unknowns, are called after them, thus from ἀριθμός we name the fraction τὸ ἀριθμοστόν [i.e. $\frac{1}{x}$ from x], τὸ δυναμοστόν from δύναμις, τὸ κυβοστόν from κύβος, τὸ δυναμοδυναμοστόν from δυναμοδύναμις, τὸ δυναμοκυβοστόν from δυναμόκυβος, and τὸ κυβοκυβοστόν from κυβόκυβος. And every such fraction shall have its symbol after the homonymous number with a line to indicate the species" (i.e. the order or power)[1]. Thus we find, for example, IV. 3, $\bar{\eta}^{a\varsigma^\backprime}$ corresponding to $\frac{8}{x}$, or with the genitive termination of ἀριθμοστοῦ, e.g., IV. 16, $\overline{\lambda\epsilon}^{\sigma o\hat{v}.\bar{a}}$ or $\frac{35}{x}$. Cf. $\sigma\bar{v}^{\delta\hat{v}.\bar{a}}$ or $\frac{250}{x^2}$. Side by side with the employment of the symbols to express fractions corresponding to $\frac{1}{x}$, $\frac{1}{x^2}$, &c., we find the terms ἀριθμοστόν, δυναμοστόν κ.τ.λ. used in full: this is regularly the case when the numerator of the fraction itself contains a numerical fraction. Thus in v. 31 ἀριθμοστοῦ $\bar{a}$ $\bar{a}^\beta$ corresponds to $\frac{1\frac{1}{2}}{x}$ and δυναμοστὸν $\bar{\varsigma}$ $\bar{a}^\delta$ to $\frac{6\frac{1}{4}}{x^2}$.

Diophantos extends his use of fractions still further to more complicated cases in which the numerator and denominator

---

[1] The meaning of the last sentence is not quite clear. I am inclined to think there is something wrong with the text, which stands in Bachet as follows: ἕξει δὲ ἕκαστον αὐτῶν ἐπὶ τοῦ ὁμωνύμου ἀριθμοῦ σημεῖον γράμμην ἔχον διαστέλλουσαν τὸ εἶδος. This he translates, "Habebit autem quaelibet pars à sibi cognomine numero notam et literam superscriptam quae speciem à specie distinguat." Here apparently *literam* corresponds to γράμμην.

may be compound expressions themselves, involving the un-
known quantity.   Thus, IV. 37, we have $\mu^{\hat{o}}\ \bar{\theta}\ \pitchfork\ \varsigma^{o\bar{\upsilon}}\ \bar{\alpha}^{\varsigma o\bar{\upsilon}.\bar{\alpha}}$, i.e.
$\dfrac{9-x}{x}$.   When, however, the denominator is a compound ex-
pression Diophantos uses the expedient which he adopts in the
case of large numbers occurring as numerator or denominator,
namely, the insertion between the expressions denoting the
numerator and denominator of the term ἐν μορίῳ or μορίου.
Thus in VI. 13 we find, $\delta^{\bar{\upsilon}}\ \bar{\xi}.\mu^{\hat{o}}\ \bar{\beta\phi\kappa}$ ἐν μορίῳ $\delta^{\bar{\upsilon}}\delta^{\bar{\upsilon}}\ \bar{\alpha}\ \mu^{\hat{o}}$ ↗ λείψει
$\delta^{\bar{\upsilon}}\ \bar{\xi}$, i.e. $\dfrac{60x^2+2520}{x^4+900-60x^2}$, and in VI. 21 $\kappa^{\bar{\upsilon}}\ \bar{\beta}.\delta^{\bar{\upsilon}}\bar{\epsilon}.\bar{\varsigma\varsigma}^{o\grave{\iota}}\ \bar{\delta}\ \mu^{\hat{o}}\ \bar{\alpha}.$ ἐν
μορίῳ $\delta^{\bar{\upsilon}}\ \bar{\alpha}\ \bar{\varsigma\varsigma}\ \bar{\beta}\ \mu^{\hat{o}}\ \bar{\alpha}$ corresponding to $\dfrac{2x^3+5x^2+4x+1}{x^2+2x+1}$.

To connect the two sides of an equation Diophantos uses
words ἴσος or ἴσος ἐστι, or the oblique cases of ἴσος when they
are made necessary by grammatical construction.   It would
appear, at least from Bachet's edition of Diophantos, that the
equations were put down in the ordinary course of writing,
and that they were not placed in separate lines for each step
in the process of simplification, being in fact written in the
same way as the propositions of Euclid.   We have, however,
signs of a system by which the steps were *tabulated* in a
manner very similar to that of modern algebraical work, so
that by means of a sort of skeleton of the procedure we get a
kind of bird's-eye view of its course, in the manuscript of Diophantos which Bachet himself used.   We have it on the
authority of M. Rodet, who in an article in the *Journal Asiatique*[1] has occasion to quote certain passages from the text of
Diophantos, that to certain problems is attached a tabular
view of the whole process, which Bachet has not in his edition
reproduced at all.   M. Rodet gives from the MS. several instances.   In these we have equations set down in a form very
like the modern, the two members being connected by the
letter *i* (abbreviated for ἴσοι) as the sign of equality[2].   Besides

---

[1] Janvier, 1878.

[2] Here again the abbreviation is explicable on the same principle as those
which I have previously discussed.   ι by itself means 10, but a distinguishing
mark is ready to hand in the breathing placed over it.

the equations written in this form there are on the left side words signifying the nature of the operation in passing from one particular step to the next. To illustrate this I will give the table after Rodet for the very simple problem I. 32. "To find two numbers whose sum, and the difference of whose squares are given." (The sum is supposed to be 20, the difference of squares is 80.) Diophantos assumes the difference of the two numbers themselves to be two ἀριθμοί. I will put the Greek table on the left side, and on the right the modern equivalent. The operations will be easily understood.

ἔκθεσις	ςᾱ μο ῑ	⋮ μο ῑ ⑁ ςᾱ]	Put for the numbers $x+10$, $10-x$.	
τετράγωνος	δῦ ᾱ ςςοὶ κ̄μο͂.ρ̄	⋮ δῐ ᾱ.μο͂ρ⑁ ςςκ̄	Squaring we have $x^2 + 20x + 100$,	
				$x^2 + 100 - 20x$.
ὑπεροχή	ςς μ̄	ι μο͂.π̄	The diff., $40x = 80$.	
μερισμός	ς ᾱ	ι μο͂.β̄	Dividing, $x = 2$.	
ὕπαρξις	ψ μο͂.ῑβ	εᾺ μο͂.η̄	Result, greater is 12, less is 8.	

The comparison of these two forms under which the same operations appear is most interesting. It is indeed obvious that if we take the skeletons of work given in the MS. the similarity is most striking. It is true that the Greek notation for the equations is very much inferior to the modern, but on the other hand the words indicating the operations make the whole very little less concise than the modern work. The omission of these tabular skeletons supplied in the MS. is a very grave defect in Bachet's edition, and thanks are due to M. Rodet for his interesting quotations from the original source. The same writer quotes two other such tables, which, however, for brevity's sake, we omit here. Though in the MS. the sign ι is used to denote equality, Bachet makes no use of any symbol for the purpose in his Latin translation. He uses throughout the full Latin word. It is interesting however to observe that in his earlier translation (1575) Xylander does use a symbol to denote equality, namely ‖, two short vertical parallel lines, in his notes to Diophantos. Thus we find, for example (p. 76) $1Q + 12 ‖ 1Q + 6N + 9$, which we ·should express by $x^2 + 12 = x^2 + 6x + 9$.

§ 5. Now that we have described in detail Diophantos' method of expressing algebraical quantities and relations, we may remark on the general system which he uses that it is essentially different in its character from the modern notation. While in modern times signs and symbols have been developed which have no intrinsic relationship to the things which they symbolise, but depend for their use upon convention, the case is quite different with Diophantos, where algebraic notation takes the form of mere abbreviation of words which are considered as pronounced or implied. This is partly proved by the symbols themselves, which in general consist of the first letter or letters of words (so written as to avoid confusion), the only possible exception being the supposed final sigma, ς, for ἀριθμός or the unknown quantity. Partly also it is proved by the fact that Diophantos uses the symbol and the complete word very often quite indifferently. Thus we find often in the same sentence ς or ςς and ἀριθμός, ἀριθμοί, δ⁰ and δύναμις, ⋔ and λείψει, and so on. The strongest proof, however, that Diophantos' algebraic notation was mere abbreviation is found in the fact that the abbreviations, which are his algebraical symbols, are used for the corresponding words even when those words have a quite different signification. So in particular the symbol ς is used as an abbreviation for ἀριθμός, when the word is used, not in its technical Diophantine sense for the unknown, but in its ordinary meaning of *a number*, especially in enunciations where ἀριθμός in its ordinary sense naturally occurs oftenest. Similarly ⋔ is not used only for λείψει but also for other inflexional forms of the stem of this word, e.g. for λιπόν or λείψας in III. 3: Εὑρεῖν τρεῖς ἀριθμοὺς ὅπως ὁ ἀπὸ τοῦ συγκειμένου ἐκ τῶν τριῶν ⋔ ἕκαστον ποιῇ τετράγωνον. Other indications are (1) the separation of the symbols and coefficients by particles [cf. I. 43, ςς⁰ⁱ ἄρα ῑ]; (2) the addition of terminations to the symbol to represent the different cases. Nesselmann gives a good instance in which many of these peculiarities are combined, ςς⁰ⁱ ἄρα ῑ μ⁰ λ ἴσοι εἰσὶν ςς⁰ⁱˢ ῑα μονάσι ῑε. I. ad fin.

In order to determine in what place, in respect of systems of algebraic notation, Diophantos stands, Nesselmann observes that we can, as regards the form of exposition of algebraic operations and equations, distinguish three historical stages of development, well marked and easily discernible. 1. The first stage Nesselmann represents by the name *Rhetoric Algebra*, or "reckoning by complete words." The characteristic of this stage is the absolute want of all symbols, the whole of the calculation being carried on by means of complete words, and forming in fact continuous prose. As representatives of this first stage Nesselmann mentions Iamblichos (of whose algebraical work he quotes a specimen in his fifth chapter) "and all Arabian and Persian algebraists who are at present known." In their works we find no vestige of algebraic symbols; the same may be said of the oldest Italian algebraists and their followers, and among them Regiomontanus. 2. The second stage Nesselmann proposes to call the *Syncopated Algebra*. This stage is essentially *rhetorical* and therein like the first in its treatment of questions, but we now find for often-recurring operations and quantities certain abbreviational symbols. To this stage belongs Diophantos and after him all the later Europeans until about the middle of the seventeenth century (with the exception of the isolated case of Vieta, who, as we have seen, initiated certain changes which anticipated later notation to some extent; we must make an exception too, though Nesselmann does not mention these cases, in favour of certain symbols used by Xylander and Bachet, ‖ being used by the former to express equality, + and − by both, as also the ordinary way of representing a fraction by placing the numerator above the denominator separated by a line drawn horizontally[1]). 3. To the third stage Nesselmann gives the name *Symbolic Algebra*, which uses a complete system of notation by signs having no visible connection with the words or things which they represent, a complete language of symbols, which supplants entirely the *rhetorical* system, it being possible to work out a solution without using a single word of the ordinary written language, with the exception (for clearness' sake) of

[1] These are only a few scattered instances. Nesselmann, though he does not mention Xylander's and Bachet's symbols, gives other instances of isolated or common uses of signs, as showing that the division between the different stages is not *sharply* marked. He instances the use of one operational algebraic symbol by Diophantos, namely ⋔, for which Lucas de Burgo uses *m* (and *p* for *plus*), Targalia φ. Vieta has + and −, also = for ~. Oughtred uses ×, and Harriot expresses multiplication by juxtaposition.

a conjunction here and there, and so on. Neither is it the Europeans posterior to the middle of the seventeenth century who were the first to use *Symbolic* forms of Algebra. In this they were anticipated many centuries by the Indians.

As examples of these three stages Nesselmann gives three instances quoting word for word the solution of a quadratic equation by Mohammed ibn Mūsā as an example of the first stage, and the solution of a problem from Diophantos to illustrate the second. Thus:

First Stage. Example from Mohammed ibn Mūsā (ed. Rosen, p. 5). "A *square* and ten of its *roots* are equal to nine and thirty dirhems, that is, if you add ten *roots* to one *square*, the sum is equal to nine and thirty. The solution is as follows: halve the number of *roots*, that is in this case five; then multiply this by itself, and the result is five and twenty. Add this to the nine and thirty, which gives sixty-four; take the square root, or eight, and subtract from it half the number of *roots,* namely five, and there remain three: this is the *root* of the *square* which was required and the square itself is *nine*[1]."

Here we observe that not even are symbols used for numbers, so that this example is even more "*rhetorical*" than the work of Iamblichos who does use the Greek symbols for his numbers.

Second stage. As an example of Diophantos I give a translation word for word[2] of II. 8. So as to make the symbols correspond exactly I use S (*Square*) for $\delta^{\ddot{v}}$ ($\delta\acute{v}\nu\alpha\mu\iota\varsigma$), N (*Number*) for ς, U for *Units* ($\mu o\nu\acute{a}\delta\varepsilon\varsigma$).

"To divide the proposed square into two squares. Let it be proposed then to divide 16 into two squares. And let the first

[1] Thus Mohammed ibn Mūsā states in words the solution
$$x^2 + 10x = 39,$$
$$x^2 + 10x + 25 = 64,$$
therefore $\qquad x + 5 = 8,$
$$x = 3.$$

[2] I have used the full words whenever Diophantos does so, and to avoid confusion have written *Square* and *Number* in the technical sense with a capital letter, and italicised them.

be supposed to be One *Square*. Thus 16 minus One *Square* must be equal to a square. I form the square from any number of N's minus as many U's as there are in the side of 16 U's. Suppose this to be 2 N's minus 4 U's. Thus the square itself will be 4 *Squares*, 16 U. minus 16 N.'s. These are equal to 16 *Units* minus One *Square*. Add to each the negative term (λεῖψις, deficiency) and take equals from equals. Thus 5 *Squares* are equal to 16 *Numbers ;* and the *Number* is 16 fifths. One [square] will be 256 twenty-fifths, and the other 144 twenty-fifths, and the sum of the two makes up 400 twenty-fifths, or 16 *Units*, and each [of the two found] is a square.

Of the *third stage* any exemplification is unnecessary.

§ 6. To the form of Diophantos' notation is due the fact that he is unable to introduce into his questions more than one unknown quantity. This limitation has made his procedure often very different from our modern work. In the first place he performs eliminations, which we should leave to be done in the course of the work, before he prepares to work out the problem, by expressing everything which occurs in such a way as to contain only one unknown. This is the case in the great majority of questions of the first Book, which are cases of the solution of determinate simultaneous equations of the first order with two, three, or four variables; all these Diophantos expresses in terms of one unknown, and then proceeds to find it from a simple equation. In cases where the relations between these variables are complicated, Diophantos shows extraordinary acuteness in the selection of an unknown quantity. Secondly, however, this limitation affects much of Diophantos' work injuriously, for while he handles problems which are by nature indeterminate and would lead with our notation to an indeterminate equation containing two or three unknowns, he is compelled by limitation of notation to assign to one or other of these arbitrarily-chosen numbers which have the effect of making the problem a determinate one. However it is but fair to say that Diophantos in assigning an arbitrary value to a quantity is careful to tell us so, saying " for such and such a quantity we put any number whatever, say such and such a one." Thus it can hardly be said that there is (in general) any loss of universality. We may say, then, that in general Diophantos is obliged to express all his unknowns in terms, or as functions, of one variable. There is something excessively interesting in the clever devices by which he contrives so to express them in terms of his single unknown, ς, as that by that very expression of them all conditions of the problem are satisfied except one, which serves to complete the solution by determining the value of ς. Another consequence of Diophantos' want of other symbols besides ς to express more variables than one is that, when (as often happens) it is necessary in the course of a problem to work out a subsidiary problem in order to obtain the coefficients &c. of the functions of ς which express the quantities to be found, in this case the required unknown which is used for the solution of the new subsidiary problem is denoted by the same symbol ς; hence we have often in the same problem the same variable ς used with two different meanings. This is an obvious inconvenience and might lead to confusion in the mind of a careless reader. Again we find two cases, II. 29 and 30, where for the proper working-out of the problem two unknowns are imperatively necessary. We should of course use x and y; but Diophantos calls the first ς as usual; the second, for want of a term, he agrees to call "*one unit*," i.e. 1. Then, later, having completed the part of the solution necessary to find ς he substitutes its value, and uses ς over again to denote what he had originally called "1"—the second variable—and so finds it. This is the most curious case I have met with, and the way in which Diophantos after having worked with this "1" along with other numerals is yet able to pounce upon the particular place where it has passed to, so as to substitute ς for it, is very remarkable. This could only be possible in particular cases such as those which I have mentioned : but, even here, it seems scarcely possible now to work out the problem using x and 1 for the variables as originally taken by Diophantos without falling into confusion. Perhaps, however, it may not be impossible that Diophantos in working out the problems before writing them down as we have them may have given the "1" which stood for a variable some mark by which

H. D.   6

he could recognise it and distinguish it from other numbers. For the problems themselves see Appendix.

It may be in some measure due to the defects of notation in his time that Diophantos will have in his solutions no numbers whatever except *rational* numbers, in which, in addition to surds and imaginary quantities, he includes *negative* quantities. Of a negative quantity *per se*, i.e. without some positive quantity to subtract it from, Diophantos had apparently no conception. Such equations then as lead to surd, imaginary, or negative roots he regards as useless for his purpose : the solution is in these cases ἀδύνατος, impossible. So we find him describing the equation $4 = 4x + 20$ as ἄτοπος because it would give $x = -4$. Diophantos makes it throughout his object to obtain solutions in rational numbers, and we find him frequently giving, as a preliminary, conditions which must be satisfied, which are the conditions of a result rational in Diophantos' sense. In the great majority of cases when Diophantos arrives in the course of a solution at an equation which would give an irrational result he retraces his steps and finds out how his equation has arisen, and how he may by altering the previous work substitute for it another which shall give a rational result. This gives rise, in general, to a subsidiary problem the solution of which ensures a rational result for the problem itself. Though, however, Diophantos has no notation for a surd, and does not admit surd results, it is scarcely true to say that he makes no use of quadratic equations which lead to such results. Thus, for example, in v. 33 he solves such an equation so far as to be able to see to what integers the solution would approximate most nearly.

CHAPTER V.

§ **1.** Before I give an account in detail of the different methods which Diophantos employs for the solution of his problems, so far as they can be classified, I must take exception to some remarks which Hankel has made in his account of Diophantos (*Zur Geschichte der Mathematik in Alterthum und Mittelalter*, Leipzig, 1874, pp. 164—5). This account does not only possess literary merit: it is the work of a man who has read Diophantos. His remarks therefore possess exceptional value as those of a man particularly well qualified to speak on matters relating to the history of mathematics, and also from the contrast to the mass of writers who have thought themselves capable of pronouncing upon Diophantos and his merits, while they show unmistakeably that they have not studied his work. Hankel, who has read Diophantos with appreciation, says in the place referred to, "The reader will now be desirous to become acquainted with the classes of indeterminate problems which Diophantos treats of, and his methods of solution. As regards the first point, we must observe that in the 130 (or so) indeterminate questions, of which Diophantos treats in his great work, there are over 50 different classes of questions, which are arranged one after the other without any recognisable classification, except that the solution of earlier questions facilitates that of the later. The first Book only contains determinate algebraic equations; Books II. to V. contain for the most part indeterminate questions, in which expressions which involve in the first or second degree two or more variables are to be made squares or cubes. Lastly, Book VI. is concerned

6—2

with right-angled triangles regarded purely arithmetically, in which some one linear or quadratic function of the sides is to be made a square or a cube. *That is all that we can pronounce about this elegant series of questions without exhibiting singly each of the fifty classes.* Almost more different in kind than the questions are their solutions, and we are completely unable to give an even tolerably exhaustive review of the different varieties in his procedure. *Of more general comprehensive methods there is in our author no trace discoverable : every question requires an entirely different method, which often, even in the problems most nearly related to the former, refuses its aid. It is on that account difficult for a more modern mathematician even after studying* 100 *Diophantine solutions to solve the* 101*st question ;* and if we have made the attempt and after some vain endeavours read Diophantos' own solution, we shall be astonished to see how suddenly Diophantos leaves the broad high-road, dashes into a side-path and with a quiet turn reaches the goal : often enough a goal with reaching which we should not be content ; we expected to have to climb a difficult path, but to be rewarded at the end by an extensive view ; instead of which our guide leads by narrow, strange, but smooth ways to a small eminence ; he has finished ! He lacks the calm and concentrated energy for a deep plunge into a single important problem : and in this way the reader also hurries with inward unrest from problem to problem, as in a succession of riddles, without being able to enjoy the individual one. Diophantos dazzles more than he delights. He is in a wonderful measure wise, clever, quick-sighted, indefatigable, but does not penetrate thoroughly or deeply into the root of the matter. As his questions seem framed in obedience to no obvious scientific necessity, often only for the sake of the solution, the solution itself also lacks perfection and deeper signification. He is a brilliant performer in the *art* of indeterminate analysis invented by him, but the *science* has nevertheless been indebted, at least directly, to this brilliant genius for few methods, because he was deficient in speculative thought which sees in the True more than the Correct. That is the general impression, which I have gained from a thorough and repeated study of Diophantos' arithmetic."

Now it will be at once obvious that, if Hankel's representation is correct, any hope of giving a general account of Diophantos' methods such as I have shown in the heading of this chapter would be perfectly illusory. Hankel clearly asserts that there are no general methods distinguishable in the *Arithmetics*. On the other hand we find Nesselmann saying (pp. 308—9) that the use of determinate numerals in Diophantos' problems constitutes no loss of generality, for throughout he is continually showing how other numerals than those which he takes will satisfy the conditions of the problem, showing "that his whole attention is directed to the explanation of the *method*, for which purpose numerical examples only serve as means"; this is proved by his frequently stopping short, when the method has been made sufficiently clear, and the remainder of the work is mere straightforward calculation. Cf. v. 14, 18, 19, 20 &c. It is true that this remark may only apply to the isolated "method" employed in one particular problem and in no other; but Nesselmann goes on to observe that, though the Greeks and Arabians used only numerical examples, yet they had general rules and methods for the solution of equations, as we have, only expressed in words. "So also Diophantos, whose methods have, it is true, in the great majority of cases no such universal character, gives us a perfectly general rule for solving what he calls a double-equation." These remarks Nesselmann makes in the 7th chapter of his book; the 8th chapter he entitles "Diophantos' treatment of equations[1]," in which he gives an account of Diophantos' solutions of (1) Determinate, (2) Indeterminate equations, classified according to their kind. Chapter 9 of his book Nesselmann calls "Diophantos' methods of solution[2]." These "methods" he gives as follows[3]: (1) "The adroit assumption of unknowns." (2) "Method of reckoning

[1] "Diophant's Behandlung der Gleichungen."
[2] "Diophant's Auflösungsmethoden."
[3] (1) "Die geschickte Annahme der Unbekannten." (2) "Methode der Zurückrechnung und Nebenaufgabe." (3) "Gebrauch des Symbols für die Unbekannte in verschiedenen Bedeutungen." (4) "Methode der Grenzen." (5) "Auflösung durch blosse Reflexion." (6) "Auflosung in allgemeinen Ausdrücken." (7) "Willkührliche Bestimmungen und Annahmen." (8) "Gebrauch des rechtwinkligen Dreiecks."

backwards and auxiliary questions." (3) "Use of the symbol for the unknown in different significations." (4) "Method of Limits." (5) "Solution by mere reflection." (6) "Solution in general expressions." (7) "Arbitrary determinations and assumptions." (8) "Use of the right-angled triangle."

At the end of chapter 8 Nesselmann observes that it is not the solution of equations that we have to wonder at, but the perfect art which enabled Diophantos to avoid such equations as he could not technically solve. We look (says Nesselmann) with astonishment at his operations, when he reduces the most difficult questions by some surprising turn to a simple equation. Then, when in the 9th chapter Nesselmann passes to the "methods," he prefaces it by saying : "To represent perfectly Diophantos' methods in all their completeness would mean nothing else than copying his book outright. The individual characteristics of almost every question give him occasion to try upon it a peculiar procedure or found upon it an artifice which cannot be applied to any other question....... Meanwhile, though it may be impossible to exhibit all his methods in any short space, yet I will try to give some operations which occur more often or are by their elegance particularly noticeable, and (where possible) to make clear their scientific principle by a general exposition from common stand-points." Now the question whether Diophantos' methods can be exhibited briefly, and whether there can be said to be any methods in his work, must depend entirely upon the meaning we attach to the word "method." Nesselmann's arrangement seems to me to be faulty inasmuch as (1) he has treated Diophantos' solution of equations—which certainly proceeded on fixed rules, and therefore by "*method*"—separately from what he calls "methods of solution," thereby making it appear as though he did not look upon the "treatment of equations" as "methods." Now certainly the "treatment of equations" should, if anything, have come under the head of "methods of solution"; and obviously the very fact that Diophantos solved equations of various kinds by fixed rules itself disproves the assertion that no *methods* are discernible. (2) The classification under the head of "Methods of solution" seems unsatisfactory. In the first

place, some of the classes can hardly be said to be *methods* of
solution at all; thus the third, "Use of the symbol for the
unknown in different significations", might be more justly
described as a "hindrance to the solution"; it is an *inconvenience* to which Diophantos was reduced owing to the want of
notation. Secondly, on the assumption of the eight "methods"
as Nesselmann describes them, it is really not surprising that
"no complete account of them could be given without copying
the whole book." To take the first, "the adroit assumption of
unknowns." Supposing that a number of distinct, different
problems are proposed, the existence of such differences makes
a different assumption of an unknown in each case absolutely
necessary. That being so, how could it be possible to give a
rule for all cases? The best that can be done is an enumeration of typical instances. The assumption that the methods
of Diophantos cannot be tabulated, on the evidence of this
fact, i.e., because no rule can be given for the "adroit assumption of unknowns" which Nesselmann classes as a "method," is
entirely unwarranted. Precisely the same may be said of
"methods" (2), (5), (6), (7). For these, by the very nature of
things, no rule can be given: they bear in their names so much
of *rule* as can be assigned to them. The case of (4), "the
Method of Limits", is different; here we have the only class
which exemplifies a "method" in the true sense of the term,
i.e. as an *instrument* for solution. And accordingly in this case
the method can be exhibited, as I hope to show later on:
(8) also deserves to some extent the name of a "method."

I think, therefore, that neither Nesselmann nor Hankel has
treated satisfactorily the question of Diophantos' methods, the
former through a faulty system of classification, the latter by
denying that general methods are anywhere discernible in
Diophantos. It is true that we cannot find in Diophantos' work
statements of method put generally as book-work to be applied
to examples. But it was not Diophantos' object to write a text-
book of Algebra. For this reason we do not find the separate
rules and limitations for the solution of different kinds of equations systematically arranged, but we have to seek them out
laboriously from the whole of his work, gathering scattered

indications here and there, and so formulate them in the best
way we can. Such being the case, I shall attempt in the following pages of this chapter to give a detailed account of what may
be called general methods running through Diophantos. For
the reasons which I have stated, my arrangement will be different
from that of Nesselmann, who is the only author who has
attempted to give a complete account of the methods. I shall
not endeavour to describe as methods such classes of solutions as
are some which are, by Nesselmann, called "methods of solution":
and, in accordance with his remark that these "methods" can
only be adequately described by a transcription of the entire
work, I shall leave them to be gathered from a perusal of
my reproduction of Diophantos' book which is given in my
Appendix.

§ 2.   I shall begin my account with

DIOPHANTOS' TREATMENT OF EQUATIONS.

This subject falls naturally into two divisions : (A) Determinate equations of different degrees.   (B)   Indeterminate
equations.

(A.) Determinate equations.

Diophantos was able without difficulty to solve determinate
equations of the first and second degree ; of a cubic equation we
find in his *Arithmetics* only one example, and that is a very
special case. The solution of simple equations we may pass
over ; hence we must separately consider Diophantos' method
of solution of (1) Pure equations, (2) Adfected, or mixed
quadratics.

(1)   *Pure determinate equations.*

By *pure* equations I mean those equations which contain
only one power of the unknown, whatever the degree. The
solution is effected in the same way whatever the exponent of
the term in the unknown; and Diophantos regards pure equations
of any degree as though they were simple equations of the first

degree[1]. He gives a general rule for this case without regard to the degree : "If we arrive at an equation containing on each side the same term but with different coefficients, we must take equals from equals, until we get one term equal to another term. But, if there are on one or on both sides negative terms, the deficiencies must be added on both sides until all the terms on both sides are positive. Then we must take equals from equals until one term is left on each side." After these operations have been performed, the equation is reduced to the form $Ax^m = B$ and is considered solved. The cases which occur in Diophantos are cases in which the value of x is found to be a rational number, integral or fractional. Diophantos only recognise one value of x which satisfies this equation; thus if m is even, he gives only the positive value, a negative value *per se* being a thing of which he had no conception. In the same way, when an equation can be reduced in degree by dividing throughout by any power of x, the possible values, $x = 0$, thus arising are not taken into account. Thus an equation of the form $x^2 = ax$, which is of common occurrence in the earlier part of the book, is taken to be merely equivalent to the simple equation $x = a$.

It may be observed that the greater proportion of the problems in Book I. are such that more than one unknown quantity is sought. Now, when there are two unknowns and two conditions, both unknowns can be easily expressed in terms of one symbol. But when there are three or four quantities to be found this reduction is much more difficult, and Diophantos manifests peculiar adroitness in effecting it : the result being that it is only necessary to solve a simple equation with one unknown quantity. With regard to *pure* equations, some have asserted that pure quadratics were the only form of quadratic

---

[1] Def. 11: Μετὰ δὲ ταῦτα ἐὰν ἀπὸ προβλήματός τινος γένηται ὕπαρξις εἴδεσι τοῖς αὐτοῖς μὴ ὁμοπληθῆ δὲ ἀπὸ ἑκατέρων τῶν μερῶν, δεήσει ἀφαιρεῖν τὰ ὅμοια ἀπὸ τῶν ὁμοίων, ἕως ἂν ἑνὸς (?) εἶδος ἑνὶ εἴδει ἴσον γένηται. ἐὰν δέ πως ἐν ὁποτέρῳ ἐνυπάρχῃ (?) ἢ ἐν ἀμφοτέροις ἐνελλείψῃ τινὰ εἴδη, δεήσει προσθεῖναι τὰ λείποντα εἴδη ἐν ἀμφοτέροις τοῖς μέρεσιν, ἕως ἂν ἑκατέρῳ τῶν μερῶν τὰ εἴδη ἐνυπάρχοντα γένηται. καὶ πάλιν ἀφελεῖν τὰ ὅμοια ἀπὸ τῶν ὁμοίων ἕως ἂν ἑκατέρῳ τῶν μερῶν ἓν εἶδος καταλειφθῇ. Bachet's text (1621). p. 10.

solved in Diophantos[1]: a statement entirely without foundation. We proceed to consider

(2) *Mixed quadratic equations.*

After the remarks in Def. 11 upon the reduction of pure equations until we have one term equal to another term, Diophantos adds[2]: "But we will show you afterwards how, in the case also when two terms are left equal to a single term, such an equation can be solved." That is to say, he promises to explain the solution of a mixed quadratic equation. In the *Arithmetics,* as we possess the book, this promise is not fulfilled. The first indications we have on the subject are a number of cases in which the equation is given, and the solution written down, or stated to be rational without any work being shown. Thus, IV. 23, "$x^2 = 4x - 4$, therefore $x = 2$": VI. 7, "$84x^2 - 7x = 7$, hence $x = \frac{1}{3}$": VI. 9, "$630x^2 - 73x = 6$, therefore $x = \frac{6}{35}$": and, VI. 8, "$630x^2 + 73x = 6$, and x is rational." These examples, though proving that somehow Diophantos had arrived at the result, are not a sufficient proof to satisfy us that he necessarily was acquainted with a regular method for the solution of quadratics; these solutions might (though their variety makes it somewhat unlikely) have been obtained by mere *trial.* That, however, Diophantos' solutions of mixed quadratics were not merely empirical, is shown by instances in V. 33. In this problem he shows pretty plainly that his method was scientific, in that he indicates that he could approximate to the root in cases where it is not rational. As this is an important point, I give the substance of the passage in question : "x has to be so determined that it must be $> \dfrac{x^2 - 60}{8}$ and $< \dfrac{x^2 - 60}{5}$, i.e. $x^2 - 60 > 5x$, and $x^2 - 60 < 8x$.

Therefore $x^2 = 5x +$ some number > 60, therefore x must be not less than 11, and $x^2 < 8x + 60$, therefore x must be not greater than 12."

---

[1] Cf. Reimer, translation of Bossut's *Gesch. d. Math.* I. 55.   Klügel's *Dictionary.*   Also Dr Heinrich Suter's doubts in *Gesch. d. Math.* Zürich, 1873.

[2] ὕστερον δέ σοι δείξομεν καὶ πῶς δύο εἰδῶν ἴσων ἑνὶ καταλειφθέντων τὸ τοιοῦτον λύεται.

Now by examining the roots of these two equations we find

$$x > \frac{5 + \sqrt{255}}{2} \text{ and } x < 4 + \sqrt{76},$$

or $x > 10\cdot6394$ and $x < 12\cdot7178$.

It is clear therefore that x *may* be < 11 or > 12, and therefore Diophantos' limits are not strictly accurate. As however it was doubtless his object to find *integral* limits, the limits 11 and 12 are those which are obviously adapted for his purpose, and are *a fortiori* right. Later in the same problem he makes an auxiliary determination of x, which must be such that

$$x^2 + 60 > 22x, \quad x^2 + 60 < 24x,$$

which give $x > 11 + \sqrt{61}, \quad x < 12 + \sqrt{84}.$

Here Diophantos says x must be > 19, < 21, which again are clearly the nearest integral limits.

The occurrence of these two examples which we have given of equations whose roots are irrational, and therefore could not be hit upon by trial, shows that in such cases Diophantos must have had a method by which he approximated to these roots. Thus it may be taken for granted that Diophantos had a definite rule for the solution of mixed quadratic equations.

We are further able to make out the formula or rule by which Diophantos solved such equations. Take, for example, the equation $ax^2 + bx + c = 0$. In our modern method of solution we divide by a and write the result originally in the form

$x = -\dfrac{b}{2a} \pm \sqrt{\dfrac{b^2}{4a^2} - \dfrac{c}{a}}.$ It does not appear that Diophantos divided throughout by a. Rather he first multiplied by a so as to bring the equation into the form $a^2x^2 + abx + ac = 0$; then solving he found $ax = -\frac{1}{2}b \pm \sqrt{\frac{1}{4}b^2 - ac}$, and regarded the result in the[1] form $x = \dfrac{\frac{1}{2}b \pm \sqrt{\frac{1}{4}b^2 - ac}}{a}$. Whether the intermediate procedure was as we have described it is not certain; but it is certain that he used the result in the form given. One remark however must be made upon the form of the root.

---

[1] Nesselmann, p. 319. Also Rodet, *Journal Asiatique*, Janvier, 1878.

Diophantos takes no account of the existence of *two* roots, according to the sign taken before the radical. Diophantos ignores always the negative sign, and takes the positive one as giving the value of the root. Though this perhaps might not surprise us in cases where one of the roots obtained is negative, yet neither does Diophantos use both roots when both are positive in sign. In contrast to this Nesselmann points out that the Arabians (as typified by Mohammed ibn Mūsā) and the older Italians do in this latter case recognise both roots. M. Rodet, however, remarks upon this comparison between Diophantos and the Arabians, so unfavourable to the former, as follows   (*a*) Diophantos did not write a text-book on Algebra, and in the cases where the equation arrived at gives two positive solutions one of them is excluded *a priori*, as for example in the case quoted by him, v. 13. Here the inequality $72x > 17x^2 + 17$ would give $x < \frac{67}{17}$ or else $x < \frac{5}{17}$. But the other inequality to be satisfied is $72x < 19x^2 + 19$, which gives $x > \frac{66}{19}$ or $x > \frac{6}{19}$. As however $\frac{5}{17} < \frac{6}{19}$, the limits $x < \frac{5}{17} > \frac{6}{19}$ are impossible. Hence the roots of the equations corresponding to the negative sign of the radical must necessarily be rejected. (*b*) Mohammed ibn Mūsā, although recognising *in theory* two roots of the equation $x^2 + c = bx$, *in practice* only uses one of the two, and, curiously enough, always takes the value corresponding to the negative sign before the radical, whereas Diophantos uses the positive sign. But see Chapter VIII.

From the rule given in Def. 11 for compensating by addition any negative terms on either side of an equation and taking equals from equals (operations called by the Arabs *aljabr* and *almukābala*) it is clear that as a preliminary to solution Diophantos so arranged his equation that all the terms were positive. Thus of the mixed quadratic equation we have three cases of which we may give instances : thus,

Case 1.   Form $mx^2 + px = q$; the root is $\dfrac{-\frac{1}{2}p + \sqrt{\frac{1}{4}p^2 + mq}}{m}$

according to Diophantos. An instance is afforded by VI. 6. Diophantos arrives namely at the equation $6x^2 + 3x = 7$, which, if it is to be of any service to his solution, should give a rational value of x; whereupon Diophantos says "the square of half the coefficient[1] of x together with the product of the absolute term and the coefficient of x^2 must be a square number; but it is not," i.e. $\frac{1}{4}p^2 + mq$, or in this case $(\frac{3}{2})^2 + 42$, must be a square in order that the root may be rational, which in this case it is not.

Case 2.   Form · $mx^2 = px + q$.   Diophantos takes $x = \dfrac{\frac{1}{2}p + \sqrt{\frac{1}{4}p^2 + mq}}{m}$. An example is IV. 45, where $2x^2 > 6x + 18$. Diophantos says : " To solve this take the square of half the co-efficient of x, i.e. 9, and the product of the absolute term and the coefficient of x^2, i.e. 36.   Adding, we have 45, the square root[2] of which is not[3] < 7.   Add half the coefficient of x and divide by the coefficient of x^2; whence $x < 5$." Here the form of the root is given completely; and the whole operation by which Diophantos found it is revealed.

Case 3.   Form $mx^2 + q = px$:   Diophantos' root is $\dfrac{\frac{1}{2}p + \sqrt{\frac{1}{4}p^2 - mq}}{m}$. Cf. in V. 13 the equation already mentioned, $17x^2 + 17 < 72x$.   Diophantos says: "Multiply half the coefficient of x into itself and we have 1296 : subtract the product of the coefficient of x^2 and the absolute term, or 289.   The remainder is 1007, the square root of which is not[4] > 31.   Add half the coefficient of x, and the result is not > 67.   Divide by the coefficient of x^2, and x is not $> \frac{67}{17}$." Here again we have the complete solution given.

(3) *Cubic equation.*

There is no ground for supposing that Diophantos was acquainted with the solution of a cubic equation.   It is true there is one cubic equation which occurs in the *Arithmetics*, but it is only a very particular case.   In VI. 19 the equation arises, $x^2 + 2x + 3 = x^3 + 3x - 3x^2 - 1$, and Diophantos says simply, " whence x is found to be 4."   All that can be said of

---

[1] For "coefficient" Diophantos uses simply πλῆθος, number: thus "number of ἀριθμοί" = coeff. of x.

[2] Diophantos calls the "square root" πλευρά or *side*.

[3] 7, though not accurate, is clearly the nearest integral limit which will serve the purpose.

[4] As before, the nearest *integral* limit.

this is that if we write the equation in true Diophantine fashion, so that all terms are positive,

$$x^3 + x = 4x^2 + 4.$$

This equation being clearly equivalent to $x(x^2+1) = 4(x^2+1)$, Diophantos probably detected the presence on both sides of the equation of a common factor. The result of dividing by it is $x = 4$, which is Diophantos' solution. Of the two other roots $x = \pm\sqrt{-1}$ no account is taken, for reasons stated above.

From this single example we have no means of judging how far Diophantos was acquainted with the solutions of equations of a degree higher than the second.

I pass now to the second general division of equations.

(B.)   Indeterminate equations.

As has been already stated, Diophantos does not in his *Arithmetics*, as we possess them, treat of indeterminate equations of the first degree. Those examples in the First Book which would lead to such equations are, by the arbitrary assumption of one of the required numbers as if known, converted into determinate equations. It is possible that the treatment of indeterminate equations belonged to the missing portion which (we have reason to believe) has been lost between Books I. and II. But we cannot with certainty dispute the view that Diophantos never gave them at all. For (as Nesselmann observes) as with indeterminate quadratic equations our object is to obtain a *rational* result, so in indeterminate simple equations we seek to find a result *in whole numbers*. But the exclusion of fractions as inadmissible results is entirely foreign to our author; indeed we do not find the slightest trace that he ever insisted on such a condition. We take therefore as our first division indeterminate equations of the second degree.

I.   *Indeterminate equations of the second degree.*

The form in which these equations occur in Diophantos is universally this : one or two (and never more) functions of the unknown quantity of the form $Ax^2 + Bx + C$ are to be made rational square numbers by finding a suitable value for x.

Thus we have to deal with one or two equations of the form $Ax^2 + Bx + C = y^2$.

(1) Single equation.

The single equation of the form $Ax^2 + Bx + C = y^2$ takes special forms when one or more of the coefficients vanish, or are subject to particular conditions. It will be well to give in order the different forms as they can be identified in Diophantos, and to premise that for " $= y^2$ " Diophantos simply uses the formula ἴσον τετραγώνῳ.

1. Equations which can always be solved rationally. This is the case when A or C or both vanish.

Form $Bx = y^2$. Diophantus puts $y^2 =$ any arbitrary square number $= m^2$, say therefore $x = \dfrac{m^2}{B}$. Cf. III. 5 : $2x = y^2$, $y^2 = 16$, $x = 8$.

Form $Bx + C = y^2$. Diophantos puts for y^2 any value m^2, and $x = \dfrac{m^2 - C}{B}$. He admits fractional values of x, only taking care that they are "rational," i.e. rational and positive. Ex. III. 7.

Form $Ax^2 + Bx = y^2$. For y Diophantos puts any multiple of x, $\dfrac{m}{n}x$; whence $Ax + B = \dfrac{m^2}{n^2}x$, the factor x disappearing and the root $x = 0$ being neglected as usual. Therefore $x = \dfrac{Bn^2}{m^2 - An^2}$. Exx. II. 22, 34.

2. Equations whose rational solution is only possible under certain conditions. The cases occurring in Diophantos are

Form $Ax^2 + C = y^2$. This can be rationally solved according to Diophantos

(a) When A is positive and a square, say a^2.

Thus $a^2x^2 + C = y^2$. In this case y^2 is put $= (ax \pm m)^2$; therefore $a^2x^2 + C = (ax \pm m)^2$,

$$x = \pm \frac{C - m^2}{2ma}$$

(m and the doubtful sign being always assumed so as to give x a positive value).

(β) When C is positive and a square number, say c^2.

Thus $Ax^2 + c^2 = y^2$. Here Diophantos puts $y = (mx \pm c)$;
therefore $\qquad\qquad Ax^2 + c^2 = (mx \pm c)^2$,

$$x = \pm \frac{2mc}{A - m^2}.$$

(γ) When one solution is known, any number of other solutions can be found. This is enunciated in VI. 16 thus, though only for the case in which C is negative: "when two numbers are given such that when one is multiplied by some square, and the other is subtracted from the product, the result is a square number; another square also can be found, greater than the first taken square, which will have the same effect." It is curious that Diophantos does not give a general enunciation of this proposition, inasmuch as not only is it applicable to the cases $\pm Ax^2 \pm C^2 = y^2$, but to the general form $Ax^2 + Bx + C = y^2$.

In the Lemma at VI. 12 Diophantos does prove that the equation $Ax^2 + C = y^2$ can be solved when $A + C$ is a square, i.e. in the particular case when the value $x = 1$ satisfies the equation. But he does not always bear this in mind, for in III. 12 the equation $52x^2 + 12 = y^2$ is pronounced to be impossible of solution, although $52 + 12 = 64$, a square, and a rational solution is therefore possible. So, III. 13, $266x^2 - 10 = y^2$ is said to be impossible, though $x = 1$ satisfies it.

It is clear that, if $x = 0$ satisfies the equation, C is a square, and therefore this case (γ) includes the previous case (β).

It is interesting to observe that in VI. 15 Diophantos states that a rational solution of the equation

$$Ax^2 - c^2 = y^2$$

is impossible *unless* A *is the sum of two squares*[1].

---

[1] Nesselmann compares Legendre, *Théorie des Nombres*, p. 60.

Lastly, we must consider the

$$\text{Form } Ax^2 + Bx + C = y^2.$$

This equation can be reduced by means of a change of variable to the previous form, wanting the second term. Thus if we put $x = z - \dfrac{B}{2A}$, the transformation gives

$$Az^2 + \frac{4AC - B^2}{4A} = y^2.$$

Diophantos, however, treats this form of the equation quite separately from the other and less fully. According to him the rational solution is only possible in the following cases.

(α) When A is positive and a square, or the equation is $a^2x^2 + Bx + C = y^2$; and Diophantos puts $y^2 = (ax + m)^2$, whence

$$x = \frac{C - m^2}{2am - B}. \qquad \text{Exx. II. 20, 21 \&c.}$$

(β) When C is positive and a square, or the equation is $Ax^2 + Bx + c^2 = y^2$; and Diophantos writes $y^2 = (mx + c)^2$, whence

$$x = \frac{2mc - B}{A - m^2}. \qquad \text{Exx. IV. 9, 10 \&c.}$$

(γ) When $\frac{1}{4}B^2 - AC$ is positive and a square number. Diophantos never expressly enunciates the possibility of this case: but it occurs, as it were unawares, in IV. 33. In this problem $3x + 18 - x^2$ is to be made a square, and the equation $3x + 18 - x^2 = y^2$ comes under the present form.

To solve this Diophantos assumes $3x + 18 - x^2 = 4x^2$ which leads to the quadratic $3x + 18 - 5x^2 = 0$, and "the equation is not rational". Hence the assumption $4x^2$ will not do : "and we must seek a square [to replace 4] such that 18 times (this square $+ 1$) $+ (\frac{3}{2})^2$ may be a square". Diophantos then solves this auxiliary equation $18(x^2 + 1) + \frac{9}{4} = y^2$, finding $x = 18$. Then he assumes

$$3x + 18 - x^2 = (18)^2x^2,$$

which gives $325x^2 - 3x - 18 = 0$, whence $x = \frac{78}{325}$.

H. D.   **7**

It is interesting to observe that from this example of Diophantos we can obtain the reduction of this general case to the
form $Ax^2 + C^2 = y^2$, wanting the middle term.

Thus, assume with Diophantos that $Ax^2 + Bx + C = m^2x^2$,
therefore by solution we have

$$x = \frac{-\dfrac{B}{2} \pm \sqrt{\dfrac{B^2}{4} - AC + Cm^2}}{A - m^2},$$

and x is rational provided $\dfrac{B^2}{4} - AC + Cm^2$ is a square. This
condition can be fulfilled if $\dfrac{B^2}{4} - AC$ be a square by a previous
case. Even if that is not the case, we have to solve (putting,
for brevity, D for $\dfrac{B^2}{4} - AC$) the equation

$$D + Cm^2 = y^2.$$

Hence the reduction is effected, by the aid of Diophantos alone.

(2)   Double-equation.

By the name "double-equation" Diophantos designates the
problem of finding one value of the unknown quantity x which
will make two functions of it simultaneously rational square
numbers. The Greek term for the "double-equation" occurs
variously as διπλοϊσότης or διπλῆ ἰσότης. We have then to
solve the equations

$$\left.\begin{aligned} mx^2 + ax + a &= u^2 \\ nx^2 + \beta x + b &= w^2 \end{aligned}\right\}$$

in rational numbers. The necessary preliminary condition is
that each of the two expressions can severally be made squares.
This is always possible when the first term (in x^2) is wanting.
This is the simplest case, and we shall accordingly take it first.

1. *Double equation of the first degree.*

Diophantos has *one distinct method* of solving the equations

$$\left. \begin{array}{l} ax + a = u^2 \\ \beta x + b = w^2 \end{array} \right\},$$

taking slightly different forms according to the nature of the coefficients.

(*a*) First method of solution of

$$\left. \begin{array}{l} ax + a = u^2 \\ \beta x + b = w^2 \end{array} \right\}.$$

This method depends upon the equation

$$\left(\frac{p+q}{2}\right)^2 - \left(\frac{p-q}{2}\right)^2 = pq.$$

If the difference between the two functions can be separated into two factors p, q, the functions themselves are equated to $\left(\frac{p \pm q}{2}\right)^2$. Diophantos himself states his rule thus, in II. 12: "Observing the difference between the two expressions, seek two numbers whose product is equal to this difference; then either equate the square of half the difference of the factors to the smaller of the expressions, or the square of half the sum to the greater." We will take the general case, and investigate what particular cases the method is applicable to, from Diophantos' point of view, remembering that his cases are such that the final quadratic equation for x arising reduces always to a simple one.

Take the equations

$$ax + a = u^2,$$
$$\beta x + b = w^2,$$

and subtracting we have $(a - \beta) x + (a - b) = u^2 - w^2$.

Let $a - \beta = \delta$, $a - b = \epsilon$ for brevity, then $\delta x + \epsilon = u^2 - w^2$.

7—2

We have then to separate $\delta x + \epsilon$ into two factors; let these factors be $p,\ \dfrac{\delta x}{p} + \dfrac{\epsilon}{p}$, and we accordingly write

$$u \pm v = \frac{\delta x}{p} + \frac{\epsilon}{p},$$

$$u \mp v = p.$$

Thus
$$u^2 = ax + a = \left(\frac{\frac{\delta x}{p} + \frac{\epsilon}{p} + p}{2}\right)^2,$$

therefore
$$\frac{\delta^2 x^2}{p^2} + \frac{2\delta x}{p}\left(\frac{\epsilon}{p} + p\right) + \left(\frac{\epsilon}{p} + p\right)^2 = 4\,(ax + a).$$

Now in order that this equation may reduce to a simple one, either

(1) the coefficient of x^2 must vanish or $\delta = 0$, therefore $\alpha = \beta$, or

(2) the absolute term must vanish.

Therefore
$$\left(\frac{\epsilon}{p} + p\right)^2 = 4a,$$

or
$$p^4 + 2\epsilon p^2 + \epsilon^2 = 4ap^2,$$

i.e.
$$p^4 + 2(a - b - 2a)\,p^2 + (a - b)^2 = 0.$$

Therefore
$$(p^2 - \overline{a + b})^2 = 4ab,$$

whence ab must be a square number.

Therefore either both a and b are squares, in which case we may substitute for them c^2 and d^2, p being then equal to $c \pm d$, or the ratio $a : b$ is the ratio of a square to a square.

With respect to (1) we observe that on one condition it is not necessary that δ should vanish, i.e. provided we can, before solving the equations, make the coefficients of x^2 in both equal by multiplying either equation or both by a square number, an operation which does not affect the problem, for a square multiplied by a square is still a square.

Thus if $\dfrac{\alpha}{\beta} = \dfrac{m^2}{n^2}$ or $\alpha n^2 = \beta m^2$, the condition $\delta = 0$ will be satisfied by multiplying the equations respectively by n^2 and m^2; and thus we can also solve the equations

$$\left.\begin{array}{l} \alpha m^2 x + a = u^2 \\ \alpha n^2 x + b = w^2 \end{array}\right\}$$

like the equations

$$\left.\begin{array}{l} \alpha x + a = u'^2 \\ \alpha x + b = w' \end{array}\right\}$$

in an infinite number of ways.

Again the equations under (2),

$$\alpha x + c^2 = u^2,$$
$$\beta x + d^2 = w^2,$$

can be solved in two different ways, according as we write them in this form or in the form

$$\left.\begin{array}{l} \alpha d^2 x + c^2 d^2 = u'^2 \\ \beta c^2 x + c^2 d^2 = w'^2 \end{array}\right\},$$

obtained by multiplying them respectively by d^2, c^2 in order that the absolute terms may be equal.

We now give those of the possible cases which are found solved in Diophantos' own work. These are equations

(1)   of the form
$$\left.\begin{array}{l} \alpha m^2 x + a = u^2 \\ \alpha n^2 x + b = w^2 \end{array}\right\},$$

a case which includes the more common ·one, when the co-efficients of x in both are *equal*.

(2)   of the form
$$\left.\begin{array}{l} \alpha x + c^2 = u^2 \\ \beta x + d^2 = w^2 \end{array}\right\},$$

solved in two different ways according as they are thus written, or in the alternative form,

$$\left.\begin{array}{l} \alpha d^2 x + c^2 d^2 = u'^2 \\ \beta c^2 x + c^2 d^2 = w'^2 \end{array}\right\}.$$

General solution of Form (1), or,

$$\left.\begin{array}{l} am^2x + a = u^2 \\ an^2x + b = w^2 \end{array}\right\}.$$

Multiplying respectively by n^2, m^2, we have to solve the equations,

$$\left.\begin{array}{l} am^2n^2x + an^2 = u'^2 \\ am^2n^2x + bm^2 = w'^2 \end{array}\right\}.$$

The difference $= an^2 - bm^2$. Suppose this separated into two factors p, q.

Put $u' \pm w' = p,$

                               $u' \mp w' = q,$

whence $u'^2 = \left(\dfrac{p+q}{2}\right)^2,\ w'^2 = \left(\dfrac{p-q}{2}\right)^2,$

therefore $am^2n^2x + an^2 = \left(\dfrac{p+q}{2}\right)^2,$

or $am^2n^2x + bm^2 = \left(\dfrac{p-q}{2}\right)^2.$

Either equation will give the same value of x, and

$$x = \frac{\dfrac{p^2+q^2}{4} - \dfrac{an^2+bm^2}{2}}{am^2n^2},$$

since $pq = an^2 - bm^2$.

Any factors p, q may be chosen provided the value of x obtained is *positive*.

Ex. from Diophantos.

$$\left.\begin{array}{l} 65 - 6x = u^2 \\ 65 - 24x = w^2 \end{array}\right\},$$

therefore $\left.\begin{array}{l} 260 - 24x = u'^2 \\ 65 - 24x = w^2 \end{array}\right\}.$

The difference $= 195 = 15 \cdot 13$ say,

therefore $\left(\dfrac{15-13}{2}\right)^2 = 65 - 24x,\ 24x = 64,\ \text{or}\ x = \tfrac{8}{3}.$

General solution (first method) of Form (2), or,

$$\begin{aligned} \alpha x + c^2 &= u'^2 \\ \beta x + d^2 &= w'^2 \end{aligned} \Big\} .$$

In order to solve by this method, we multiply by d^2, c^2 respectively and write

$$\begin{aligned} \alpha d^2 x + c^2 d^2 &= u^2 \\ \beta c^2 x + c^2 d^2 &= w^2 \end{aligned} \Big\} ,$$

u being the greater.

The diff. $= (\alpha d^2 - \beta c^2)\, x$.   Let the factors of this be px, q,

therefore

$$u^2 = \left(\frac{px + q}{2} \right)^2 ,$$

$$v^2 = \left(\frac{px - q}{2} \right)^2 .$$

Hence x is found from the equation

$$\alpha d^2 x + c^2 d^2 = \left(\frac{px + q}{2} \right)^2 .$$

This equation gives

$$p^2 x^2 + 2x\,(pq - 2\alpha d^2) + q^2 - 4c^2 d^2 = 0,$$

or, since $\qquad\qquad pq = \alpha d^2 - \beta c^2,$

$$p^2 x^2 - 2x\,(\alpha d^2 + \beta c^2) + q^2 - 4c^2 d^2 = 0.$$

In order that this may reduce to a simple equation, as Diophantos requires, the absolute term must vanish.

Therefore $\qquad\qquad q^2 - 4c^2 d^2 = 0,$

whence $\qquad\qquad q = 2cd.$

Thus our method in this case furnishes us with only *one* solution of the double-equation, q being restricted to the value $2cd$, and this solution is

$$x = \frac{2\,(\alpha d^2 + \beta c^2)}{p^2} = \frac{8 c^2 d^2\,(\alpha d^2 + \beta c^2)}{(\alpha d^2 - \beta c^2)^2} .$$

Ex. from Diophantos.   This method is only used in one particular case, IV. 45, where $c^2 = d^2$ as the equations originally stand, namely

$$\begin{aligned} 8x + 4 &= u^2 \\ 6x + 4 &= w^2 \end{aligned} \Big\} ,$$

the difference is $2x$ and q is necessarily taken $= 2\sqrt{4} = 4$, and the factors are $\dfrac{x}{2}$, 4,

therefore $\qquad 8x + 4 = \left(\dfrac{x}{4} + 2\right)^2$ and $x = 112$.

General solution (second method) of Form (2), or
$$\left.\begin{aligned} \alpha x + c^2 &= u^2 \\ \beta x + d^2 &= w^2 \end{aligned}\right\}.$$
Here the difference $= (\alpha - \beta)\, x + (c^2 - d^2) = \delta x + \epsilon$ say, for brevity.

Let the factors of $dx + \epsilon$ be p, $\dfrac{\delta x}{p} + \dfrac{\epsilon}{p}$. Then, as before proved (p. 100), p must be equal to $(c \pm d)$.

Therefore the factors are
$$\frac{\alpha - \beta}{c \pm d} x + c \mp d, \; c \pm d,$$
and we have finally
$$\alpha x + c^2 = \tfrac{1}{4}\left(\frac{\alpha - \beta}{c \pm d}\, x + c \mp d + c \pm d\right)^2$$
$$= \tfrac{1}{4}\left\{\left(\frac{\alpha - \beta}{c \pm d}\right)x + 2c\right\}^2,$$

therefore $\qquad \left(\dfrac{\alpha - \beta}{c \pm d}\right)^2 x^2 + 4x\left\{\dfrac{c\,(\alpha - \beta)}{c \pm d} - \alpha\right\} = 0,$

which equation gives two possible values for x. Thus in this case we can find by our method *two* values of x, since one of the factors, p, may be $c \pm d$.

Ex. from Diophantos, III. 17 : to solve the equations
$$\left.\begin{aligned} 10x + 9 &= u^2 \\ 5x + 4 &= w^2 \end{aligned}\right\}.$$

The difference is here $5x + 5$, and Diophantos chooses as the factors 5, $x + 1$. This case therefore corresponds to the value $c + d$ of p. The solution is given by
$$\left(\frac{x}{2} + 3\right)^2 = 10x + 9, \text{ whence } x = 28.$$

The other value $c - d$ of p is in this case excluded, because it would lead to a negative value of x.

The possibility of deriving any number of solutions of a double-equation when one solution is known does not seem to have been noticed by Diophantos, though he uses the principle in certain special cases of the single equation. Fermat was the first, apparently, to discover that this might always be done, if one value a of x were known, by substituting in the equations $x + a$ for x. By this means it is possible to find a positive solution even if a is negative, by successive applications of the principle.

But nevertheless Diophantos had certain peculiar artifices by which he could arrive at a second value. One of these artifices (which is made necessary in one case by the unsuitableness of the value found for x by the ordinary method), employed in IV. 45, gives a different way of solving a double-equation from that which has been explained, used only in a special case.

(β)   Second method of solution of a double-equation of the first degree.

Consider only the special case

$$hx + n^2 = u^2,$$

$$(h + f) x + n^2 = w^2.$$

Take these expressions, and n^2, and write them in order of magnitude, denoting them for convenience by A, B, C.

$$A = (h + f) x + n^2, \quad B = hx + n^2, \quad C = n^2,$$

therefore $\qquad \dfrac{A - B}{B - C} = \dfrac{f}{h}$ and $\left. \begin{array}{l} A - B = fx \\ B - C = hx \end{array} \right\}$.

Suppose now $\qquad hx + n^2 = (y + n)^2$,

therefore $\qquad hx = y^2 + 2ny,$

therefore $\qquad A - B = \dfrac{f}{h} (y^2 + 2ny),$

or $\qquad A = (y + n)^2 + \dfrac{f}{h} (y^2 + 2ny),$

thus it is only necessary to make this expression a square.

Write therefore

$$\left(1 + \frac{f}{h}\right)y^2 + 2n\left(\frac{f}{h} + 1\right)y + n^2 = (py - n)^2,$$

whence any number of values for y, and therefore for x, can be found, by varying p.

Ex. The only example in the *Arithmetics* is in IV. 45. There is the additional condition in this case of a limit to the value of x. The double-equation

$$\left. \begin{array}{l} 8x + 4 = u^2 \\ 6x + 4 = w^2 \end{array} \right\},$$

has to be solved in such a manner that $x < 2$.

Here $\dfrac{A - B}{B - C} = \frac{1}{3}$, and B is taken[1] to be $(y + 2)^2$,

therefore $\qquad A - B = \dfrac{y^2 + 4y}{3}$,

therefore $\qquad A = \dfrac{y^2 + 4y}{3} + y^2 + 4y + 4 = \dfrac{4y^2}{3} + \dfrac{16y}{3} + 4$

which must be made a square, or, multiplying by $\frac{9}{4}$,

$$3y^2 + 12y + 9 = \text{a square},$$

where y must be < 2.

Diophantos assumes

$$3y^2 + 12y + 9 = (my - 3)^2,$$

whence $\qquad y = \dfrac{6m + 12}{m^2 - 3}$,

and the value of m is then determined so that $y < 2$.

As we find only a special case in Diophantos solved by this method, it would be out of place to investigate the con-

---

[1] Of course Diophantos uses the same variable x where I have for clearness used y.

Then, to express what I have called m later, he says:

"I form a square from 3 minus *some number* of x's and x becomes *some number* multiplied by 6 together with 12 and divided by the difference by which the square of *the number* exceeds *three*."

ditions under which more general cases might be solved in this manner[1].

2. Double equation of the second degree,

or the general form

$$Ax^2 + Bx + C = u^2,$$
$$A'x^2 + B'x + C' = w^2.$$

These equations are much less thoroughly treated in Diophantos than those of the first degree. Only such special instances occur as can be easily solved by the methods which we have described for those of the first degree.

One separate case must be mentioned, which cannot be solved, from Diophantos' standpoint, by the preceding method, but which sometimes occurs and is solved by a peculiar method.

The form of double-equation being

$$\alpha x^2 + ax = u^2 \rbrace \dots\dots\dots\dots\dots(1),$$
$$\beta x^2 + bx = w^2 \rbrace \dots\dots\dots\dots\dots(2),$$

Diophantos assumes $\quad u^2 = m^2 x^2,$

whence from (1)

$$x = \frac{a}{m^2 - \alpha},$$

and by substitution in (2)

$$\beta \left(\frac{a}{m^2 - \alpha} \right)^2 + \frac{ba}{m^2 - \alpha} \text{ must be a square,}$$

or $\quad \dfrac{a^2\beta + ba(m^2 - \alpha)}{(m^2 - \alpha)^2}$ is a square.

Therefore we have to solve the equation

$$abm^2 + a(\beta a - \alpha b) = y^2,$$

and this form can or cannot be solved by processes already given according to the nature of the coefficients[2].

---

[1] Bachet and after him Cossali proved the possibility of solving $\dfrac{ax+b}{cx+d}\rbrace$ by this method under two conditions.

[2] Diophantos did not apparently observe that this form of equation could be

II. *Indeterminate equations of a degree higher than the second.*

(1) *Single Equations.*

These are properly divided by Nesselmann into two classes; the first of which comprises those questions in which it is required to make a function of x of a higher degree than the second a square; the second comprises those in which a rational value of x has to be found which will make any function of x, not a square, but a higher power of some number. The first class of problems is the solution in rational numbers of

$$Ax^n + Bx^{n-1} + \ldots\ldots + Kx + L = y^2,$$

the second the solution of

$$Ax^n + Bx^{n-1} + \ldots\ldots + Kx + L = y^3,$$

for Diophantos does not go beyond making a function of x a *cube*. Also in no instance of the first class does the index n exceed 6, nor in the second class (except in a special case or two) exceed 3.

First class. Equation

$$Ax^n + Bx^{n-1} + \ldots\ldots + Kx + L = y^2.$$

We give now the forms found in Diophantos.

1. Equation $Ax^3 + Bx^2 + Cx + d^2 = y^2.$

Here we might (the absolute term being a square) put for y the expression $mx + d$, and determine m so that the coefficient of x in the resulting equation vanishes, in which case

$$2md = C, \quad m = \frac{C}{2d},$$

and we obtain in Diophantos' manner a simple equation for x, giving

$$x = \frac{C^2 - 4d^2 B}{4d^2 A}.$$

reduced to one of the first degree by dividing by x^2 and putting y for $\frac{1}{x}$, in which case it becomes

$$\left. \begin{array}{l} a + ay = u'^2 \\ \beta + by = w'^2 \end{array} \right\}.$$

This reduction was given by Lagrange.

Or we might put for y an expression $m^2x^2 + nx + d$, and determine m, n so that the coefficients of x, x^2 in the resulting equation both vanish, whence we should again have a simple equation for x. Diophantos, in the only example of this form of equation which occurs, makes the first supposition. Thus in VI. 20 the equation occurs,

$$x^3 - 3x^2 + 3x + 1 = y^2,$$

and Diophantos assumes $y = \frac{3}{2}x + 1$, whence $x = \frac{21}{4}$.

2. Equation $Ax^4 + Bx^3 + Cx^2 + Dx + E = y^2$.

In order that this equation may be solved by Diophantos' method, either A or E must be a square. If A is a square and equal to a^2 we may assume $y = ax^2 + \dfrac{B}{2a}x + n$, determining n so that the term in x^2 vanishes. If E is a square (e^2) we may write $y = mx^2 + \dfrac{D}{2e}x + e$, determining m so that the term in x^2 may vanish in the resulting equation. We shall then in either case obtain a simple equation for x, in Diophantos' manner.

The examples of this form in Diophantos are of the kind,

$$a^2x^4 + Bx^3 + Cx^2 + Dx + e^2 = y^2,$$

where we can assume $y = \pm ax^2 + kx \pm e$, determining k so that in the resulting equation (in addition to the coefficient of x^4, and the absolute term) the coefficient of x^3, or that of x, may vanish, after which we again have a simple equation.

Ex. IV. 29: $9x^4 - 4x^3 + 6x^2 - 12x + 1 = y^2$. Here Diophantos assumes $y = 3x^2 - 6x + 1$, and the equation reduces to

$$32x^3 - 36x^2 = 0 \text{ and } x = \tfrac{9}{8}.$$

Diophantos is guided in his choice of signs in the expression $\pm ax^2 + kx \pm e$ by the necessity for obtaining a "rational" result.

But far more difficult to solve are those equations in which (the left expression being bi-quadratic) the odd powers of x are wanting, i.e. the equations $Ax^4 + Cx^2 + E = y^2$, and $Ax^4 + E = y^2$,

even when A or E is a square, or both are so. These cases
Diophantos treats more imperfectly.

3.   Equation $Ax^4 + Cx^2 + E = y^2$.

Of this form we find only very special cases. The type is

$$a^2x^4 - c^2x^2 + e^2 = y^2,$$

which is written

$$a^2x^2 - c^2 + \frac{e^2}{x^2} = y^2.$$

Here y is assumed to be ax or $\dfrac{e}{x}$, and in either case we
have a rational value of x.

Exx. v. 30 : $25x^2 - 9 + \dfrac{25}{4x^2} = y^2$. This is assumed to be
equal to $25x^2$.

v. 31 : $\dfrac{25}{4}x^2 - 25 + \dfrac{25}{4x^2} = y^2$. y^2 assumed to be $= \dfrac{25}{4x^2}$.

4.   Equation $Ax^4 + E = y^2$.

The case occurring in Diophantos is $x^4 + 97 = y^2$. Diophantos
tries one assumption, $y = x^2 - 10$, and finds that this gives
$x^2 = \frac{3}{20}$, which leads to no rational result. Instead however
of investigating in what cases this equation can be solved, he
simply shirks the equation and seeks by altering his original
assumptions to obtain an equation in the place of the one first
found, which can be solved in rational numbers. The result is
that by altering his assumptions and working out the question
by their aid he replaces the refractory equation, $x^4 + 97 = y^2$, by
the equation $x^4 + 337 = y^2$, and is able to find a suitable substitution for y, namely $x^2 - 25$. This gives as the required
solution $x = \frac{12}{5}$. For this case of Diophantos' characteristic
artifice of retracing his steps [1]—" back-reckoning," as Nesselmann calls it, see Appendix V. 32.

5.   Equation of sixth degree in the special form

$$x^6 - Ax^3 + Bx + c^2 = y^2.$$

---

[1] "Methode der Zurückrechnung und Nebenaufgabe."

It is only necessary to put $y = x^3 + c$, whence $- Ax^2 + B = 2cx^2$ and $x^2 = \dfrac{B}{A + 2c}$. This gives Diophantos a rational solution if $\dfrac{B}{A + 2c}$ is a square.

6. If however this last condition does not hold, as in the case occurring IV. 19, $x^6 - 16x^3 + x + 64 = y^2$, Diophantos employs his usual artifice of "back-reckoning," by which he is enabled to replace this equation by $x^6 - 128x^3 + x + 4096 = y^2$, which satisfies the condition, and (assuming $y = x^3 + 64$) x is found to be $\frac{1}{16}$.

Second Class. Equation of the form

$$Ax^n + Bx^{n-1} + \ldots\ldots + Kx + L = y^3.$$

Except for such simple cases as $Ax^2 = y^3$, $Ax^4 = y^3$, where it is only necessary to assume $y = mx$, the only cases which occur in Diophantos are $Ax^2 + Bx + C = y^3$, $Ax^3 + Bx^2 + Cx + D = y^3$.

1. Equation $\qquad Ax^2 + Bx + C = y^3.$

There are of this form only two examples. First, in VI. 1 $x^2 - 4x + 4$ is to be made a cube, being at the same time already a square. Diophantos therefore naturally assumes $x - 2 =$ a cube number, say 8, whence $x = 10$.

Secondly, in VI. 19 a peculiar case occurs. A cube is to be found which exceeds a square by 2. Diophantos assumes $(x - 1)^3$ for the cube, and $(x + 1)^2$ for the square, obtaining $x^3 - 3x^2 + 3x - 1 = x^2 + 2x + 3$, or the equation

$$x^3 + x = 4x^2 + 4,$$

previously mentioned (pp. 36, 93), which is satisfied by $x = 4$. The question here arises: Was it accidentally or not that this cubic took so special and easy a form? Were $x - 1, x + 1$ assumed with the knowledge and intention of finding such an equation? Since 27 and 25 are so near each other and are, as Fermat observes[1], the only integral numbers which satisfy the

---

[1] Note to VI. 19. Fermatii *Opera Math.* p. 192.

conditions, it seems most likely that it was in view of these numbers that Diophantos hit upon the assumptions $x+1$, $x-1$, and employed them to lead back to a known result with all the air of a general proof. Had this not been so, we should probably have found, as elsewhere in the work, Diophantos first leading us on a false tack and then showing us how we can in all cases correct our assumptions. The very fact that he takes the right assumptions to begin with makes us suspect that the solution is not based upon a general principle, but is empirical merely.

2. The equation

$$Ax^3 + Bx^2 + Cx + D = y^3.$$

If A or D is a cube number this equation is easy of solution. For, first, if $A = a^3$ we have only to write $y = ax + \dfrac{B}{3a^2}$, and we arrive in Diophantos' manner at a simple equation.

Secondly, if $D = d^3$, we put $y = \dfrac{C}{3d^2}x + d$.

If the equation is $a^3x^3 + Bx^2 + Cx + d^3 = y^3$, we can use either assumption, or put $y = ax + d$, obtaining as before a simple equation.

Apparently Diophantos only used the last assumption; for he rejects as impossible the equation $y^3 = 8x^3 - x^2 + 8x - 1$ because $y = 2x - 1$ gives a negative value $x = -\frac{2}{11}$, whereas either of the other assumptions give rational values[1].

(2) *Double-equation.*

There are a few examples in which of two functions of x one is to be made a square, the other a cube, by one and the same rational value of x. The cases are for the most part very simple, e.g. in VI. 21 we have to solve

$$\left. \begin{array}{l} 4x + 2 = y^3 \\ 2x + 1 = z^2 \end{array} \right\},$$

therefore $y^3 = 2z^2$, and z is assumed to be 2.

---

[1] There is a special case in which C and D vanish, $Ax^3 + Bx^2 = y^3$. Here y is put $= mx$ and $x = \dfrac{B}{m^3 - A}$. Cf. IV. 6, 30.

A rather more complicated case is VI. 23, where we have the double equation

$$2x^2 + 2x = y^2 \atop x^3 + 2x^2 + x = z^3 \Big\} \, .$$

Diophantos assumes $y = mx$, whence $x = \dfrac{2}{m^2 - 2}$, and we have to solve the single equation

$$\left(\frac{2}{m^2 - 2}\right)^3 + 2\left(\frac{2}{m^2 - 2}\right)^2 + \frac{2}{m^2 - 2} = z^3,$$

or $$\frac{2m^4}{(m^2 - 2)^3} = z^3.$$

To make $2m^4$ a cube, we need only make $2m$ a cube, or put $m = 4$. This gives for x the value $\frac{1}{7}$.

The general case

$$Ax^3 + Bx^2 + Cx = z^3,$$
$$bx^2 + cx = y^2,$$

would, of course, be much more difficult; for, putting $y = mx$,

we find $$x = \frac{c}{m^2 - b},$$

and we have to solve

$$A\left(\frac{c}{m^2 - b}\right)^3 + B\left(\frac{c}{m^2 - b}\right)^2 + C\left(\frac{c}{m^2 - b}\right) = z^3,$$

or $$Ccm^4 + c(Bc - 2bC)m^2 + bc(bC - Bc) + Ac^3 = u^3,$$

of which equation the above corresponding one is a very particular case.

§ 3. *Summary of the preceding investigation.*

We may sum up briefly the results of our investigation of Diophantos' methods of dealing with equations thus.

1. Diophantos solves completely equations of the first degree, but takes pains beforehand to secure that the solution shall be positive. He shows remarkable address in reducing a number of simultaneous equations of the first degree to a single equation in *one* variable.

2.   For determinate equations of the second degree Diophantos has a general method or rule of solution.   He takes
however in the *Arithmetics* no account of more than *one* root,
even when both roots are positive rational numbers.   But his
object is always to secure *a* solution in rational numbers, and
therefore we need not be surprised at his ignoring one root of a
quadratic, even though he knew of its existence.

3.   No equations of a higher degree than the second are
found in the book except a particular case of a cubic.

4.   Indeterminate equations of the first degree are not
treated in the work as we have it, and indeterminate equations
of the second degree, e.g. $Ax^2 + Bx + C = y^2$, are only fully treated
in the case where A or C vanishes, in the more general cases
more imperfectly.

5.   For "double-equations" of the second degree he has a
definite method when the coefficient of x^2 in both expressions
vanishes; this however is not of quite general application, and is
supplemented in one or two cases by another artifice of particular
application.   Of more complicated cases we have only a few
examples under conditions favourable for solution by his
method.

6.   Diophantos' treatment of indeterminate equations of
higher degrees than the second depends upon the particular
conditions of the problems, and his methods lack generality.

7.   After all, more wonderful than his actual treatment of
equations are the extraordinary artifices by which he contrives
to avoid such equations as he cannot theoretically solve, e.g. by
his device of "Back-reckoning," instances of which, however,
would have been out of place in this chapter, and can only
be studied in the problems themselves.

§ 4.   I shall, as I said before, not attempt to class as methods
what Nesselmann has tried so to describe, e.g. "Solution by mere
reflection," "solution in general expressions," of which there
are few instances definitely described as such by Diophantos,
and "arbitrary determinations and assumptions."   It is clear that
the most that can be done to formulate these "methods" is the

enumeration of a few instances. This is what Nesselmann
has done, and he himself regrets at the end of his chapter on
"Methods of solution" that it must of necessity be so incomplete.
To understand and appreciate these artifices of Diophantos it is
necessary to read the problems themselves singly, and for these
I refer to the abstract of them in the Appendix. As for the
"Use of the right-angled triangle," all that can be said of a
general character is that rational right-angled triangles (whose
sides are all rational numbers) are alone used in Diophantos,
and that accordingly the introduction of such a right-angled
triangle is merely a convenient device to express the problem of
finding two square numbers whose sum is also a square number.
The general forms for the sides of a right-angled triangle are
$a^2 + b^2$, $a^2 - b^2$, $2ab$, which clearly satisfy the condition

$$(a^2 + b^2)^2 = (a^2 - b^2)^2 + (2ab)^2.$$

The expression of the sides in this form Diophantos calls "forming a right-angled triangle from the numbers a and b." It is
by this time unnecessary to observe that Diophantos does not
use general numbers such as a, b but particular ones. "Forming
a right-angled triangle from 7, 2" means taking a right-angled
triangle whose sides are $7^2 + 2^2$, $7^2 - 2^2$, $2 \cdot 7 \cdot 2$, or 53, 45, 28.

§ 5. METHOD OF LIMITS.

As Diophantos often has to find a series of numbers in
ascending or descending order of magnitude: as also he does
not admit negative solutions, it is often necessary for him to
reject a solution which he has found by a straightforward method,
in order to satisfy such conditions; he is then very frequently
obliged to find solutions of problems which lie within certain
limits in order to replace the ones rejected.

1. A very simple case is the following : Required to find a
value of x such that some power of it, x^n, shall lie between two
assigned limits, given numbers. Let the given numbers be a, b.
Then Diophantos' method is : Multiply a and b both successively
by 2^n, 3^n, and so on until some $(n)^{th}$ power is seen which lies between the two products. Thus suppose c^n lies between ap^n and bp^n;

then we can put $x = \dfrac{c}{p}$, in which case the condition is satisfied,

for $\left(\dfrac{c}{p}\right)^n$ lies between a and b.

Exx. In IV. 34 Diophantos finds a square between $\frac{5}{4}$ and 2 thus: he multiplies by a square, 64; thus we have the limits 80 and 128; 100 is clearly a square lying between these limits; hence $(\frac{10}{8})^2$ or $\frac{25}{16}$ satisfies the condition of lying between $\frac{5}{4}$ and 2.

Here of course Diophantos might have multiplied by any other square, as 16, and the limits would then have become 20 and 32, between which there lies the square 25, and so we should have $\frac{25}{16}$ again as the square required.

In VI. 23 a sixth power (a "cube-cube") is required which lies between 8 and 16. Now the sixth powers of the first natural numbers are 1, 64, 729, 4096...Multiply 8 and 16 (as in rule) by 2^6 or 64 and we have as limits 512 and 1024, and 729 lies between them; therefore $\frac{729}{64}$ is a sixth power such as was required. To multiply by 729 in this case would not give us a result.

2. Other problems of finding values of x agreeably to certain limits cannot be reduced to a general rule. By giving, however, a few instances, we may give an idea of Diophantos' methods in general.

Ex. 1. In IV. 26 it is necessary to find x so that $\dfrac{8}{x^2 + x}$ lies between x and $x + 1$. The first condition gives $8 > x^3 + x^2$. Diophantos accordingly assumes

$$8 = (x + \tfrac{1}{3})^3 = x^3 + x^2 + \dfrac{x}{3} + \tfrac{1}{27},$$

which is $> x^3 + x^2$. Thus $x = \frac{5}{3}$ satisfies one condition. It also is seen to satisfy the second, or $\dfrac{8}{x^2 + x} < x + 1$; but Diophantos practically neglects this condition, though it turns out to be satisfied. The method is, therefore, here imperfect.

Ex. 2. Find a value of x such that

$$x > \tfrac{1}{8}(x^2 - 60) < \tfrac{1}{5}(x^2 - 60),$$
or $\qquad x^2 - 60 > 5x, \quad x^2 - 60 < 8x.$

Hence, says Diophantos, x is $\not< 11$ nor > 12. We have
already spoken (pp. 90, 91) of the reasoning by which he
arrives at this result (by taking only one root of the quadratic,
and taking the nearest integral limits). It is also required
that $x^2 - 60$ shall be a square. Assuming then

$$x^2 - 60 = (x - m)^2, \quad x = \frac{m^2 + 60}{2m},$$

which must be $> 11 < 12$, whence

$$m^2 + 60 > 22m, \quad m^2 + 60 < 24m,$$

and (says Diophantos) m must therefore lie between 19 and 21.
Accordingly he writes $x^2 - 60 = (x - 20)^2$, and $x = 11\frac{1}{2}$, which is
a value of x satisfying the conditions.

§ 6. METHOD OF APPROXIMATION TO LIMITS.

We come now to a very distinctive method called by Diophantos παρισότης or παρισότητος ἀγωγή. The object of this
is to find two or three square numbers whose sum is a given
number, and each of which approximates as closely as possible
to one and the same number and therefore to each other.

This method can be best explained by giving Diophantos'
two instances, in the first of which *two* such squares, and in the
second *three* are required. In cases like this the principles
cannot be so well described with general symbols as with concrete numbers, whose properties are immediately obvious, and
render separate expression of conditions unnecessary.

Ex. 1. Divide 13 into two squares each of which > 6.

Take $\frac{13}{2}$ or $6\frac{1}{2}$ and find what small fraction $\frac{1}{x^2}$ added to it
makes it a square: thus $6\frac{1}{2} + \frac{1}{x^2}$ must be a square, or $26 + \frac{1}{y^2}$
is a square. Diophantos puts

$$26 + \frac{1}{y^2} = \left(5 + \frac{1}{y}\right)^2, \text{ or } 26y^2 + 1 = (5y + 1)^2,$$

whence $y = 10$ and $\frac{1}{y^2} = \frac{1}{100}$, or $\frac{1}{x^2} = \frac{1}{400}$, and $6\frac{1}{2} + \frac{1}{400} = $ a square $= (\frac{51}{20})^2$. [The assumption of $(5y+1)^2$ is not arbitrary, for assume $26y^2 + 1 = (py+1)^2$, therefore $y = \dfrac{2p}{26-p^2}$, and, since $\dfrac{1}{y}$ should be a *small* proper fraction, therefore 5 is the most suitable and the smallest possible value for p, $26 - p^2$ being $< 2p$ or $p^2 + 2p + 1 > 27$.] It is now necessary (says Diophantos) to divide 13 into two squares whose sides are each as near as possible to $\frac{51}{20}$.

Now the sides of the two squares of which 13 is by nature compounded are 3 and 2, and

$$\left.\begin{array}{l} 3 \text{ is } > \tfrac{51}{20} \text{ by } \tfrac{9}{20} \\ 2 \text{ is } < \tfrac{51}{20} \text{ by } \tfrac{11}{20} \end{array}\right\}.$$

Now if $3 - \frac{9}{20}$, $2 + \frac{11}{20}$ were taken as the sides of two squares their sum would be

$$2\left(\tfrac{51}{20}\right)^2 = \frac{2 \cdot 2601}{400},$$

which is > 13.

Accordingly Diophantos puts

$$3 - 9x, \quad 2 + 11x,$$

for the sides of the required squares, where x is therefore not exactly $\frac{1}{20}$ but near it.

Thus, assuming

$$(3 - 9x)^2 + (2 + 11x)^2 = 13,$$

Diophantos obtains $x = \frac{5}{101}$.

Thus the sides of the required squares are $\frac{257}{101}$, $\frac{258}{101}$.

Ex. 2. Divide 10 into three squares such that each square is > 3.

Take $\frac{10}{3}$ or $3\frac{1}{3}$ and find what fraction of the form $\dfrac{1}{x^2}$ added to it will make it a square, i.e. make $30 + \dfrac{9}{x^2}$ a square or $30y^2 + 1$, where $\dfrac{3}{x} = \dfrac{1}{y}$.

Diophantos writes $30y^2 + 1 = (5y + 1)^2$, whence $y = 2$ and $\frac{1}{x^2} = \frac{1}{36}$.

And $3\frac{1}{3} + \frac{1}{36} = $ a square $= \frac{121}{36}$.

[As before, if we assume $30y^2 + 1 = (py + 1)^2$, $y = \dfrac{2p}{30 - p^2}$, and since $\frac{1}{y}$ must be a small proper fraction, $30 - p^2$ should $< 2p$ or $p^2 + 2p + 1 > 31$, and 5 is the smallest possible value of p. For this reason Diophantos chooses it.]

We have now (says Diophantos) to make the sides of the required squares as near as may be to $\frac{11}{6}$.

Now $\qquad 10 = 9 + 1 = 3^2 + (\frac{3}{5})^2 + (\frac{4}{5})^2$,

and 3, $\frac{3}{5}$, $\frac{4}{5}$ are the sides of three squares whose sum $= 10$. Bringing $(3, \frac{3}{5}, \frac{4}{5})$ and $\frac{11}{6}$ to a common denominator, we have

$$(\tfrac{90}{30}, \tfrac{18}{30}, \tfrac{24}{30}) \text{ and } \tfrac{55}{30}.$$

Now $\qquad\qquad 3$ is $> \frac{55}{30}$ by $\frac{35}{30}$,

$\qquad\qquad\qquad \frac{3}{5}$ is $< \frac{55}{30}$ by $\frac{37}{30}$,

$\qquad\qquad\qquad \frac{4}{5}$ is $< \frac{55}{30}$ by $\frac{31}{30}$.

If then we took $3 - \frac{35}{30}$, $\frac{3}{5} + \frac{37}{30}$, $\frac{4}{5} + \frac{31}{30}$ for the sides, the sum of their squares would be $3 (\frac{11}{6})^2$ or $\frac{363}{36}$, which is > 10. Diophantos accordingly assumes as the sides of the three required squares

$$3 - 35x, \quad \tfrac{3}{5} + 37x, \quad \tfrac{4}{5} + 31x,$$

where x must therefore be not exactly $\frac{1}{30}$, but near it.

Solving $\quad (3 - 35x)^2 + (\tfrac{3}{5} + 37x)^2 + (\tfrac{4}{5} + 31x)^2 = 10$,

or $\qquad\qquad 10 - 116x + 3555x^2 = 10$,

we have $\qquad\qquad x = \frac{116}{3555}$;

the required sides are therefore found to be

$$\tfrac{1321}{711}, \quad \tfrac{1285}{711}, \quad \tfrac{1288}{711},$$

and the squares $\qquad \frac{1745041}{505521}, \frac{1651225}{505521}, \frac{1658944}{505521}$.

The two instances here given, though only instances, serve perfectly to illustrate the method of Diophantos. To have put them generally with the use of algebraical symbols, instead of

concrete numbers, would have rendered necessary the introduction of a large number of such symbols, and the number of
conditions (e.g. that such and such an expression shall be a
square) which it would have been necessary to express would
have nullified all the advantages of this general treatment.

As it only lies within my scope to explain what we actually
find in Diophantos' work, I shall not here introduce certain
investigations embodied by Poselger in his article "Beiträge zur
Unbestimmten Analysis," published in the *Abhandlungen
der Königlichen Akademie der Wissenschaften zu Berlin Aus dem
Jahre* 1832, Berlin, 1834. One section of this paper Poselger
entitles "Annäherungs-methoden nach Diophantus," and obtains
in it, upon Diophantos' principles [1], a method of approximation
to the value of a surd which will furnish the same results as the
method by means of continued fractions, except that the approximation by what he calls the "Diophantine method" is quicker
than the method of continued fractions, so that it may serve to
expedite the latter [2].

[1] "Wenn wir den Weg des Diophantos verfolgen."
[2] "Die Diophantische Methode kann also dazu dienen, die Convergenz der
Partialbrüche des Kettenbruchs zu beschleunigen."

CHAPTER VI.

§ 1. THE PORISMS OF DIOPHANTOS.

WE have already spoken (in the Historical Introduction) of the *Porisms* of Diophantos as having probably formed a distinct part of the work of our author. We also discussed the question as to whether the *Porisms* now lost formed an integral portion of the *Arithmetics* or whether it was a completely separate treatise. What remains for us to do under the head of Diophantos' *Porisms* is to collect such references to them and such enunciations of definite porisms as are directly given by Diophantos. If we confine our list of Porisms to those given under that name by Diophantos, it does not therefore follow that many other theorems enunciated, assumed or implied in the extant work, but not distinctly called Porisms, may not with equal propriety be supposed to have been actually propounded in the *Porisms*. For distinctness, however, and in order to make our assumptions perfectly safe, it will be better to separate what are actually called porisms from other theorems implied and assumed in Diophantos' problems.

First then with regard to the actual *Porisms*. I shall not attempt to discuss here the nature of the proposition which was called a porism, for such a discussion would be irrelevant to my purpose. The *Porisms* themselves too have been well enumerated and explained by Nesselmann in his tenth chapter; he has also given, with few omissions, the chief of the other theorems assumed by Diophantos as known. Of necessity, therefore, in this section and the next I shall have to cover very much the same ground, and shall accordingly be as brief as may be.

Porism 1.   The first porism enunciated by Diophantos occurs in v. 3.   He says "We have from the *Porisms* that if each of two numbers and their product when severally added to the same number produce squares, the numbers are the squares of two consecutive numbers[1]."   This theorem is not correctly enunciated, for two consecutive squares are not the only two numbers which will satisfy the condition.   For suppose

$$x + a = m^2, \quad y + a = n^2, \quad xy + a = p^2.$$

Now by help of the first two equations we find

$$xy + a = m^2 n^2 - a (m^2 + n^2 - 1) + a^2,$$

and this is equal to p^2.   In order that

$$m^2 n^2 - a (m^2 + n^2 - 1) + a^2$$

may be a square certain conditions must be satisfied.   One sufficient condition is

$$m^2 + n^2 - 1 = 2mn,$$

or $m - n = \pm 1,$

and this is Diophantos' condition.

But we may also regard

$$m^2 n^2 - a (m^2 + n^2 - 1) + a^2 = p^2$$

as an indeterminate equation in m of which we know one solution, namely $m = n \pm 1.$

Other solutions are then found by substituting $z + (n \pm 1)$ for m, whence we have the equation

$$(n^2 - a) z^2 + 2 \{n^2 (n \pm 1) - a (n \pm 1)\} z + (n^2 - a) (n \pm 1)^2$$
$$- a (n^2 - 1) + a^2 = p^2,$$

or $(n^2 - a) z^2 + 2 (n^2 - a) (n \pm 1) z + \{n (n \pm 1) - a\}^2 = p^2,$

which is easy to solve in Diophantos' manner, the absolute term being a square.

But in the problem v. 3 *three* numbers are required such that each of them, and the product of each pair, severally added

---

[1] καὶ ἐπεὶ ἔχομεν ἐν τοῖς πορίσμασιν, ὅτι ἐὰν δύο ἀριθμοὶ ἑκάτερός τε καὶ ὁ ὑπ᾽ αὐτῶν μετὰ τοῦ αὐτοῦ δοθέντος ποιῇ τετράγωνον, γεγόνασιν ἀπὸ δύο τετραγώνων τῶν κατὰ τὸ ἑξῆς.

to a given number produce squares. Thus, if the third number be z, three more conditions must be added, namely, $z + a$, $zx + a$, $yz + a$ should be squares. The two last conditions are satisfied, if $m + 1 = n$, by putting

$$z = 2(x+y) - 1 = 4m^2 + 4m + 1 - 4a,$$

when

$$xz + a = \{m(2m+1) - 2a\}^2,$$

$$yz + a = \{m(2m+3) - (2a-1)\}^2,$$

and this means of satisfying the conditions may have affected the formulating of the Porism.

v. 4 gives another case of the Porism with $-a$ for $+a$.

Porism 2. In v. 5 Diophantos says[1], "We have in the *Porisms* that in addition to any two consecutive squares we can find another number which, being double of the sum of both and increased by 2, makes up three numbers, the product of any pair of which *plus* the sum of that pair or the third number produces a square," i.e.

$$m^2, \quad m^2 + 2m + 1, \quad 4(m^2 + m + 1),$$

are three numbers which satisfy the conditions.

The same porism is assumed and made use of in the following problem, v. 6.

Porism 3 occurs in v. 19. Unfortunately the text of the enunciation is corrupt, but there can be no doubt that the correct statement of the porism is " The difference of two cubes can be transformed into the sum of two cubes." Diophantos contents himself with the mere enunciation and does not proceed to effect the actual transformation. Thus we do not know his method, or how far he was able to prove the porism as a perfectly general theorem. The theorems upon the transformation of sums and differences of cubes were investigated by Vieta, Bachet and Fermat.

---

[1] καὶ ἔχομεν πάλιν ἐν τοῖς πορίσμασιν ὅτι πᾶσι δύο τετραγώνοις τοῖς κατὰ τὸ ἑξῆς προσευρίσκεται ἕτερος ἀριθμὸς ὃς ὢν διπλασίων συναμφοτέρου καὶ δυάδι μείζων, τρεῖς ἀριθμοὺς ποιεῖ ὧν ὁ ὑπὸ ὁποιωνοῦν ἐάντε προσλάβῃ συναμφότερον, ἐάντε λοιπὸν ποιεῖ τετράγωνον.

Vieta gives three problems on the subject [1] (*Zetetica* IV.).

1.   Given two cubes, to find in rational numbers two others whose sum equals the difference of the two given ones.   As a solution of $a^3 - b^3 = x^3 + y^3$, he finds

$$x = \frac{a\,(a^3 - 2b^3)}{a^3 + b^3}, \qquad y = \frac{b\,(2a^3 - b^3)}{a^3 + b^3}\,.$$

2.   Given two cubes, to find in rational numbers two others, whose difference equals the sum of the given ones;

$$a^3 + b^3 = x^3 - y^3, \qquad x = \frac{a\,(a^3 + 2b^3)}{a^3 - b^3}, \qquad y = \frac{b\,(2a^3 + b^3)}{a^3 - b^3}\,.$$

3.   Given two cubes, to find in rational numbers two others, whose difference equals the difference of the given ones;

$$a^3 - b^3 = x^3 - y^3, \qquad x = \frac{b\,(2a^3 - b^3)}{a^3 + b^3}, \qquad y = \frac{a\,(2b^3 - a^3)}{a^3 + b^3}\,.$$

In 1 clearly x is negative if $2b^3 > a^3$; therefore, to secure a "rational" result, $\left(\dfrac{a}{b}\right)^3 > 2$.   But for a "rational" result in 3 we must have exactly the opposite condition, $\dfrac{a^3}{b^3} < 2$.   Fermat, who apparently was the first to notice this, remarked that in consequence the processes 1 and 3 exactly supplement each other,

[1] Poselger (*Berlin Abhandlungen*, 1832) has obtained these results.   He gets, e.g. the first as follows:

Assume two cubes $(a - x)^3$, $(mx - \beta)^3$, which are to be taken so that their sum $= a^3 - \beta^3$.

Now
$$(a - x)^3 = a^3 - 3a^2x + 3ax^2 - x^3,$$
$$(mx - \beta)^3 = -\beta^3 + 3m\beta^2 x - 3m^2\beta x^2 + m^3 x^3.$$

If then
$$m = \left(\frac{a}{\beta}\right)^2,$$

$$x = \frac{3\,(m^2\beta - a)}{m^3 - 1} = \frac{3a\beta^3}{a^3 + \beta^3},$$

$$(a - x)^3 + (mx - \beta)^3 = a^3 - \beta^3,$$

and
$$a - x = \frac{a\,(a^3 - 2\beta^3)}{a^3 + \beta^3}$$

$$\left. mx - \beta = \frac{\beta\,(2a^3 - \beta^3)}{a^3 + \beta^3} \right\}.$$

so that by employing them successively we can effect the transformation of 1, even when

$$\left(\frac{a}{b}\right)^3 \not> 2.$$

Process 2 is always possible, therefore by the suitable combination of processes the transformation of a sum of two cubes into a difference, or a difference of two cubes into a sum of two others, is always practicable.

Besides the *Porisms*, there are many other propositions assumed or implied by Diophantos which are not definitely called porisms, though some of them are very similar to the porisms just described.

§ 2.   THEOREMS ASSUMED OR IMPLIED BY DIOPHANTOS.

Of these Nesselmann rightly distinguishes two classes, the first being of the nature of *identical formulae*, the second theorems relating to the sums of two or more square numbers, &c.

1.   The first class do not require enumeration in detail. We may mention one or two examples, e.g. that the expressions $\left(\frac{a+b}{2}\right)^2 - ab$ and $a^2(a+1)^2 + a^2 + (a+1)^2$ are squares, and that $a(a^2 - a) + a + (a^2 - a)$ is always a cube.

Again, Nesselmann thinks that Diophantos made use of the separation of $a^3 - b^3$ into factors in the solution of v. 8, in which he gives the result without clearly showing his mode of procedure in obtaining it; though its separability into factors is nowhere expressly mentioned, and is not made use of in certain places where we should most naturally expect to find it, e.g. in IV. 12.

2.   But far more important than these identical formulae are the numerous propositions in the Theory of Numbers which we find stated or assumed as known in the *Arithmetics*. It is, in general, in explanation or extension of these that Fermat wrote his famous notes. So far as Diophantos is concerned it is extremely difficult, or rather impossible, to say how far these

propositions rested for him upon rigorous mathematical demonstration, and how far, on the other hand, his knowledge of them
was merely empirical and derived only from trial in particular
cases, whereas he enunciates them or assumes them to hold
in all possible cases. But the objection to assuming that
Diophantos had a completely scientific system of investigating
these propositions, as opposed to a merely empirical knowledge
of them, on the ground that' he does not prove them in the
present treatise, would seem to apply equally to Fermat's own
theorems set forth in these notes, except in so far as we might
be inclined to argue that Diophantos could not, in the period
to which he belongs, have possessed such machinery of demonstration as Fermat. Even supposing this to be true, we should
be very careful in making assertions as to what the ancients
could or could not prove, when we consider how much they
did actually accomplish. And, secondly, as regards machinery
of proof, we have seen that up to Fermat's time there had
been very little advance upon Diophantos in the matter of
notation.

It will be best to enumerate here in order the principal
propositions of this kind which we find in Diophantos, observing
in each case any indication, which is perceptible, of the extent
which we may suppose Diophantos' knowledge of the Theory of
Numbers to have reached. It will be necessary and useful
to refer to Fermat's notes occasionally.

The question of the merits of Fermat's notes themselves
this is not the place to inquire into. It is well known
that he almost universally enunciates the theorems contained
in these notes without proof, and gives as his reason for not
inserting the proofs that his margin was too small, and so on.
It is considered, however, that as his theorems are always *true*,
he must necessarily have proved them rigorously. Concerning
this statement I will only remark that in the note to v. 25
Fermat addresses himself to the solution of a problem which
was "most difficult and had troubled him a long time," and
says that he has at last found a general solution. Of this
he gives a demonstration which is hopelessly wrong, and which
vitiates the solution completely.

(a)   *Theorems in Diophantos respecting the composition of numbers as the sum of two squares.*

1.   *Any square number can be resolved into two squares in any number of ways,* II. 8, 9.

2.   *Any number which is the sum of two squares can be resolved into two other squares in any number of ways,* II. 10.

N.B. It is implied throughout that the squares may be fractional, as well as integral.

3.   *If there are two whole numbers each of which is the sum of two squares, their product can be resolved into the sum of two squares in two ways,* III. 22.

The object of III. 22 is to find four rational right-angled triangles having the same hypotenuse. The method is this. Form two right-angled triangles from (a, b), (c, d) respectively, viz.

$$a^2 + b^2, \quad a^2 - b^2, \quad 2ab,$$
$$c^2 + d^2, \quad c^2 - d^2, \quad 2cd.$$

Multiplying all the sides of each by the hypotenuse of the other, we have two triangles having the same hypotenuse,

$$(a^2 + b^2)(c^2 + d^2), \quad (a^2 - b^2)(c^2 + d^2), \quad 2ab(c^2 + d^2),$$
$$(a^2 + b^2)(c^2 + d^2), \quad (a^2 + b^2)(c^2 - d^2), \quad 2cd(a^2 + b^2).$$

Two other triangles having the same hypotenuse are got by using the theorem enunciated, viz.

$$(a^2 + b^2)(c^2 + d^2) = (ac \pm bd)^2 + (ad \mp bc)^2,$$

and the triangles are formed from $ac \pm bd$, $ad \mp bc$, being

$$(a^2 + b^2)(c^2 + d^2), \quad 4abcd + (a^2 - b^2)(c^2 - d^2), \quad 2(ac + bd)(ad - bc),$$
$$(a^2 + b^2)(c^2 + d^2), \quad 4abcd - (a^2 - b^2)(c^2 - d^2), \quad 2(ac - bd)(ad + bc).$$

In Diophantos' case

$$a^2 + b^2 = 1^2 + 2^2 = 5,$$
$$c^2 + d^2 = 2^2 + 3^2 = 13 ;$$

and the triangles are

$$(65, 52, 39), \quad (65, 60, 25), \quad (65, 63, 16), \quad (65, 56, 33).$$

[If certain relations hold between a, b, c, d this method fails. Diophantos has provided against them by taking two right-angled triangles ὑπὸ ἐλαχίστων ἀριθμῶν (3, 4, 5), (5, 12, 13)].

Upon this problem Fermat remarks that (1) a prime number of the form $4n+1$ can only be the hypotenuse of a right-angled triangle in one way, the square of it in two ways, &c.

(2) If a prime number made up of two squares be multiplied by another prime also made up of two squares, the product can be divided into two squares in two ways; if the first is multiplied by the square of the second, in three ways, &c.

Now we observe that Diophantos has taken for the hypotenuse of the first two right-angled triangles *the first two prime numbers of the form* $4n+1$, viz. 5 and 13, both of which numbers are the sum of two squares, and, in accordance with Fermat's remark, they can each be the hypotenuse of one single right-angled triangle only. It does not, of course, follow from this selection of 5 and 13 that Diophantos was acquainted with the theorem that *every prime number of the form* $4n+1$ *is the sum of two squares.* But, when we remark that he multiplies 5 and 13 together and observes that the product can form the hypotenuse of a right-angled triangle in four ways, it is very hard to resist the conclusion that he was acquainted with the mathematical facts stated in Fermat's second remark on this problem. For clearly 65 is the smallest number which can be the hypotenuse of four rational right-angled triangles; also Diophantos did not find out this fact simply by *trying* all numbers up to 65 ; on the contrary he obtained it by multiplying together the first two prime numbers of the form $4n+1$, in a perfectly scientific manner.

This remarkable problem, then, serves to show pretty conclusively that Diophantos had considerable knowledge of the properties of numbers which are the sum of two squares.

4. Still more remarkable is a condition of possibility of solution prefixed to the problem v. 12. The object of this problem is "to divide 1 into two parts such that, if a given number is added to either part, the result will be a square." Unfortunately the text of the added condition is very much

corrupted. There is no doubt, however, about the first few words, " *The given number must not be odd.*" i.e. *No number of the form* $4n + 3$ [*or* $4n - 1$] *can be the sum of two squares.* The text, however, of the latter half of the condition is, in Bachet's edition, in a hopeless state, and the point cannot be settled without a fresh consultation of the MSS.[1] The true condition is given by Fermat thus. "*The given number must not be odd, and the double of it increased by one, when divided by the greatest square which measures it, must not be divisible by a prime number of the form* $4n - 1$." (Note upon v. 12; also in a letter to Roberval). There is, of course, room for any number of conjectures as to what may have been Diophantos' words[2]. There would seem to be no doubt that in Diophantos' condition there was something about "double the number" (i.e. a number of the form $4n$), also about "greater by unity" and "a prime number." From our data, then, it would appear that, if Diophantos did not succeed in giving the complete sufficient and necessary condition stated by Fermat, he must at all events have made a close approximation to it.

[1] Bachet's text has δεῖ δὴ τὸν διδόμενον μήτε περισσὸν εἶναι, μήτε ὁ διπλασίων αὐτοῦ ή μ°ᾱ. μείζονα ἔχῃ μέρος δ̄.ἢ μετρεῖται ὑπὸ τοῖ ᾱ°ὖ. ϛ°ὖ.

He also says that a Vatican MS. reads μήτε ὁ διπλασίων αὐτοῦ ἀριθμὸν μονάδα ᾱ. μείζονα ἔχῃ μέρος τέταρτον, ἢ μετρεῖται ὑπὸ τοῦ πρώτου ἀριθμοῦ.

Neither does Xylander help us much. He frankly tells us that he cannot understand the passage. "Imitari statueram bonos grammaticos hoc loco, quorum (ut aiunt) est multa nescire. Ego verò nescio heic non multa, sed paene omnia. Quid enim (ut reliqua taceam) est μήτε ὁ διπλασίων αὐτοῦ ἀρ̄ μō ᾱ, &c. quae causae huius προσδιορισμοῦ, quae processus? immo qui processus, quae operatio, quae solutio?"

[2] Nesselmann discusses an attempt made by Schulz to correct the text, and himself suggests μήτε τὸν διπλασίονα αὐτοῦ ἀριθμὸν μονάδι μείζονα ἔχειν, ὃς μετρεῖται ὑπὸ τινος πρώτου ἀριθμοῦ. But this ignores μέρος τέταρτον and is not satisfactory.

Hankel, however (*Gesch. d. Math.* p. 169), says: "Ich zweifele nicht, dass die von den Msscr. arg entstellte Determination so zu lesen ist: Δεῖ δὴ τὸν διδόμενον μήτε περισσὸν εἶναι, μήτε τὸν διπλασίονα αὐτοῦ ἀριθμὸν μονάδι ᾱ μείζονα μετρεῖσθαι ὑπό του πρώτου ἀριθμοῦ, ὃς ἂν μονάδι ᾱ μείζων ἔχῃ μέρος τέταρτον." Now this correction, which exactly gives Fermat's condition, seems a decidedly probable one. Here the words μέρος τέταρτον find a place; and, secondly, the repetition of μονάδι ᾱ μείζων might well confuse a copyist. του for τοῦ is of course natural enough; Nesselmann reads τινος for του.

H. D.   9

We thus see (a) that Diophantos certainly knew that no number of the form $4n + 3$ could be the sum of two squares, and (b) that he had, at least, advanced a considerable way towards the discovery of the true condition of this problem, as quoted above from Fermat.

(b)   On numbers which are the sum of three squares.

In the problem v. 14 a condition is stated by Diophantos respecting the form of a number which added to three parts of unity makes each of them a square. If a be this number, clearly $3a + 1$ must be divisible into three squares.

Respecting the number a Diophantos says " It must not be 2 or any multiple of 8 increased by 2."

i.e. *a number of the form* $24n + 7$ *cannot be the sum of three squares*. Now the factor **3** of 24 is irrelevant here, for with respect to *three* this number is of the form $3m + 1$, and this so far as **3** is concerned might be a square or the sum of two or three squares. Hence we may neglect the factor **3** in $24n$.

We must therefore credit Diophantos with the knowledge of the fact that *no number of the form* $8n + 7$ *can be the sum of three squares*.

This condition is true, but does not include *all* the numbers which cannot be the sum of three squares, for it is not true that all numbers which are not of the form $8n + 7$ are made up of three squares. Even Bachet remarked that the number a might not be of the form $32n + 9$, or a number of the form $96n + 28$ cannot be the sum of three squares.

Fermat gives the conditions to which a must be subject thus:

Write down two geometrical series (common ratio of each 4), the first and second series beginning respectively with 1, 8,

1	4	16	64	256	1024	4096
8	32	128	512	2048	8192	32768

then a must not be (1) any number obtained by taking twice any term of the upper series and adding all the preceding terms, or (2) the number found by adding to the numbers so obtained any multiple of the corresponding term of the second series.

Thus (a) must not be,

$$
\begin{aligned}
8n + 2.1 &= 8n + 2, \\
32n + 2.4 + 1 &= 32n + 9, \\
128n + 2.16 + 4 + 1 &= 128n + 37, \\
512n + 2.64 + 16 + 4 + 1 &= 512n + 149, \\
&\text{&c.}
\end{aligned}
$$

Again there are other problems, e.g. V. 22, in which, though conditions are necessary for the possibility of solution, none are mentioned; but suitable assumptions are tacitly made, without rules by which they must be guided. It does not follow from the omission to state such rules that Diophantos was ignorant of even the minutest points connected with them ; as however we have no definite statements, it is best to desist from speculation in cases of doubt.

(c) *Composition of numbers as the sum of four squares.*

Every number is either a square or the sum of two, three or four squares. This well-known theorem, enunciated by Fermat in his note to Diophantos IV. 31, shows at once that any number can be divided into four squares either integral or fractional, since any square number can be divided into two other squares, integral or fractional. We have now to look for indications in the *Arithmetics* as to how far Diophantos was acquainted with the properties of numbers as the sum of four squares. Unfortunately it is impossible to decide this question with anything like certainty. There are three problems [IV. 31, 32 and V. 17] in which it is required to divide a number into four squares, and from the absence of mention of any condition to which the number must conform, considering that in both cases where a number is to be divided into *three* or *two* squares [V. 14 and 12] he *does* state a condition, we should probably be right in inferring that Diophantos was aware, at least *empirically,* if not scientifically, that *any* number could be divided into four squares. That he was able to prove the theorem scientifically it would be rash to assert, though it is not impossible. But we may at least be certain that Diophantos came as near to the proof of it as did Bachet, who takes all the natural numbers up to 120 and finds by trial that all of them can actually be expressed as squares, or as the sum of two, three or four squares in whole numbers. So much we may be sure that Diophantos could do, and hence he might have empirically satisfied himself that in any case occurring in practice it is possible to divide any number into four squares, integral or fractional, even if he could not give a rigorous mathematical demonstration of the general theorem. Here again we must be content, at least in our present state of knowledge of Greek mathematics, to remain in doubt.

CHAPTER VII.

§ **1.** Of the many vexed questions relating to Diophantos none is more difficult to pronounce upon than that which we propose to discuss in the present chapter. Here, as in so many other cases, diametrically opposite views have been taken by authorities equally capable of judging as to the merits of the case. Thus Bachet calls Diophantos "optimum praeclarissimumque Logisticae parentem," though possibly he means no more by this than what he afterwards says, "that he was the first algebraist of whom we know." Cossali quotes "l' abate Andres" as the most thoroughgoing upholder of the originality of Diophantos. M. Tannery, however, whom we have before had occasion to mention, takes a completely opposite view, being entirely unwilling to credit Diophantos with being anything more than a learned compiler. Views intermediate between these extremes are those of Nicholas Saunderson, Cossali, Colebrooke and Nesselmann; and we shall find that, so far as we are able to judge from the data before us, Saunderson's estimate is singularly good. He says in his *Elements of Algebra* (1740), "Diophantos is the first writer on Algebra we meet with among the ancients; not that the invention of the art is particularly to be ascribed to him, for he has nowhere taught the fundamental rules and principles of Algebra; he treats it everywhere as an art already known, and seems to intend, not so much to teach, as to cultivate and improve it, by applying it to certain indeterminate problems concerning square and cube numbers, right-angled triangles, &c., which till that time seemed to have been either not at all considered, or at least not regularly treated of. These

problems are very curious and entertaining; but yet in the
resolution of them there frequently occur difficulties, which
nothing less than the nicest and most refined Algebra, applied
with the utmost skill and judgment, could ever surmount: and
most certain it is that, in this way, no man ever extended the
limits of analytic art further than Diophantos has done, or discovered greater penetration and judgment; whether we consider
his wonderful sagacity and peculiar artifice in forming such
proper positions as the nature of the questions under consideration required, or the more than ordinary subtilty of his reasoning upon them.   Every particular problem puts us upon a new
way of thinking, and furnishes a fresh vein of analytical treasure,
which, considering the vast variety there is of them, cannot but
be very instructive to the mind in conducting itself through
almost all difficulties of this kind, wherever they occur."

§ 2. We will now, without anticipating our results further,
proceed to consider the arguments for and against Diophantos'
originality. But first we may dispose of the supposition that
Greek algebra may have been derived from Arabia. This is
rendered inconceivable by what we know of the state of learning
in Arabia at different periods. Algebra cannot have been
developed in Arabia at the time when Diophantos wrote;
the claim of Mohammed ibn Mūsā to be considered the first
important Arabian algebraist, if not actually the first, is apparently not disputed. On the other hand Rodet has shown
that Mohammed ibn Mūsā was largely indebted to Greece.
There is moreover great dissimilarity between Greek and Indian
algebra ; this would seem to indicate that the two were evolved
independently. We may also here dispose of Bombelli's strange
statement that he found that Diophantos very often quoted
Indian authors[1]. We do not find in Diophantos, as we have
him, a single reference to any Indian author whatever. There
is therefore some difficulty in understanding Bombelli's positive
statement. It is at first sight a tempting hypothesis to suppose
that the "frequent quotations" occurred in parts of Diophantos'

---

[1] "Ed in detta opera abbiamo ritrovato, ch' egli assai volte cita gli autori
indiani, col che mi ha fatto conoscere, che questa disciplina appo gl' indiani
prima fu che agli arabi."

work contained only in the MS. which Bombelli used.   But we
know that not a single Indian author is mentioned in that MS.
We can only explain the remark by supposing that Bombelli
confused the text and the scholia of Maximus Planudes; for in
the latter mention is made of an " Indian method of multiplication."   Such must be considered the meagre foundation for
Bombelli's statement.

There is not, then, much doubt that, if we are to find any
writers on algebra earlier than Diophantos to whom he was
indebted, we must seek for them among his own countrymen.

§ 3.   Let us now consider the indications bearing upon the
present question which are to be found in Diophantos' own work.
Distinct allusions to previous writers there are none with the
sole exception of the two references to Hypsikles which occur
in the fragment on *Polygonal Numbers*.   These references, however, are of little or no importance as affecting the question of
Diophantos' originality; for, so far as they show anything, they
show that Diophantos was far in advance of Hypsikles in his
treatment of polygonal numbers.   And, so far as we can judge
of the progress which had been made in their theoretical treatment by writers anterior to Diophantos from what we know of
such arithmeticians as Nikomachos and Theon of Smyrna, we
must conclude that (even if we assume that the missing part of
Diophantos' tract on this subject was insignificant as compared
with the portion which has survived) Diophantos made a great
step in advance of his predecessors.   His method of dealing
with polygonal numbers is new; and we look in vain among
his precursors for equally general propositions with regard to
such numbers or for equally scientific proofs of known properties.   Not that previous arithmeticians were unacquainted
with Diophantos' propositions as applied to particular polygonal
numbers, and even as applicable generally; but of their general
application they convinced themselves only empirically, and by
the successive evolution of higher and higher orders of such
numbers.

We may here remark, with respect to the term "arithmetic"
which Diophantos applies to his whole work, that he is making
a new use of the term.   According to the previously accepted

distinction of ἀριθμητική and λογιστική the former treats of the
abstract properties of numbers, considered apart from their
mutual relations, λογιστική of problems involving the relations
of concrete numbers. λογιστική, then, includes algebra. According to the distinction previously in vogue the term ἀριθμητική would properly apply only to Diophantos' tract on
Polygonal Numbers; but, as in the six books of Diophantos the
numbers are treated as abstract, he drops the distinction.

§ 4. Next to direct references to the names of predecessors,
we must look to the language of Diophantos, in order to see
whether there is any implication that anything which he teaches
is new. And in this regard we might naturally expect that
the preface or dedication to Dionysios would be important. It
is as follows: Τὴν εὕρεσιν τῶν ἐν τοῖς ἀριθμοῖς προβλημάτων,
τιμιώτατέ μοι Διονύσιε, γινώσκων σε σπουδαίως ἔχοντα μαθεῖν,
ὀργανῶσαι τὴν μέθοδον ἐπειράθην, ἀρξάμενος ἀφ᾽ ὧν συνέστηκε
τὰ πράγματα θεμελίων, ὑποστῆσαι τὴν ἐν τοῖς ἀριθμοῖς φύσιν
τε καὶ δύναμιν. ἴσως μὲν οὖν δοκεῖ τὸ πρᾶγμα δυσχερέστερον,
ἐπειδὴ μήπω γνώριμόν ἐστι, δυσέλπιστοι γὰρ εἰς κατόρθωσίν
εἰσιν αἱ τῶν ἀρχομένων ψυχαί, ὅμως δ᾽ εὐκατάληπτόν σοι γενή-
σεται διὰ τὴν σὴν προθυμίαν καὶ τὴν ἐμὴν ἀπόδειξιν· ταχεῖα
γὰρ εἰς μάθησιν ἐπιθυμία προσλαβοῦσα διδαχήν. The first
expression which would seem to carry with it an indication of
the nature of the work as conceived by Diophantos himself is
ὀργανῶσαι τὴν μεθοδόν. The word ὀργανῶσαι has of itself been
enough to convince some that the whole matter and method of
the *Arithmetics* were original[1]. Cossali and Colebrooke are of
opinion that the language of the preface implies that some part
of what Diophantos is about to teach is new[2]. But Montucla

---

[1] Cf. the view of "l' abate Andres" as stated by Cossali: "Diofanto stesso
parla in guisa, che sembra mostrare assai chiaramente d' essere stata sua inven-
zione la dottrina da lui proposta, e spiegata nella sua opera."

[2] "A me par troppo il dire, che da quelle espressioni non ne esca alcun
lume; mi pare troppo il restingere la novità, che annunziano, al metodo, che nell'
opera di Diofanto regnas si mira; ma parmi anche troppo il dedurne essere stato
Diofanto in assoluto senso inventor dell' analisi." Cossali.
"He certainly intimates that some part of what he proposes to teach is new:
ἴσως μὲν οὖν δοκεῖ τὸ πρᾶγμα δυσχερέστερον ἐπειδὴ μήπω γνώριμόν ἐστι: while in
other places (Def. 10) he expects the student to be previously exercised in the

does not go too far when he says that the preface does not give us any clue. The word ὀργανῶσαι is translated by Bachet as "fabricari," but this can hardly be right. It means "to set forth in order", to "systematise"; and such an expression may perfectly well apply if there were absolutely nothing new in the work, and Diophantos were merely writing a text-book simply giving in a compact and systematic form the sum and substance of previous labours. The words ἐπειδὴ μήπω γνώριμόν ἐστιν have also been made use of by advocates of Diophantos' claim to originality; but, looked at closely, they clearly imply no more than that the methods were unknown to Dionysios. The phrase is subjective, as is shown by the following words, δυσέλπιστοι γὰρ εἰς κατόρθωσίν εἰσιν αἱ τῶν ἀρχομένων ψυχαί. The language of the definitions also has been variously understood. "L' abate Andres" concluded from their very presence at the beginning of the book that Diophantos is minutely explaining preliminary matter as if he were speaking of a new science as yet unknown to others. But the fact is that he does *not* minutely explain preliminary matter; he gives an extremely curt summary of the necessary preliminaries. Moreover he makes no stipulations as to what he will choose to call by a certain name. Thus a square καλεῖται δύναμις : the unknown quantity *is called* ἀριθμός, and its sign *is* ςο. Again, he says λεῖψις ἐπὶ λεῖψιν πολλαπλασιασθεῖσα ποιεῖ ὕπαρξιν, *Minus multiplied by minus gives plus*[1]. In the 10th

algorithm of Algebra. The seeming contradiction is reconciled by conceiving the principles to have been known, but the application of them to a certain class of problems concerning numbers to have been new." Colebrooke.

[1] I adhere to this translation of the Greek because, though not quite literal, it serves to convey the meaning intended better than any other version. It is not easy to translate it literally. Mr James Gow (*History of Greek Mathematics*, p. 108), says that it should properly be translated "A difference multiplied by a difference makes an addition." This translation seems unfortunate, because (1) it is difficult, if not impossible, to attach any meaning to it, (2) λεῖψις and ὕπαρξις are correlatives, whereas "difference" and "addition" are not. If either of these words are used at all, we should surely say either "A difference multiplied by a difference makes a sum", or "A subtraction multiplied by a subtraction makes an addition." The true meaning of λεῖψις must be "a falling-short" or "a wanting", and that of ὕπαρξις "a presence" or "a forthcoming". If, therefore, a literal translation is desired, I would suggest "A wanting multi-

Definition he says how important it is that the beginner should
be familiar with the operations of Addition, Subtraction, &c.;
and in the 11th Definition the rules for reducing a quadratic to
its simplest form are given in a dogmatic authoritative manner
which would only be appropriate if the operation were generally
known : in fine, the definitions, in so far as they have any bearing on the present question, seem to show that Diophantos does
not wish it to be understood that they contain anything new.
He gives them as a short but necessary resumé of known principles, more for the purpose of a reminder than as laying any
new foundation.

To assert, then, that Diophantos invented algebra is, to say
the least, an exaggeration, as we can even now see from the
indications above mentioned. His notation, so far as it is a notation, is apparently new; but, as it is merely in the nature of
abbreviations for complete words, it cannot be said to constitute
any great advance in algebra.

§ 5. I may here mention a curious theory propounded by
Wallis, that algebra was not a late invention at all, but that it
was in common use by the Greeks from the time of their earliest
discoveries in the field of geometry, that in fact they discovered their geometrical theorems by algebra, but were extremely
careful to conceal the fact. But to believe that the great Greek
geometers were capable of this systematic imposition is scarcely
possible[1].

plied by a wanting makes a forthcoming". But, though this would be correct,
it loses by obscurity more than it gains by accuracy.

[1] "De Algebra, prout apud Eucliden Pappum Diophantum et scriptores
habetur. Mihi quidem extra omne dubium est, veteribus cognitam fuisse et
usu comprobatam istiusmodi artem aliquam Investigandi, qualis est ea quam
nos Algebram dicimus: Indeque derivatas esse quae apud eos conspiciuntur
prolixiores et intricatae Demonstrationes. Aliosque ex recentioribus mecum
hae in re sentire comperio....Hanc autem artem Investigandi Veteres occu-
luerunt sedulo: contenti, per demonstrationes *Apagogicas* (ad absurdum seu
impossibile ducentes si quod asserunt negetur) assensum cogere; potius quam
directum methodum indicare, qua fuerint inventae propositiones illae quas ipsi
aliter et per ambages demonstrant." (Wallis, *Opera*, Vol. II.)

Bossut is certainly right in his criticism of this theory. "Si cette opinion
était vraie, elle inculperait ces grands hommes d'une charlatanerie systématique
et traditionelle, ce qui est invraisemblable en soi-même et ne pourrait être admis
sans les preuves les plus évidentes. Or, sur quoi une telle opinion est-elle

§ 6. What remains to be said may, perhaps, be best arranged under the principal of Diophantos' methods as headings; and it will be advisable to take them in order, and consider in each case whether anything is anticipated by Greek authors whose works we know. For it would seem useless to speculate on what they might have written. If we once leave the safe ground of positive proveable fact, such an investigation as the present could lead to no useful result. It is this fact which makes so much of what M. Tannery has written on this subject seem unsatisfactory. He states that Diophantos was no more than a learned compiler, like Pappos: though it may be observed that this is a comparison by no means discreditable to the former; he does not think it necessary to explain the complete want of any other works on the same subject previous to Diophantos. The scarcity of information respecting similar previous labours, says M. Tannery, is easily explicable on other grounds which do not concern us here[1]. The nature of the work joined to what we know of Diophantos would seem to prove his statement, thinks M. Tannery; thus the work is very unequal, some operations being even clumsy[2]. But we are not likely to admit that inequality in a work is any evidence against originality; for what great genius always equalled himself? Certainly, if we cannot find any certain traces of anticipation of Diophantos by his predecessors, he is entitled to the benefit of any doubt. Besides, given that Diophantos was not the inventor of any considerable portion of his science, the merit of having made it known and arranged it scientifically is little less than that of the discoverer of the whole, and very much greater than that of the discoverer of a small fraction of it.

First with regard to the use of the unknown quantity by

fondée? Sur quelques anciennes propositions, tirées principalement du treizième livre d'Euclide, où l'on a cru reconnaître l'algèbre, mais qui ne supposent réellement que l'analyse géométrique, dans laquelle les anciens étaient fort exercés, comme je l'ai déjà marqué. Il paraît certain que les Grecs n'ont commencé à connaître l'algèbre qu'au temps de Diophante." (*Histoire Générale des Mathématiques* par Charles Bossut, Paris, 1810.) The truth of the last sentence is not so clear.

[1] *Bulletin des Sciences mathématiques et astronomiques*, 1879, p. 261.
[2] *Ibid.*

Diophantos.   There is apparently no indication that ἀριθμός, in the restricted sense appropriated to it by Diophantos, was employed by any other extant writer without an epithet to mark the use, and certainly δύναμις as restricted to the square *of the unknown* is Diophantine.   But the employment of an unknown quantity and calculations in terms of it are found before Diophantos' time.   To find a thing in general expressions is, with Diophantos, to find it ἐν ἀορίστῳ.   Cf. the problem IV. 20. But the same word is used in the same sense by Thymaridas in his *Epanthema*.   We know of him only through Iamblichos, but he probably belongs to the same period as Theon of Smyrna. Not only does Thymaridas distinguish between numbers which are ὡρισμένοι (known) and ἀόριστοι (unknown), but the *Epanthema* gives a rule for solving a particular set of simultaneous equations of the first degree with any number of variables. The artifice employed is the same as in I. 16, 17, of Diophantos. This account which Iamblichos gives of the *Epanthema* of Thymaridas is important for the history of algebra.   For the essence of algebra is present here as much as in Diophantos, the "notation" employed by him showing only a very slight advance. Thus we have here another proof, if one were needed, that Diophantos did not invent algebra.

Diophantos was acquainted with the solution of a mixed or complete quadratic.   This solution he promises in the 11th Definition to explain later on.   But, as we have before remarked, the promised exposition never comes, at least in the part of his work which we possess.   He shows, however, sufficiently plainly in a number of problems the exact rule which he followed in the solution of such equations.   The question therefore arises : Did Diophantos himself discover and formulate his purely arithmetical rule for solving complete determinate quadratics, or was the method in use before his time ?   Cossali points out that the propositions 58, 59, 84 and 85 of Euclid's δεδομένα give in a geometrical form the solution of the equations

$$ax - x^2 = b, \ ax + x^2 = b, \text{ and of } \left.\begin{array}{l} x \pm y = a \\ xy = b \end{array}\right\} .$$

It was only necessary to transform the geometry into algebra, in order to obtain Diophantos' rule ; and this might have been done by some mathematician intermediate between Euclid and Diophantos, or by Diophantos himself. It is quite possible that it may have been in this manner that the rule arose ; and, if that is the case, it is probable that the transformation referred to was accomplished by some mathematician not much later than Euclid himself ; for Heron of Alexandria (*circa* 100 B.C.) already used a similar rule[1]. We hear moreover of a work on quadratic equations by Hipparchos (probably *circa* 161—126 B.C.)[2]. Thus we may conclude that Diophantos' rule for solving complete quadratics was not his discovery.

§ 7.   But it is not upon Diophantos' solution of determinate equations that the supporters of his claim to originality rely ; it is rather that part of his work which forms its main subject, namely, Indeterminate or Semi-determinate Analysis. Accordingly it is to that that the term *Diophantine* analysis is applied. We should therefore look more especially for anticipations of Diophantine analysis, if we would be in a position to judge as to Diophantos' originality.

The foundation of semi-determinate analysis was laid by Pythagoras. Not only did he propound the geometrical theorem that in a right-angled triangle the square on the hypotenuse is equal to the sum of the squares on the other two sides, but he applied it to numbers and gave a rule—of somewhat narrow application, it is true—for finding an infinite number of right-angled triangles whose sides are all rational numbers. His rule, expressed in algebraical form, asserts that if there are three numbers of the form $2m^2 - 2m + 1$, $2m^2 - 2m$, and $2m - 1$, they form a right-angled triangle. This rule applies clearly to that particular case only in which two of the numbers differ by unity, i.e. that particular case of Diophantos' general form for a right-angled triangle $(m^2 + n^2,\ m^2 - n^2,\ 2mn)$ in which $m - n = 1$. But Pythagoras' rule is an attempt to deal with the general problem of Diophantos, II. 8, 9.   Plato gives another form for a

---

[1] Cf. Cantor, pp. 341, 342. The solution of a quadratic was for Heron no more than a matter of arithmetical calculation. He solved such equations by making both sides complete squares.

[2] Cf. Cantor, p. 313.

rational right-angled triangle, namely $(m^2+1, m^2-1, 2m)$, which is that particular case of the form used by Diophantos in which $n=1$. Euclid, Book X. prop. 29 is the same problem as Dioph. II. 8, 9, Diophantos improving upon Euclid's solution. In comparing, however, Euclid's arithmetic with that of Diophantos we should remember that with Euclid arithmetic is still geometry: a fact which accounts for his marvellously-developed doctrine of irrational and incommensurable numbers. In Diophantos the connection with arithmetic and geometry is severed, and irrational numbers are studiously avoided throughout his work.

There is another certain case of the solution of an indeterminate equation of the second degree in rational numbers before Diophantos. Theon of Smyrna, in his work Τῶν κατὰ μαθηματικὴν χρησίμων εἰς τὴν τοῦ Πλάτωνος ἀνάγνωσιν [sc. expositio, say the editors], gives a theorem περὶ πλευρικῶν καὶ διαμετρικῶν ἀριθμῶν. From this theorem we derive immediately any number of solutions of the equations

$$\left.\begin{array}{c} 2t^2 + 1 = u^2 \\ 2x^2 - 1 = y^2 \end{array}\right\},$$

provided that we can find, by trial or otherwise, one solution of either. Theon does not make this application of his theorem: he solved a somewhat important problem of the second degree in indeterminate analysis without knowing it. There is an allusion to the doctrine of Side- and Diagonal-numbers in Proclus, *Comment. on Euclid* IV. p. 111.

§ 8. Such are the data upon which Nesselmann founded his view as to the originality of our author. But M. Tannery has tried to show, by reference to a famous problem, that still more difficult questions in indeterminate analysis had been propounded before the time of Diophantos. This problem is known by the name of the "Cattle-problem"; it is an epigram, and is commonly attributed to Archimedes. It was discovered by Lessing, and his discussion of it may be found in *Zur Geschichte und Litteratur* (Braunschweig, 1773), p. 421 seqq. I have quoted it below according to the text given by Lessing[1]. The title does

[1] I have unfortunately not been able to consult the critical work on this epigram by Dr J. Struve and Dr K. L. Struve, father and son (Altona, 1821).

not actually imply that Archimedes was the author. Of the
two divisions into which it falls the second leads to an indeter-

My information about it is derived at second-hand from Nesselmann. Lessing's
text can hardly be perfect, but it seems better to give it as it is without emendation.

ΠΡΟΒΛΗΜΑ

ὅπερ ᾿ΑΡΧΙΜΗΔΗΣ ἐν ἐπιγράμμασιν εὑρὼν
τοῖς ἐν ᾿Αλεξανδρείᾳ περὶ ταῦτα πραγματουμένοις ζητεῖν ἀπέστειλεν
ἐν τῇ πρὸς ᾿Ερατοσθένην τὸν Κυρηναῖον
ἐπιστολῇ.

Πληθὺν ἠελίοιο βοῶν, ὦ ξεῖνε, μέτρησον,
φροντίδ᾽ ἐπιστήσας, εἰ μετέχεις σοφίης,
πόσση ἄρ᾽ ἐν πεδίοις Σικελῆς ποτ᾽ ἐβόσκετο νήσου
Θρινακίης, τετραχῇ στίφεα δασσαμένη
χροιὴν ἀλλάσσοντα· τὸ μὲν λευκοῖο γάλακτος,
κυανέῳ δ᾽ ἕτερον χρώματι λαμπόμενον,
ἄλλογε μὲν ξανθὸν, τὸ δὲ ποικίλον. ᾿Εν δὲ ἑκάστῳ
στίφει ἔσαν ταῦροι πλήθεσι βριθόμενοι,
συμμετρίης τοιῆσδε τετευχότες· ἀργότριχας μὲν
κυανέων ταύρων ἡμίσει ἠδὲ τρίτῳ,
καὶ ξανθοῖς σύμπασιν ἴσους, ὦ ξεῖνε, νόησον.
Αὐτὰρ κυανέους τῷ τετράτῳ μέρεϊ
μικτοχρόων καὶ πέμπτῳ, ἔτι ξανθοῖσί τε πᾶσι.
Τοὺς δ᾽ ὑπολειπομένους ποικιλόχρωτας ἄθρει
ἀργεννῶν ταύρων ἕκτῳ μέρει, ἑβδομάτῳ τε
καὶ ξανθοῖς αὐτοὺς πᾶσιν ἰσαζομένους.
Θηλείαισι δὲ βουσὶ τάδ᾽ ἔπλετο· λευκότριχες μὲν
ἦσαν συμπάσης κυανέης ἀγέλης
τῷ τριτάτῳ τε μέρει καὶ τετράτῳ ἀτρεκὲς ἶσαι.
Αὐτὰρ κυάνεαι τῷ τετράτῳ τε πάλιν
μικτοχρόων καὶ πέμπτῳ ὁμοῦ μέρει ἰσάζοντο
σὺν ταύροις πάσης εἰς νόμον ἐρχομένης.
Ξανθοτρίχων ἀγέλης πέμπτῳ μέρει ἠδὲ καὶ ἕκτῳ
ποικίλαι ἰσάριθμον πλῆθος ἔχον. Τετραχῇ
ξανθαὶ δ᾽ ἠριθμεῦντο μέρους τρίτου ἡμίσει ἶσαι
ἀργεννῆς ἀγέλης ἑβδομάτῳ τε μέρει.
Ξεῖνε, σὺ δ᾽ ἠελίοιο βόες πόσαι ἀτρεκὲς εἰπών·
χωρὶς μὲν ταύρων ζατρεφέων ἀριθμόν,
χωρὶς δ᾽ αὖ θηλεῖαι ὅσαι κατὰ χροιὰν ἕκασται,
οὐκ ἄϊδρίς κε λέγοι, οὐδ᾽ ἀριθμῶν ἀδαής,

οὐ μὴν πώγε σοφοῖς ἐν ἀριθμοῖς· ἀλλ᾽ ἴθι φράζευ
καὶ τάδε πάντα βόων ἠελίοιο πάθη.
᾿Αργότριχες ταῦροι μὲν ἐπεὶ μιξαίατο πληθὺν
κυανέοις ἵσταντ᾽ ἔμπεδον ἰσόμετροι
εἰς βάθος εἰς εὖρος τε· τὰ δ᾽ αὖ περιμήκεα πάντη
πίμπλαντο πλίνθου Θρινακίης πεδία.
Ξανθοὶ δ᾽ αὖ τ᾽ εἰς ἓν καὶ ποικίλοι ἀθροισθέντες

minate equation of the second degree. In view of this fact it is important for us to discuss briefly the matter and probable date of this epigram. Struve does not admit that it can pretend to that antiquity which is claimed for it in the title. This we may allow without going so far as Klügel, who makes it as late as the introduction of the present decimal system of numeration. Nesselmann's view is that the heterogeneous conditions, which are thrown together to render the problem difficult, show that the author (if the whole is due to one author) could have had no idea how to solve it. Nesselmann is of opinion that the editors of the anthology were justified in refusing a place to this epigram, that the most one could do would be to admit the first part and condemn the latter part as corrupt, and that we might fairly regard the whole as unauthentic because even the first part could not belong to the age of Archimedes. The first part, which falls into two divisions, gives seven equations of the first degree for determining eight unknown quantities, namely the number of bulls and cows of each of four colours. The solution of the first part gives, if $(X\,Y Z\,W)$ are the numbers of the bulls, $(xyzw)$ the corresponding numbers of cows,

$$
\begin{aligned}
X &= 10366482\,n, & x &= 7206360\,n, \\
Y &= 7460514\,n, & y &= 4893246\,n, \\
Z &= 7358060\,n, & z &= 3515820\,n, \\
W &= 4149387\,n, & w &= 5439213\,n,
\end{aligned}
$$

where n is an integer. If we take the smallest possible value the number of cattle is sufficiently enormous. The Scholiast's solution corresponds to the value 80 of n, the result being "truly," as Lessing observes, "a tolerably large herd for Sicily." The same might be said of the solution arising from putting $n = 1$ above. This is surely a curious commentary on M. Tannery's theory above alluded to (pp. 6, 7), that the price of the wine in VI. 33 of Diophantos is a sufficient evidence of the

ἵσταντ' ἀμβολάδην ἐξ ἑνὸς ἀρχόμενοι
σχῆμα τελειοῦντες τὸ τρικράσπεδον· οὔτε προσόντων
ἀλλοχρόων ταύρων, οὔτ' ἐπιλειπομένων.
Ταῦτα συνεξευρὼν καὶ ἐνὶ πραπίδεσσιν ἀθροίσας
καὶ πληθέων ἀποδοὺς, ὦ ξένε, πάντα μέτρα
ἔρχεο κυδιόων νικηφόρος· ἴσθι τε πάντως
κεκριμένος ταύτῃ ὄμπνιος ἐν σοφίῃ.

date of the epigram. If the " Cattle-problem " of which we are
now speaking were really due to Archimedes, we should, supposing M. Tannery's theory to hold good, scarcely have found
the result in such glaring contradiction to what cannot but
have been the facts of the case. Nesselmann further argues in
favour of his view by pointing out (1) that the problem is
clearly at an end, when it is said that he who solves the
problem must be not unskilled in numbers, i.e. where I have
shown the division; and the addition of two new conditions
with the preface "And yet he could not pretend to proficiency
in wise calculations" unless he could solve the rest, shows
the marks of the interpolator on the face of it, and, moreover,
of a clumsy interpolator who could neither solve the complete
problem itself, nor even conceal his patchwork. (2) The language and versification are against the authenticity. (3) The
Scholiast's solution does not, as it claims, satisfy the whole
problem, but only the first part. (4) The impossibility of
solution with the Greek numeral notation and the absurdly
large numbers show that the author, or authors, could not
have seen what the effect of the many heterogeneous conditions
would be. Nesselmann draws the conclusion above stated; and
we may safely assume, as he says, that this epigram is from the
historical point of view worthless, and could not, even if it
were shown to be earlier than the date of Diophantos, be held
to prove anything against his originality.

M. Tannery takes the opposite view and uses the epigram
for the express purpose of proving his assumption that Diophantos was not an original writer. M. Tannery takes a passage
attributed to Geminos in which he is describing the distinction
between λογιστική and ἀριθμητική. λογιστική according to
Geminos θεωρεῖ τὸ μὲν κληθὲν ὑπ' Ἀρχιμήδους βοϊκὸν πρόβλημα, τοῦτο¹ δὲ μηλίτας καὶ φιαλίτας ἀριθμούς. Of the two

¹ I do not read τοὺς as M. Tannery does. He alters τοῦτο, the original
reading, into τοὺς, simply remarking that τοῦτο is an "inadmissible reading."
τοῦτο δὲ is certainly a reading which needs no defence, being exactly what we
should expect to have. The passage appears to be taken from the Scholia to
Plato's *Charmides*, where, however, Stallbaum and Heiberg read θεωρεῖ οὖν τοῦτο
μὲν τὸ κληθὲν ὑπ' Ἀρχιμήδους βοεικὸν πρόβλημα, τοῦτο δὲ μηλίτας καὶ φιαλίτας

H. D.   10

kinds of problems which are here distinguished as falling within the province of λογιστική M. Tannery understands the first to be indeterminate problems, the type taken (κληθὲν ὑπ' 'Αρχιμήδους βοϊκὸν πρόβλημα) being nothing more or less than the very problem we have been speaking of. He states that Nesselmann has not appreciated the problem properly, and finally that we have here an indubitable reference to an indeterminate problem of the second degree (viz. the equation $8Ax^2 + 1 = y^2$, where A is a very large number) more difficult than those of Diòphantos. But this statement would seem simply to beg the question. For, if the expression of Geminos refers to the problem which we are speaking of, it may even then only refer to the first part, that is, an indeterminate problem of the first degree : M. Tannery has still to show that the whole problem is one, and a genuine product of antiquity. But I have not found that M. Tannery makes any attempt to answer Nesselmann's arguments; and, unless they are answered, the conclusion which the latter draws from them cannot be said to be invalidated.

But Nesselmann's view is also opposed by Heiberg (*Quaestiones Archimedeae*, 1879). I do not think, however, that his arguments in favour of the authenticity are conclusive; and, though answering some, he does not answer all of Nesselmann's objections. With regard to the language Heiberg observes that the dialect need not surprise us, for the use by Archimedes of the Ionic instead of the Doric dialect for this epigram would easily be explained by the common use of the Ionic dialect for epic and elegiac poetry[1]. And he further suggests that, even if

ἀριθμούς, which seems better than the reading quoted by M. Tannery from Hultsch, *Heronis Reliquiae*, and given above.

[1] Heiberg admits that the language of the title is not satisfactory. He points out that ἐν ἐπιγράμμασιν should go, not with εἰρὼν, but with ἀπέστειλε, though so far separated from it, and that the use of the plural ἐπιγράμμασιν is unsatisfactory. Upon the reading ποικίλαι ἰσάριθμον πλῆθος ἔχον τετραχῇ (l. 24) he observes that by symmetry z should not be equal to *four times* $(\frac{1}{6} + \frac{1}{7})(W + w)$, but to $(\frac{1}{6} + \frac{1}{7})(W + w)$ itself, and, even if that were the case, we should require τετράκις. Hence he suggests for this line ποικίλαι ἰσάριθμον πλῆθος ἔχουσ' ἐφάνη. (Apparently, to judge from his punctuation, Lessing understood τετραχῇ in the sense of "fourthly.") Heiberg explains πλίνθου (l. 36) as "quadrangulum solidum," by which is meant simply " a square," as is clearly indicated by l. 34.

the difficulties as to the language are considered too great, we
may suppose the problem itself to have been the work of
Archimedes, the language of it that of some later author. But,
if Heiberg will go so far as to admit that the language may be
the work of a later author than Archimedes, it would be no
more unnatural to suppose that the matter itself of the latter
part of the problem was also of later date. The suggestion that
Archimedes could not have solved the whole problem (as completed by the two last conditions) Heiberg meets with arguments which appear to be extremely unsafe. He says that
Archimedes' approximations to the value of $\sqrt{3}$, although we
cannot see by what process he arrived at them, show plainly
that his arithmetic was little behind our modern arithmetic,
and that, e.g., he possessed means of approximation little inferior to the modern method by continued fractions. Heiberg
further observes that Archimedes possessed machinery for dealing with very large numbers. But we are not justified in
assuming on these two grounds that Archimedes could solve
the indeterminate equation $8Ax^2 + 1 = y^2$, where (Nesselmann,
p. 488) $A = 51285802909803$, for the solution of which we
should use continued fractions. I do not think, therefore, that
Heiberg has made out his case. Hence I should hesitate to
assume that the problem before us is an indubitable case,
previous to Diophantos, of an indeterminate equation of the
second degree more difficult than those treated by him.

The discussion of the " Cattle-problem " as possibly throwing
some light on the present question would seem to have added
nothing to the arguments previously stated ; and the question
of Diophantos' originality may be considered to be unaffected by
anything that has been said about the epigram.

We may therefore adopt, with little or no variation, Nesselmann's final result, that he is far from believing that Diophantos
merely worked up the materials of others. On the contrary he
is convinced that the greater part of his propositions and his
ingenious methods are his own. There is moreover an "Indivi-
duum" running through the whole work which strongly confirms
this conclusion.

CHAPTER VIII.

§ 1. I propose in this chapter to examine briefly the indications which are to be found in certain Arabian algebraists of in-
debtedness to, or points of contact with, Diophantos. And in
doing so I shall leave out of consideration the Arabic translations
of his work or commentaries thereupon. These are, so far as
we know, all lost, and such notices of them as we have I have
given in Chapter III. of this Essay (pp. 39—42). Our historical knowledge of the time and manner in which Diophantos
became known to the Arabs is so very scanty as to amount
almost to nothing: hence the importance of careful comparison
of the matter, methods, and mode of expression of Diophantos
with those of the important representatives of early Arabian
algebra. Now it has been argued that, since the first translation of Diophantos into Arabic that we know of was made by
Abu'l-Wafā, who lived A.D. 940—998, while Mohammed ibn
Mūsā's algebraical work belongs to the beginning of the 9th
century, Arabian algebra must have been developed independently of that of the Greeks. This conclusion, however, is
not warranted by this evidence. It does not follow from the
want of historical proof of connection between Greek and
Arabian algebra that there was no such connection; and it is to
internal evidence that we must look for the correction of this
misconception. I shall accordingly enumerate a number of
points of similarity between the Arabian algebraists and Diophantos which would seem to indicate that the Arabs were
acquainted with Diophantos and Greek algebra before the time
of Mohammed ibn Mūsā, and that in Arabian algebra generally,

at least in its beginnings, the Greek element greatly predomi-
nated, though other elements were not wanting.

§ 2. The first Arabian who concerns us here is **Mohammed
ibn Mūsā Al-Khārizmi**. He wrote a work which he called
Aljabr walmukābala, and which is, so far as we know, not only the
first book which bore such a title, but (if we can trust Arabian
notices) was the first book which dealt with the subject indicated thereby. Mohammed ibn Mūsā uses the words *aljabr* and
almukābala without explanation, and, curiously enough, there
is no application of the processes indicated by the words in the
theoretical part of the treatise: facts which must be held to
show that these processes were known, to some extent at least,
even before his time, and were known by those names. A mere
translation of the two terms *jabr* and *mukābala* does not of itself
give us any light as to their significance. *Jabr* has been translated in Latin by the words *restauratio* and *restitutio*, and in
German by "Wiederherstellung"; *mukābala* by *oppositio*, or
"comparison," and in German by "Gegenüberstellung." Fortunately, however, we have explanations of the two terms given
by later Arabians, who all agree as to the meaning conveyed by
them[1]. When we have an algebraical equation in which terms
affected with a negative sign occur on either side or on both
sides, the process by which we make all the terms positive, i.e.
adding to both sides of the equation such positive terms as will
make up the deficiencies, or absorb the negative ones, is *jabr* or
restauratio. When, again, we have by *jabr* transformed our
equation into one in which all the terms are positive, the
process by which we strike out such terms as occur on both
sides, with the result that there is, finally, only one term con-

---

[1] Rosen gives, in his edition of *The Algebra of Mohammed ben Musa*, a
number of passages from various authors explaining *aljabr* and *almukābala*.
I shall give only one, as an example. Rosen says "In the Kholāset al Hisāb, a
compendium of arithmetic and geometry by Baha-Eddin Mohammed ben Al
Hosain, who died A.H. 1031, i.e. 1575 A.D., the Arabic text of which, together
with a Persian commentary by Roshan Ali, was printed at Calcutta (1812, 8vo),
the following explanation is given: ' The side (of the equation) on which something is to be subtracted, is made complete, and as much is to be added to the
other side; this is *jebr*; again those cognate quantities which are equal on both
sides are removed, and this is *mokābalah* '."

taining each power of the unknown, i.e. subtracting equals from
equals, is *mukābala, oppositio* or "comparison." Such was the
meaning of the terms *jabr* and *mukābala*; and the use of these
words together as the title of Mohammed ibn Mūsā's treatise is
due to the continual occurrence in the science there expounded
of the processes so named. It is true that in the theoretical
part of it he assumes that the operations have been already
completed, and accordingly divides quadratic equations at once
into six classes, viz.

$$ax^2 = bx, \quad ax^2 = c, \quad bx = c,$$
$$x^2 + bx = c, \quad x^2 + c = bx, \quad x^2 = bx + c,$$

but the operations are nevertheless an essential preliminary.
Now what does Diophantos say of the necessary preliminaries
in dealing with an equation? "If the same powers of the unknown with positive but different coefficients occur on both
sides, we must take like from like until we have one single expression equal to another. If there are on both sides, or on
either side, negative terms, the defects must be added on both
sides, until the different powers occur on both sides with positive coefficients, when we must take like from like as before.
We must contrive always, if possible, to reduce our equations so
that they may contain one single term equated to one other.
But afterwards we will explain to you how, when two terms are
left equal to a third, such an equation is solved." (Def. 11.)
Here we have an exact description of the operations called by
the Arabian algebraists *aljabr* and *almukābala*. And, as we
said, these operations must have been familiar in Arabia before
the date of Mohammed ibn Mūsā's treatise. This comparison
would, therefore, seem to suggest that Diophantos was well
known in Arabia at an early date.

Next, with regard to the names used by Mohammed ibn
Mūsā for the unknown quantity and its powers, we observe that
the known quantity is called the "Number"; hence it is no
matter for surprise that he has not used the word corresponding
to ἀριθμός for his unknown quantity. He uses *shai* ("thing")
for this purpose or *jidr* ("root"). This last word may be a
translation of the Indian *mūla*, or it may be a recollection of the

ῥίζη of Nikomachos. But we can say nothing with certainty as to the connection of the three words. For the square of the unknown he uses *māl* (translated by Cantor as "Vermögen," "Besitz," equivalent to "power"), which may very well be a translation of the δύναμις of Diophantos.

M. Rodet comments in his article *L'algèbre d'Al-Khârizmi* (*Journal Asiatique*, 1878) upon the expression used by Mohammed ibn Mūsā for *minus*, with the view of proving that it is as likely to be a reminiscence of Diophantos as a term derived from India[1].

The most important point, however, for us to examine here is the solution of the complete quadratic equation as given by Diophantos and as given by Mohammed ibn Mūsā. The latter gives rules for the solution of each of the forms of the quadratic according to his distinction; and each of these forms we find in Diophantos. After the rules for the three forms of the complete quadratic Mohammed ibn Mūsā gives geometrical proofs of them. Now in Greece it was the practice to work out theorems

---

[1] He says (pp. 31, 32) "Le mot dont il se sert pour désigner les termes d'une équation affectés du signe – est *nâqis*, qui signifie, comme on le sait, 'manquant de, privé de': un amputé, par exemple, est *nâqis* de son bras ou de sa jambe; c'est donc très-improprement qu'Al-Khârizmi emploie cette expression pour désigner ' la partie enlevée'...Aussi le mot en question n'a-t-il plus été employé par ses successeurs, et Behâ ed-Dîn qui, au moment d'exposer la *règle des signes* dans la multiplication algébrique, avait dit : ' s'il y a soustraction, on appelle ce dont on soustrait *zâ'id* (additif), et ce que l'on soustrait *nâqis* (manquant de), ne nomme plus dans la suite les termes négatifs que ' les séparés, mis à part, retranchés.'

D'où vient ce mot *nâqis*? Il répond, si l'on veut, au sanscrit *ûnas* ou au préfixe *vi-* au moyen desquels on indique la soustraction : *vyêkas* ou *êkônas* veut dire 'dont on a retranché,' mais l'adjectif *ûnas* se rapporte ici au 'ce dont on a retranché' de Behâ ed-Dîn, et non à la quantité retranchée. Or, le grec possède et emploie en langage algébrique une expression tout à fait analogue, c'est l'adjectif ἐλλιπής, dont Diophant se sert, par exemple, pour définir le signe de la soustraction ⋔ : ψ ἐλλιπὲς κάτω νεῦον, 'un ψ incomplet incliné vers le bas.' L'arabe, j'en prends à témoin tous les arabisants, traduirait ἐλλιπής par *en-nâqis*. Dans l'indication des opérations algébriques Diophant lit, à la place de son signe ⋔, ἐν λείψει : μονάδες β̄ ἐν λείψει ἀριθμοῦ ἑνός, dit-il; mot-à-mot: ' 2 unités manquant d'une inconnue,' pour exprimer 2 − *x*. Donc, s'il est possible qu'Al-Khârizmi ait emprunté, sauf l'emploi qu'il en fait, son *nâqis* au sanscrit *ûnas*, il pourrait tout aussi bien se faire qu'il l'eût pris au grec ἐν λείψει."

concerned with numbers by the aid of geometry; even in Dio-phantos we find the geometrical method employed for the treatise on *Polygonal Numbers* and a trace of it even in the *Arith-metics*, although the separation between geometry and algebra is there complete. On the other hand, the Indian method was to employ algebra for working out geometrical propositions, and algebra reached a far higher degree of development in India than in Greece, though it is probable that even India was in-debted to Greece for the first principles. Hence we should naturally consider the geometrical basis of early Arabian algebra as a sign of obligation to Greece. This supposition is supported by a very remarkable piece of evidence adduced by Cantor. It is based on the letters used by Mohammed ibn Mūsā to mark the points in the geometrical figures used to prove his rules. The very use of letters in a geometrical figure is Greek, not Indian; and the letters which are used are chosen in what appears to be, at first sight, a strange manner. The Arabic letters here used do not follow the order of the later Arabian alphabet, an order depending on the form of the letters and the mode of writing them, nor is their order quite explained by the original arrangement of the Arabian alphabet which corresponds to the order in the other Semitic languages. If however we take the Arabic letters used in the figures and change them respectively into those Greek letters which have the same nu-merical value, the series follows the Greek order exactly, and not only so, but agrees with it in excluding ϛ and ι. But what reason could an Arab have had for refusing to use the particular letters which denoted 6 and 10 for geometrical figures? None, so far as we can see. The Greek, however, had a reason for omitting the two letters ϛ and ι, the former because it was really no longer regarded as a letter, the latter because it was a mere stroke, Ι, which might have led to confusion. We can hardly refuse to admit Cantor's conclusion from this evidence that Mohammed ibn Mūsā's geometrical proofs of his rules for solving the different forms of the complete quadratic are Greek. And it is, moreover, a reasonable inference that the Greeks themselves discovered the rules for the solution of a complete quadratic by means of geometry. We thus have a confirmation of the supposition as to the origin of the rules used by Diophantos, which was mentioned above (pp. 140, 141), and we may properly conclude that algebra, as we find it in Diophantos, was the result of a continuous development which extended from the time of Euclid to that of Heron and of Diophantos, and was independent of external influences.

I now pass to the consideration of the actual rules which Mohammed ibn Mūsā gives for the solution of the complete quadratic, as compared with those of Diophantos. We remarked above (p. 91) that Diophantos would appear, when solving the ·equation $ax^2 + bx = c$, to have first multiplied by a throughout, so as to make the first term a square, and that he would, with

our notation, have given the root in the form $\dfrac{\sqrt{\dfrac{b^2}{4} + ac} - \dfrac{b}{2}}{a}$.

Mohammed ibn Mūsā, however, first divides by a throughout: "The solution is the same when two squares or three, or more or less, be specified ; you reduce them to one single square and in the same proportion you reduce also the roots and simple numbers which are connected therewith[1]." This discrepancy between the Greek and the Arabian algebraist is not a very striking or important one; but it is worth while to observe that Mohammed ibn Mūsā's rule is not the early Indian one; for Brahmagupta (born 598) sometimes multiplies throughout by a like Diophantos, sometimes by $4a$, which was also the regular practice of Çrīdhara, who thus obtained the root in the form $\dfrac{\sqrt{b^2 + 4ac} - b}{2a}$. This rule of Çrīdhara's is quoted and followed by Bhāskara. Another apparent discrepancy between Mohammed ibn Mūsā and Diophantos lies in the fact that Diophantos never shows any sign, in his book as we have it, of recognising two roots of a quadratic, even where both roots are positive and real, and not only when one of them is negative: a negative or irrational value he would, of course, not recognise; unless an equation has a real positive root it is for Diophantos "impossible." Negative and irrational roots appear to be tacitly put aside by

[1] Rosen, *The Algebra of Mohammed ben Musa*, p. 9.

Mohammed ibn Mūsā and the earliest Indian algebraists, though both Mohammed ibn Mūsā and the Indians recognise the existence of two roots. The former undoubtedly recognises two roots, at least in the case where both are real and positive. His most definite statement on this subject is given in his rule for the solution of the equation $x^2 + c = bx$, or the case of the quadratic in which we have "*Squares and Numbers equal to Roots;* for instance, ' a square and twenty-one in numbers are equal to ten roots of the same square.' That is to say, what must be the amount of a square, which when twenty-one dirhems are added to it, becomes equal to the equivalent of ten roots of that square? Solution: Halve the number of the roots ; the moiety is five. Multiply this by itself; the product is twenty-five. Subtract from this the twenty-one which are connected with the square ; the remainder is four. Extract its root; it is two. *Subtract this from the moiety of the roots,* which is five ; the remainder is three. This is the root of the square which you required, and the square is nine. *Or you may add the root to the moiety of the roots;* the sum is seven; this is the root of the square which you sought for, and the square itself is forty-nine. *When you meet with an instance which refers you to this case, try its solution by addition, and if that do not serve, then subtraction certainly will. For in this case both addition and subtraction may be employed,* which will not answer in any other of the three cases in which the number of the roots must be halved. And know that, when in a question belonging to this case you have halved the number of roots and multiplied the moiety by itself, if the product be less than the number of dirhems connected with the square, then the instance is impossible; but if the product be equal to the dirhems by themselves, then the root of the square is equal to the moiety of the roots alone, without either addition or subtraction. In every instance where you have two squares, or more or less, reduce them to one entire square, as I have explained under the first case[1]." This definite recognition of the existence of two roots, if Diophantos could be proved not to have known of it, would seem to show

[1] Quoted from *The Algebra of Mohammed ben Musa* (ed. Rosen), pp. 11, 12.

that Mohammed ibn Mūsā could here have been indebted to India only. Rodet, however, remarks that we are not justified in concluding from the evidence that Diophantos did not know of the existence of two roots: in the cases where one is negative we should not expect him to mention it, for a negative root is for him "impossible," and in certain cases mentioned above (p. 92) one of the positive roots is irrelevant. Rodet further observes that Mohammed ibn Mūsā, while recognising in theory two roots of the equation $x^2 + c = bx$, uses in practice only one, and that (curiously enough) in all instances the root corresponding to the sign *minus* of the radical. This statement however is not quite accurate, for in some examples of the rule which we quoted above he gives two possible values[1].

Mohammed ibn Mūsā, being the first writer of a treatise on algebra, so far as we know, is for obvious reasons the most important for the purposes of this chapter. If the influence of Diophantos and Greek algebra upon the earliest Arabian algebra is once established, it is clearly unnecessary to search so carefully in the works of later Arabians for points of connection with our author. For, his influence having once for all exerted itself, the later developments would naturally be the result of other and later influences, and direct reminiscences of Diophantos would disappear or be obscured. I shall, therefore, mention only a few other Arabian authors, and those with greater brevity.

§ 3. **Abu'l-Wafā Al-Būzjāni** we have already had occasion to mention (pp. 40, 41) as a translator of Diophantos and a commentator on his work. As then he studied our author so thoroughly it would be only natural to expect that his works would abound in reminiscences of Diophantos. On Abu'l-Wafā perhaps the most important authority is Wöpcke. It must suffice to refer for details to his articles[2].

§ 4. An Arabic MS. bearing the date 972 is concerned with the theory of numbers throughout and particularly with the formation of rational right-angled triangles. Unfortunately the

---

[1] Cf. Rosen's edition, p. 42.

[2] Cf. in particular the articles on *Mathématiques chez les Arabes* (*Journal Asiatique* for 1855).

beginning of it is lost, and with the beginning the name of the author. In the fragment we find the problem *To find a square which, when increased or diminished by a given number, is again a square* proposed and solved. The author of the fragment was undoubtedly an Arabian, and it would probably not be rash to say that much of it was based on Diophantos.

§ 5. Again, **Abu Ja'far Mohammed ibn Alhusain** wrote a treatise on rational right-angled triangles at a date probably not much later than 992. He gives as the object of the whole the investigation of the problem just mentioned. It is ˉnoteworthy (says Cantor) that a geometrical explanation of the solution of this problem makes use of similar principles to those which we could trace in Mohammed ibn Mūsā's geometrical proofs of the solution of the complete quadratic, and he further definitely alludes to Euclid II. 7. If we consider the use of right-angled triangles as a means of finding solutions of this problem, and c_1, c_2 be the two sides of a right-angled triangle which contain the right angle, then $c_1^2 + c_2^2$ is the square of the hypotenuse, and $c_1^2 + c_2^2 \pm 2c_1c_2$ is a square. Hence, says Ibn Alhusain, $c_1^2 + c_2^2$ is a square which, when increased or diminished by the same number $2c_1c_2$, is still a square. Diophantos says similarly that "in every right-angled triangle the square of the hypotenuse remains a square when double the product of the other two sides is added to, or subtracted from, it." (III. 22.)

§ 6. Lastly, we must consider in this connection the work of **Alkarkhī**, already mentioned (pp. 24, 25). We possess two treatises of his, of which the second is a continuation of the first. The first is called *Al-Kāfī fīl hisāb* and is arithmetical, the second is the *Fakhrī*, an algebraic treatise. Cantor points out that, when we compare Alkarkhī's arithmetic with that of certain Arabian contemporaries and predecessors of his, we see a marked contrast, in that, while others used Indian numeral signs and methods of calculation, Alkarkhī writes out all his numbers as words, and draws generally from Greek sources rather than Indian. The advantages of the Indian notation as compared with Greek in securing clearness and compactness of work were so great that we might naturally be surprised to see Alkarkhī ignoring them, and might wonder that he could have been unaware of them or have undervalued them so much. Cantor, however, thinks that the true explanation is, not that he was ignorant of the Indian arithmetical methods and notation or underestimated their advantages, but that Alkarkhī was a representative of one of two mathematical schools in Arabia, the Greek and the Indian. Alkarkhī was not the solitary representative of the Greek arithmetic; he was not merely an exception to an otherwise universal acceptation of the Indian method. He was rather, as we said, a representative of one of two schools standing in contrast to each other. Another representative of the Greek school was Abu'l-Wafā, who also makes no use of ciphers in his arithmetic. Even in Alkarkhī's arithmetical treatise, as in the works of Abu'l-Wafā, there are not wanting certain Indian elements. These could hardly by any means have been avoided, at any rate as regards the matter of their treatises; but the Greek element was so predominant that, practically, the other may be neglected.

But the real importance of Alkarkhī in this connection centres in his second treatise, the *Fakhrī*. Here again he appears as an admiring pupil of the Greeks, and especially of Diophantos, whom he often mentions by name in his book. The *Fakhrī* consists of two parts, the first of which may be said to contain the theory of algebra, the second the practice of it, or the application to particular problems. In both parts we find Diophantos largely made use of. Alkarkhī solves in this treatise not only determinate but indeterminate equations, so that he may be taken as the representative of the Arabian indeterminate analysis. In his solutions of indeterminate equations of the first and second degrees we find no trace of Indian methods. Diophantos is the basis upon which he builds, but he has also extended the Greek algebraist. If we refer to the account which the Italian algebraists give of the evolution of the successive powers of the unknown quantity in the Arabian system, we shall see (as already remarked, p. 71, n. 1) that Alkarkhī is an exception to the adoption of the Indian system of generation of powers by the *multiplication* of indices. He uses the *additive* system, like Diophantos. The square of the unknown being *māl*, and the cube *ka'b*, the succeeding powers are

$m\bar{a}l\ m\bar{a}l,\ m\bar{a}l\ ka'b,\ ka'b\ ka'b,\ m\bar{a}l\ m\bar{a}l\ ka'b,\ m\bar{a}l\ ka'b\ ka'b,\ ka'b\ ka'b$ $ka'b$, &c. Alkarkhī speaks of the six forms of the quadratic which Mohammed ibn Mūsā distinguished and explains at the same time what he understands by *jabr* and *mukābala*. He appears to include both processes under *jabr*, understanding rather by *mukābala* the resulting equation written in one of the six forms. Among the examples given by Alkarkhī are $x^2 + 10x = 39$, and $x^2 + 21 = 10x$, both of which occur in Mohammed ibn Mūsā. Alkarkhī has two solutions of both, the first geometrical, the second (as he expresses it) "after Diophantos' manner." The second of the two equations which we have mentioned he reduces to $x^2 - 10x + 25 = 4$, and then, remarking that the first member may be either $(x-5)^2$ or $(5-x)^2$, he gives the two solutions $x = 7$, and $x = 3$. The remarkable point about his treatment of this equation is his use of the expression "after Diophantos' manner" applied to it. We spoke above (p. 92) of the doubt as to whether Diophantos knew or did not know of the existence of two roots of a quadratic. But Alkarkhī's expression "after Diophantos' manner" would seem to settle this question beyond the possibility of a doubt; and perhaps it would not be going too far to take his words quite literally and to suppose that the two examples of the quadratic of which we are speaking were taken directly from Diophantos. If so, we should have still more direct proof of the Greek origin of Mohammed ibn Mūsā's algebra. On the other hand, however, it must be mentioned that of two geometrical explanations of the equation $x^2 + 10x = 39$ which Alkarkhī gives one cannot be Greek. In the first of the two he derives the solution directly from Euclid, II. 6 ; and this method is therefore solely Greek. But in the second geometrical solution he employs one line to represent x^2, another to represent $10x$, and a third to represent 100. This confusion of dimensions is alien from the Greek manner ; we must therefore suppose that this geometrical solution is an Arabian product, and probably a discovery of Alkarkhī himself.

As an instance of an indeterminate equation treated by Alkarkhī we may give the equation $mx^2 + nx + p = y^2$. He gives as a condition for the solution that either m or p must be a square. He then puts for y a binomial expression, of which one term is either $\sqrt{mx^2}$ or $\sqrt{p}$. This is, as we have seen, exactly Diophantos' procedure.

With regard to the collection of problems, which forms the second part of the *Fakhri*, we observe that Alkarkhī only admits rational and positive solutions, excluding even the value 0. In other cases the solution is for Alkarkhī as for Diophantos "impossible." Many of the problems in indeterminate analysis are taken directly from Diophantos, and are placed in the order in which they are there found. Of a marginal note by Alsirāj at the end of the fourth section of the second part of the treatise we have already spoken (p. 25).

ADDENDUM.

In the note beginning on p. 64 I discussed three objections urged by Mr James Gow in his *History of Greek Mathematics* against my suggestion as to the origin of the symbol ∽ for ἀριθμός. The second of these objections asserted that it is of very rare occurrence, and is not found in the MSS. of Nikomachos and Pappos, where it might most naturally be expected. In reply to this, I pointed out that it was not in the least necessary for my theory that it should occur anywhere except in Diophantos ; and accordingly I did not raise the question whether the symbol was found in MSS. so rarely as Mr Gow appears to suppose. Since then I have thought that it would be interesting to inquire into this point a little further, without, however, going too far afield. While reading Heiberg's *Quaestiones Archimedeae* in connection with the *Cattle-problem* discussed in chapter VIII. it occurred to me that the symbol for ἀριθμός would be likely to be found, if anywhere, in the MSS. of the *De arenae numero libellus* of Archimedes, which Heiberg gives at the end of the book, and that, if it did so occur, Heiberg's textual criticisms would place the matter beyond doubt, without the necessity of actually collating the MSS. My expectation proved to be fully justified ; for it is quite clear that the symbol occurred in the MSS. of this work of Archimedes rather frequently, and that its form had given rise to exactly the same confusion and doubt as in the case of Diophantos. I will here give references to the places where it undoubtedly occurred. See the following pages in Heiberg's book.

    p. 172.

    p. 174. Heiberg reads ἀριθμόν, with the remark "καὶ omnes." But the similarity of the signs for ἀριθμός and καί is well known, and it could hardly be anything else than this similarity which could cause such a difference of readings.

    p. 187. Heiberg's remark " ἀριθμῶν om. codd. Bas. R ; excidit ante ς (καί)" speaks for itself. Also on the same page "ἀριθμῶν] ꝰꝰ FBC."

    p. 188. ꝰꝰ three times for ἀριθμῶν.

    p. 191. Here there is a confusion between ς (six) and ἀριθμός, where Heiberg remarks, "Error ortus est ex compendio illo uerbi ἀριθμός, de quo dixi ad I, 3."

    p. 192. ἐλάττων and ἀριθμός given as alternative readings, with the observation, " Confusa sunt compendia."

Thus it is clear that the symbol in question occurs tolerably often in the MSS. of another arithmetical treatise, and that the only one which I have investigated in this connection : a fact which certainly does not support Mr Gow's statement that it is very rarely found.

APPENDIX.

ABSTRACT OF THE *ARITHMETICS* AND THE TRACT ON *POLYGONAL NUMBERS*.

DIOPHANTOS. *ARITHMETICS.*

BOOK I.

Introduction addressed to Dionysios.

Definitions.

1. " Square " and " side," " cube," " square-square," &c.
2. " Power." Notation $\delta^{\bar{v}}$, $\kappa^{\bar{v}}$, $\delta\delta^{\bar{v}}$, $\delta\kappa^{\bar{v}}$, $\kappa\kappa^{\bar{v}}$, $\mu^{\bar{v}}$, $\backsim$.
3. Corresponding fractions, the reciprocals of the former; names used corresponding to the " numbers."
4. "Number"×"Number"= square. Square × square = "square-square," &c.
5. " Number " × corresponding fraction = unit ($\mu o\nu\acute{a}s$).
6. "Species " not changed by multiplication with monads.
7.
8.$\Big\}$ Reciprocal × reciprocal = reciprocal square, &c.
9. *Minus multiplied by minus gives plus.* Notation for minus, ⋔.
10. Division. Remark on familiarity with processes.
11. Simplification of equations.

Problems.

1. Divide a given number into two having a given difference.
   Given number 100, given difference 40.
   Lesser number required x. Therefore
   $$2x + 40 = 100,$$
   $$x = 30.$$
   The required numbers are **70, 30**.

2. To divide a given number into two having a given ratio.
   Given number 60, given ratio 3 : 1.
   Two numbers x, $3x$. Therefore $x = 15$.
   The numbers are **45, 15.**

164   DIOPHANTOS OF ALEXANDRIA.

3. To divide a given number into two having a given ratio *and* difference [1].

Given number 80 ; ratio 3 : 1 ; difference 4.

Smaller number x. Therefore the larger is $3x+4$, $x=19$.

The numbers are 61, 19.

4. Find two numbers in a given ratio, their difference also being given.

Given ratio 5 : 1. Difference 20.

Numbers $5x$, x. Therefore $x=5$, and the numbers are 25, 5.

5. To divide a given number into two such that the sum of given fractions (not the same) of each is a given number.

Necessary condition. The latter given number must lie between the numbers arising when the given fractions are taken of the first given number.

First given number 100, given fractions $\frac{1}{3}$ and $\frac{1}{5}$, given sum 30.

Second part $5x$. Therefore first part $= 3\,(30-x)$.

Therefore $90+2x=100$, $x=5$.

The required parts are **75, 25**.

6. To divide a given number into two parts, such that a given fraction of one exceeds a given fraction of the other by a given difference.

Necessary condition. The latter number must be less than that which arises when that fraction of the first number is taken which exceeds the other fraction.

Given number 100 ; fractions $\frac{1}{4}$ and $\frac{1}{6}$ respectively ; excess 20.

Second part $6x$. Therefore $10x+80=100$, $x=2$, and the parts are **88, 12**.

7. From the same (required) number to take away two given numbers, so that the remainders are in a given ratio.

Given numbers 100, 20 ; ratio 3 : 1.

x required number. Therefore

$$x-100 : x-20 = 1 : 3,   x=\textbf{140}.$$

8. To two given numbers to add the same (required) number, so that the sums are in a given ratio.

[1] By this Diophantos means " such that one is so many times the other *plus* a given number."

Condition. This ratio must be less than that of the greater given number to the smaller.

Given numbers 100, 20, given ratio 3 : 1.

x required number. Therefore

$$3x + 60 = x + 100, \text{ and } x = 20.$$

9. From two given numbers to subtract the same (required) one so that the two remainders are in a given ratio.

Condition. This ratio must be greater than that of the greater given number to the smaller.

Given numbers 20, 100, ratio 6 : 1.

x required number. Therefore

$$120 - 6x = 100 - x, \text{ and } x = 4.$$

10. Given two numbers, to add the same (required) number to the smaller, and subtract it from the larger, so that the sum in the first case may have to the difference in the second a given ratio.

Given numbers 20, 100, given ratio 4 : 1.

x required number. Therefore

$$20 + x : 100 - x = 4 : 1, \text{ and } x = 76.$$

11. Of two given numbers to add the first to, and subtract the second from, the same (required) number, so that the numbers which arise may have a given ratio.

Given numbers 20, 100 respectively, ratio 3 : 1.

x required number. Therefore

$$3x - 300 = x + 20, \text{ and } x = 160.$$

12. To divide a given number twice into two parts, such that the first of the first pair may have to the first of the second a given ratio, and also the second of the first pair to the second of the second another given ratio.

Given number 100, ratio of greater of first parts to less of second 2 : 1, ratio of greater of second parts to less of first 3 : 1.

x smaller of second parts. The parts then are

$$\left. \begin{matrix} 2x \\ 100 - 2x \end{matrix} \right\} \text{ and } \left. \begin{matrix} 300 - 6x \\ x \end{matrix} \right\}. \text{ Therefore } 300 - 5x = 100, \quad x = 40,$$

and the parts are (80, 20), (60, 40).

13. To divide a given number thrice into two parts, such that one of the first parts and one of the second parts, the other of the second

parts and one of the third parts, the other of the third parts and the remaining one of the first parts, are respectively in given ratios.

Given number 100, ratio of greater of first parts to less of second 3 : 1, of greater of second to less of third 2 : 1, and of greater of third to less of first 4 : 1.

x smaller of third parts. Therefore greater of second $= 2x$, less of second $= 100 - 2x$, greater of first $= 300 - 6x$.

Therefore less of first $= 6x - 200$.

Hence greater of third $= 24x - 800$.

Therefore $25x - 800 = 100$, $x = 36$,

and the respective divisions are (**84, 16**), (**72, 28**), (**64, 36**).

14.   To find two numbers such that their product has to their sum a given ratio.   [One is arbitrarily assumed subject to the]

Condition. The assumed value of one of the two must be greater than the numerator of the ratio [the denominator being 1].

Ratio 3 : 1. x one number, the other **12** (> 3).   Therefore
$$12x = 3x + 36,   x = 4,$$
and the numbers are **4, 12**.

15.   To find two numbers such that each after receiving from the other a given number may bear to the remainder a given ratio.

Let the first receive 30 from the second, ratio being then 2 : 1, and the second 50 from the first, ratio being then 3 : 1.

$x + 30$ the second.   Therefore the first $= 2x - 30$,

and $x + 80 : 2x - 80 = 3 : 1$.

Therefore $x = 64$, and the numbers are **98, 94**.

16.   To find three numbers such that the sums of each pair are given numbers.

Condition. Half the sum of all must be greater than any one singly.

Let $(1) + (2) = 20$, $(2) + (3) = 30$, $(3) + (1) = 40$.

x the sum of the three.   Therefore the numbers are
$$x - 30, x - 40, x - 20.$$
Hence the sum $x = 3x - 90$.   Therefore $x = 45$,

and the numbers are **15, 5, 25**.

17.   To find four numbers such that the sums of all sets of three are given.

Condition. One third of the sum of all must be greater than any one singly.

Sums of threes 22, 24, 27, 20.

x the sum of all four.   Therefore the numbers are
$$x-22,\ x-24,\ x-27,\ x-20.$$
Therefore $4x-93=x,\ x=31,$
and the numbers are **9, 7, 4, 11.**

18.   To find three numbers such that the sum of any pair exceeds the third by a given number.

Given excesses 20, 30, 40.

$2x$ sum of all, $x=45$.   The numbers are **25, 35, 30.**

19.   [A different solution of the foregoing problem.]

20.   To find four numbers such that the sum of any three exceeds the fourth by a given number.

Condition.   Half the sum of the four given differences must be greater than any one of them.

Given differences 20, 30, 40, 50.

$2x$ the sum of the four required numbers.   Therefore the numbers are
$$x-10,\ x-15,\ x-20,\ x-25.$$
Therefore $4x-70=2x$, and $x=35$.

Therefore the numbers are **25, 20, 15, 10.**

21.   [Another solution of the foregoing.]

22.   To divide a given number into three, such that the sum of each extreme and the mean has to the remaining extreme a given ratio.

Given number 100 ; $(1)+(2)=3\ .\ (3),\ (2)+(3)=4\ .\ (1)$.

x the third.   Hence the sum of first and second $=3x$.   Therefore $4x=100$.

$x=25$, and the sum of the first two $=75$.

y the first [1].   Therefore $(2)+(3)=4y$.   Therefore $5y=100$,
$y=20$.   The required parts are **20, 55, 25.**

23.   To find three numbers such that the greatest exceeds the middle number by a given fraction of the least, the middle exceeds the least by the same given fraction of the greatest, but the least exceeds the same given fraction of the middle number by a given number.

---

[1] As already remarked on pp. 80, 81, Diophantos does not use a second syllable for the unknown, but uses ἀριθμός for the second operation as well as for the first.

Condition. The middle number must exceed the least by such a fraction of the greatest, that if its denominator be multiplied into the excess of the middle number over the least, the result is greater than the middle number.

Greatest exceeds middle by $\frac{1}{3}$ of least, middle exceeds least by $\frac{1}{3}$ of greatest, least exceeds $\frac{1}{3}$ of middle by 10.

$x+10$ the least. Therefore middle $= 3x$, greatest $= 6x-30$. Therefore $x = 12\frac{1}{2}$, and the numbers are 45, $37\frac{1}{2}$, $22\frac{1}{2}$.

24. [Another solution of the foregoing.]

25. To find three numbers such that, if each give to the next following a given fraction of itself, in order, the results after each has given and taken may be equal.

Let first give $\frac{1}{3}$ of itself to second, second $\frac{1}{4}$ of itself to third, third $\frac{1}{5}$ of itself to first.

Assume the second to be a number divisible by 4, say 4. $3x$ the first, and $x = 2$. The numbers are 6, 4, 5.

26. Find four numbers such that, if each give to the next following a given fraction of itself, the results may all be equal.

Let first give $\frac{1}{3}$ of itself to second, $\frac{1}{4}, \frac{1}{5}, \frac{1}{6}$ being the other fractions.

Assume the second to be a multiple of 4, say 4. $3x$ the first. The second after giving and taking becomes $x+3$.

Therefore first after giving x to second and receiving $\frac{1}{6}$ of fourth $= x+3$.

Therefore fourth $= 18 - 6x$. And fourth after giving $3-x$ to first and receiving $\frac{1}{5}$ of third $= x+3$. Therefore third $= 30x - 60$.

Lastly the third after giving $6x - 12$ to fourth and receiving 1 from second $= x+3$. Therefore

$$24x - 47 = x+3, \quad x = \frac{50}{23}.$$

Therefore the numbers are $\dfrac{150}{23}$, 4, $\dfrac{120}{23}$, $\dfrac{114}{23}$,

or, multiplying by the common denominator, **150, 92, 120, 114.**

27.   To find three numbers such that, if each receives a given fraction of the sum of the other two, the results are all equal.

The fractions being $\dfrac{1}{3}$, $\dfrac{1}{4}$, $\dfrac{1}{5}$, the sum of the second and third

is *assumed* to be 3, and x put for the first.

The numbers are, after multiplying by a common denominator, **13, 17, 19.**

28.   To find four numbers such that, if each receives a given fraction of the sum of the remaining three, the four results are equal.

The given fractions being $\dfrac{1}{3}$, $\dfrac{1}{4}$, $\dfrac{1}{5}$, $\dfrac{1}{6}$, we *assume* the sum of

the last three numbers to be 3.

Putting x for the first, Diophantos finds in like manner that numbers are **47, 77, 92, 101.**

29.   Given two numbers, to find a third which, when multiplied by each successively, makes one product a square and the other the side of that square.

Given numbers 200, 5.

x required number, $200x = (5x)^2$, $x = 8$.

30.   *To find two numbers whose sum and whose product are given.*

Condition.   *The square of half the sum must exceed the product by a square number,* ἔστι δὲ τοῦτο πλασματικόν [1].

Given sum 20, product 96.

$2x$ the difference of the required numbers.

Therefore numbers are $10 + x$, $10 - x$.

Hence $100 - x^2 = 96$.

Therefore $x = 2$, and the difference $= 4$.   The required numbers are **12, 8.**

---

[1] There has been much controversy as to the meaning of this difficult phrase. Xylander, the author of the Scholia, Bachet, Cossali, Schulz, Nesselmann, all discuss it. As I do not profess here to be commenting on the text I shall not criticise their respective views, but only remark that I think it is best to take πλασματικόν in a passive sense. "And this condition can (easily) be formed," i.e. can be investigated (and shown to be true), or *discovered*.

31. *To find two numbers, having given their sum and the sum of their squares.*

Condition. *Double the sum of the squares must exceed the square of their sum by a square,* ἔστι δὲ καὶ τοῦτο πλασματικόν.

Sum 20, sum of squares 208.

$2x$ the difference.

Therefore the numbers are $10 + x$, $10 - x$.

Thus $200 + 2x^2 = 208$. Hence $x = 2$,

and the numbers are **12, 8.**

32. To find two numbers, having given their sum and the difference of their squares.

Sum 20, difference of squares 80.

$2x$ difference of the numbers,

and we find the numbers **12, 8.**

33. *To find two numbers whose difference and product are given.*

Condition. *Four times the product together with square of difference must produce a complete square,* ἔστι δὲ καὶ τοῦτο πλασματικόν.

Difference 4, product 96.

$2x$ the sum. Therefore the numbers are found to be **12, 8.**

34. Find two numbers in a given ratio such that the sum of their squares is to their sum also in a given ratio.

Ratios 3 : 1 and 5 : 1 respectively.

x lesser number. $x = 2$; the numbers are **2, 6.**

35. Find two numbers in a given ratio such that the sum of their squares is to their difference in a given ratio.

Ratios being 3 : 1, 10 : 1, the numbers are **2, 6.**

36. Find two numbers in a given ratio such that the difference of their squares is to their sum in a given ratio.

Ratios being 3 : 1 and 6 : 1, the numbers are **3, 9.**

37. Find two numbers in a given ratio such that the difference of their squares is to their difference in a given ratio.

Ratios being 3 : 1 and 12 : 1, the numbers are **3, 9.**

Similarly by this method can be found two numbers in a given ratio (1) such that their product is to their sum in a given ratio, or (2) such that their product is to their difference in a given ratio.

38. To find two numbers in a given ratio such that the square of the smaller is to the larger in a given ratio.

Ratios 3 : 1 and 6 : 1. Numbers **54, 18.**

39.   To find two numbers in a given ratio such that the square of the smaller is to the smaller itself in a given ratio.

Ratios 3 : 1 and 6 : 1.   Numbers 18, 6.

40.   To find two numbers in a given ratio such that the square of the less has a given ratio to the sum of both.

Ratios 3 : 1, 2 : 1.   Numbers **24, 8.**

41.   To find two numbers in a given ratio such that the square of the smaller has a given ratio to their difference.

Ratios 3 : 1 and 6 : 1.   Numbers **36, 12.**

42.   Similarly can be found two numbers in a given ratio,

(1) such that square of larger has a given ratio to the smaller.

(2) such that square of larger has to larger itself a given ratio.

(3) such that square of larger has a given ratio to the sum or difference of the two.

43.   Given two numbers, to find a third such that the sums of the several pairs multiplied by the corresponding third give three numbers in A. P.

Given numbers 3, 5.

x the required number.   Therefore the three expressions are
$$3x + 15,\ 5x + 15,\ 8x.$$

Now $3x + 15$ must be either the middle or the least of the three, $5x + 15$ either the greatest or the middle.

(1) $5x + 15$ greatest, $3x + 15$ least.   Therefore $x = \dfrac{15}{4}$.

(2) $5x + 15$ greatest, $3x + 15$ middle.   Therefore $x = \dfrac{15}{7}$.

(3) $8x$ greatest, $3x + 15$ least.   Therefore $x = 15$.

BOOK II.

[The first five questions of this Book are identical with questions in
    Book I. In each case the ratio of one required number to the
    other is assumed to be 2 : 1. The enunciations only are here
    given.]

    1. To find two numbers whose sum is to the sum of their
squares in a given ratio.

    2. Find two numbers whose difference is to the difference of
their squares in a given ratio.

    3. Find two numbers whose product is to their sum or difference
in a given ratio.

    4. Find two numbers such that the sum of their squares is to
the difference of the numbers in a given ratio.

    5. Find two numbers such that the difference of their squares is
to the sum of the numbers in a given ratio.

    6. Find two numbers having a given difference, and such that
the difference of their squares exceeds the difference of the numbers
themselves by a given number.

    Condition. The square of their difference must be less than the
sum of the two given differences.

        Difference of numbers 2, the other given number 20.

        x the smaller number. Therefore $x + 2$ is the larger and
           $4x + 4 = 22$.

    $x = 4\frac{1}{2}$, and the numbers are $4\frac{1}{2}$, $6\frac{1}{2}$.

    7. Find two numbers such that the difference of their squares
may be greater than their difference by a given number and in a
given ratio (to it)[1]. [*Difference assumed.*]

    Condition. The ratio being 3 : 1, the square of the difference
of the numbers must be < sum of three times that difference and the
given number.

---

    [1] By this Diophantos means "may exceed a given proportion or fraction of
it by a given number."

Given number 10, difference of numbers required 2.

x the smaller number. Therefore the larger $= x + 2$,

and $4x + 4 = 3 \cdot 2 + 10$.

Therefore $x = 3$,

and the numbers are 3, 5.

8. *To divide a square number into two squares.*

Let the square number be 16.

x^2 one of the required squares. Therefore $16 - x^2$ must be equal to a square.

Take a square of the form[1] $(mx - 4)^2$, 4 being taken as the absolute term because the square of $4 = 16$.

i.e. take (say) $(2x - 4)^2$ and equate it to $16 - x^2$.

Therefore $\qquad 4x^2 - 16x = -x^2$.

Therefore $\qquad\qquad x = \dfrac{16}{5}$,

and the squares required are $\dfrac{256}{25}, \dfrac{144}{25}$.

9. [Another solution of the foregoing, practically equivalent.]

10. *To divide a number which is the sum of two squares into two other squares.*

Given number $13 = 3^2 + 2^2$.

As the roots of these squares are 2, 3, take $(x + 2)^2$ as the first square and $(mx - 3)^2$ as the second required, say $(2x - 3)^2$.

Therefore $\qquad (x + 2)^2 + (2x - 3)^2 = 13$.

$$x = \frac{8}{5}.$$

Therefore the required squares are $\dfrac{324}{25}, \dfrac{1}{25}$.

11. *To find two square numbers differing by a given number.*

Given difference 60.

Side of one number x, side of the other x plus any number whose square < 60, say 3.

Therefore $\qquad (x + 3)^2 - x^2 = 60$,

$$x = 8\tfrac{1}{2},$$

and the required squares are $72\tfrac{1}{4}, 132\tfrac{1}{4}$.

---

[1] Diophantos' words are: "I form the square from any number of ἀριθμοί *minus* as many units as are contained in the side of 16." The precaution implied throughout in the choice of m is that we must assume it so that the result may be *rational* in Diophantos' sense, i.e. rational and positive.

12. *To add such a number to each of two given numbers that the results shall both be squares.*

(1) Given numbers 2, 3, required number x.

Therefore $\left.\begin{array}{c} x+2 \\ x+3 \end{array}\right\}$ must each be squares.

This is called a double-equation.

To solve it, *take the difference between them, and resolve it into two factors*[1] : in this case say 4 and $\frac{1}{4}$.

Then *take either*

(a) *the square of half the difference between these factors and equate it to the smaller expression,*

or (b) *the square of half the sum and equate it to the larger.*

In this case (a) the square of half the difference $= \frac{225}{64}$.

Therefore $x + 2 = \frac{225}{64}$, and $x = \frac{97}{64}$,

while the squares are $\frac{225}{64}$, $\frac{289}{64}$.

(2) In order to avoid a double-equation,

First find a number which added to 2 gives a square, say $x^2 - 2$.

Therefore, since the same number added to 3 gives a square,
        $x^2 + 1 = \text{square} = (x - 4)^2$ say,

the absolute term (in this case 4) being so chosen that the solution may give $x^2 > 2$.

Therefore $x = \frac{15}{8}$,

and the required number is $\frac{97}{64}$, as before.

13. *From two given numbers to take the same (required) number so that both the remainders are squares.*

Given numbers 9, 21.

Assuming $9 - x^2$ as the required number we satisfy one condition, and it remains that $12 + x^2 = $ a square.

Assume as the side of this square x minus some number whose square > 12, say 4.

---

[1] We must, as usual, choose suitable factors, i.e. such as will give a "rational" result. This must always be premised.

Therefore $(x-4)^2 = 12 + x^2.$
$$x = \frac{1}{2},$$
and the required number is $8\frac{3}{4}$.

14. *From the same (required) number to subtract successively two given numbers so that the remainders may both be squares.*

6, 7 the given numbers. Then

(1) let x be required number.

Therefore $\left.\begin{array}{c} x-6 \\ x-7 \end{array}\right\}$ are both squares.

The difference $= 1$, which is the product of 2 and $\frac{1}{2}$;

and, by the rule for solving a double-equation,
$$x = \frac{121}{16}.$$

(2) To avoid a double-equation seek a number which exceeds a square by 6,

i.e. let $x^2 + 6$ be the required number.

Therefore also $x^2 - 1 = $ square $= (x-2)^2$ say.

Hence $x = \frac{5}{4},$

and the number required $= \frac{121}{16}$.

15. *To divide a given number into two parts, and to find a square number which when added to either of the two parts gives a square number.*

Given number 20. Take two numbers the sum of whose squares < 20, say 2, 3. Add x to each and square.

We then have $\left.\begin{array}{c} x^2 + 4x + 4 \\ x^2 + 6x + 9 \end{array}\right\},$

and if $\left.\begin{array}{c} 4x + 4 \\ 6x + 9 \end{array}\right\}$

are respectively subtracted the remainders are the same square.

Let then x^2 be the square required,

and therefore $\left.\begin{array}{c} 4x + 4 \\ 6x + 9 \end{array}\right\}$

the required parts of 20.

Then $10x + 13 = 20,$

and $x = \frac{7}{10}.$

Thus the required parts are $\left(\dfrac{68}{10}, \dfrac{132}{10}\right)$,

and the required square $\dfrac{49}{100}$.

16. To divide a given number into two parts and find a square which exceeds either part by a square.

Given number 20.

Take $(x + m)^2$ for the required square, where $m^2 < 20$,

i.e. let $(x + 2)^2$ be the required square (say).

This leaves a square if either $\left.\begin{array}{l} 4x + 4 \\ \text{or } 2x + 3 \end{array}\right\}$ is subtracted.

Let these be the parts of 20,

and $\qquad\qquad\qquad x = \dfrac{13}{6}$.

Therefore the parts required are $\left(\dfrac{76}{6}, \dfrac{44}{6}\right)$,

and the required square is $\dfrac{625}{36}$.

17. Find two numbers in a given ratio such that either together with an assigned square produces a square.

Assigned square 9, ratio 3 : 1.

If we take a square whose side is $mx + 3$ and subtract 9 from it, the remainder will be one of the numbers required.

Take e. g. $(x + 3)^2 - 9 = x^2 + 6x$ for the smaller number.

Therefore $3x^2 + 18x =$ the larger number,

and $3x^2 + 18x + 9$ must be made a square $= (2x - 3)^2$ say.

Therefore $\qquad\qquad x = 30$,

and the required numbers are **1080, 3240**.

18. To find three numbers such that, if each give to the next following a given fraction of itself and a given number besides, the results after each has given and taken may be equal.

First gives to second $\dfrac{1}{5}$ of itself + 6, second to third $\dfrac{1}{6}$ of itself

+ 7, third to first $\dfrac{1}{7}$ of itself + 8.

Assume that the first two are $5x$, $6x$ [equivalent to one condition], and we find the numbers to be $\dfrac{90}{7}$, $\dfrac{108}{7}$, $\dfrac{105}{7}$.

19. Divide a number into three parts satisfying the conditions of the preceding problem.

Given number 80. First gives to second $\frac{1}{5}$ of itself + 6 &c., and results are equal.

[Diophantos assumes $5x$, 12 for the first two numbers, and his result is $\frac{170}{19}$, $\frac{228}{19}$, $\frac{217}{19}$; but the solution does not correspond to the question.] (See p. 25.)

20. To find three squares such that the difference of the greatest and the second is to the difference of the second and the least in a given ratio.

Given ratio 3 : 1.

Assume the least square $= x^2$, the middle $= x^2 + 2x + 1$.

Therefore the greatest $= x^2 + 8x + 4 = $ square $= (x + 3)^2$ say.

Therefore $$x = \frac{5}{2},$$

and the squares are $30\frac{1}{4}$, $12\frac{1}{4}$, $6\frac{1}{4}$.

21. To find two numbers such that the square of either added to the other number is a square.

x, $2x + 1$ are assumed, which by their form satisfy one condition. The other condition gives
$$4x^2 + 5x + 1 = \text{square} = (2x - 2)^2 \text{ say.}$$

Therefore $$x = \frac{3}{13},$$

and the numbers are $\frac{3}{13}$, $\frac{19}{13}$.

22. To find two numbers such that the square of either *minus* the other number is a square.

$x + 1$, $2x + 1$ are assumed, satisfying one condition.

Therefore $4x^2 + 3x = $ square $= 9x^2$ say.

Therefore $$x = \frac{3}{5},$$

and the numbers are $\frac{8}{5}$, $\frac{11}{5}$.

23. To find two numbers such that the sum of the square of either and the sum of both is a square.

Assume x, $x + 1$ for the numbers. These satisfy one condition.

H. D.   12

Also $x^2 + 4x + 2$ must be a square $= (x - 2)^2$ say.

Therefore $$x = \frac{1}{4}.$$

Hence the numbers are $\frac{1}{4}, \frac{5}{4}$.

24. To find two numbers such that the difference of the square of either and the sum of both is a square.

Assume $x + 1$, x for the numbers, and we must have
$$x^2 - 2x - 1 \text{ a square} = (x - 3)^2 \text{ say.}$$
Therefore $$x = 2\tfrac{1}{2},$$
and the numbers are $3\tfrac{1}{2}, 2\tfrac{1}{2}$.

25. To find two numbers such that the sum of either and the square of their sum is a square.

Since $\qquad x^2 + 3x^2$, $x^2 + 8x^2$ are squares,
let the numbers be $3x^2$, $8x^2$ and their sum x.

Therefore $\qquad 11x^2 = x$ and $x = \dfrac{1}{11}$.

Therefore the numbers are $\dfrac{3}{121}, \dfrac{8}{121}$.

26. To find two numbers such that the difference of the square of the sum of both and either number is a square.

If we subtract 7, 12 from 16 we get squares.

Assume then $12x^2$, $7x^2$ for the numbers, $16x^2 = $ square of sum.

Therefore $\qquad 19x^2 = 4x$, $x = \dfrac{4}{19}$,

and the numbers are $\dfrac{192}{361}, \dfrac{112}{361}$.

27. To find two numbers such that the sum of either and their product is a square, and the sum of the sides of the two squares so arising equal to a given number, 6 suppose.

Since $x(4x - 1) + x = $ square, let x, $4x - 1$ be the numbers.
Therefore $4x^2 + 3x - 1$ is a square, whose side is $6 - 2x$.

Therefore $$x = \frac{37}{27},$$

and the numbers are $\dfrac{37}{27}, \dfrac{121}{27}$.

28. To find two numbers such that the difference of their product and either is a square, and the sum of the sides of the two squares so arising equal to a number, 5.

Assume $4x+1$, x for the numbers, which therefore satisfy one condition.

Also $4x^2 - 3x - 1 = (5 - 2x)^2$. Therefore $x = \dfrac{26}{17}$,

and the numbers are $\dfrac{26}{17}$, $\dfrac{121}{17}$.

29. *To find two square numbers such that the sum of the product and either is a square.*[1]

Let the numbers[1] be x^2, y^2.

Therefore $\left.\begin{array}{l} x^2y^2 + y^2 \\ x^2y^2 + x^2 \end{array}\right\}$ are both squares.

To make the first a square we make $x^2 + 1$ a square, putting

$x^2 + 1 = (x - 2)^2$. Therefore $x = \dfrac{3}{4}$.

We have now to make $\dfrac{9}{16}(y^2 + 1)$ a square [and y must be different from x].

Put $\qquad 9y^2 + 9 = (3y - 4)^2$ say.

Therefore $\qquad\qquad y = \dfrac{7}{24}$.

Therefore the numbers are $\dfrac{9}{16}$, $\dfrac{49}{576}$.

30. To find two square numbers such that the difference of their product and either is a square.

Let x^2, y^2 be the numbers.

Therefore $\left.\begin{array}{l} x^2y^2 - y^2 \\ x^2y^2 - x^2 \end{array}\right\}$ are both squares.

A solution of $x^2 - 1 = $ square is $x^2 = \dfrac{25}{16}$,

and a solution of $y^2 - 1 = $ square is $y = \dfrac{17}{8}$.

Therefore the numbers are $\dfrac{25}{16}$, $\dfrac{289}{64}$.

31. To find two numbers such that their product $\pm$ their sum gives a square.

---

[1] Diophantos does not use two unknowns, but assumes the numbers to be x^2 and 1 until he has found x. Then he uses the same unknown to find what he had first called unity, as explained above, p. 81. The same remark applies to the next problem.

$a^2 + b^2 \pm 2ab$ is a square. Put 2, 3 for a, b, and $2^2 + 3^2 \pm 2 . 2 . 3$
is a square. Assume then product $= (2^2 + 3^2) x^2 = 13x^2$,
the numbers being x, $13x$, and the sum $2 . 2 . 3x^2$ or $12x^2$.

Therefore $14x = 12x^2$, and $x = \dfrac{7}{6}$.

Therefore the numbers are $\dfrac{7}{6}$, $\dfrac{91}{6}$.

32.   To find two numbers whose sum is a square and having the
same property as the numbers in the preceding problem.

$2 . 2m . m =$ square, and $\overline{2m}\big|^2 + \overline{m}\big|^2 \pm 2 . 2m . m =$ square.
If $m = 2$, $4^2 + 2^2 \pm 2 . 4 . 2 = 36$ or 4.
Let then the product of numbers be $(4^2 + 2^2) x^2$ or $20x^2$ and
their sum $2 . 4 . 2x^2$ or $16x^2$, and let the numbers be $2x$, $10x$.

Therefore $12x = 16x^2$, $x = \dfrac{3}{4}$,

and the numbers are $\dfrac{6}{4}$, $\dfrac{30}{4}$.

33.   To find three numbers such that the sum of the square of
any one and the succeeding number is a square.

Let the first be x, the second $2x + 1$, the third $2(2x + 1) + 1$
or $4x + 3$, so that two conditions are satisfied.
Lastly $(4x + 3)^2 + x =$ square $= (4x - 4)^2$ say.

Therefore $x = \dfrac{7}{57}$,

and the numbers are $\dfrac{7}{57}$, $\dfrac{71}{57}$, $\dfrac{199}{57}$.

34.   To find three numbers such that the difference of the square
of any one and the succeeding number is a square.

Assume first $x + 1$, second $2x + 1$, third $4x + 1$.   Therefore
two conditions are satisfied, and the third gives
$16x^2 + 7x =$ square $= 25x^2$ say.

Therefore $x = \dfrac{7}{9}$,

and the numbers are $\dfrac{16}{9}$, $\dfrac{23}{9}$, $\dfrac{37}{9}$.

35.   To find three numbers such that, if the square of any one be
added to the sum of all, the result is a square.

$\left(\dfrac{m - n}{2}\right)^2 + mn$ is a square. Take a number separable into two factors (m, n) in three ways, say 12, which is the product of $(1, 12)$, $(2, 6)$, $(3, 4)$.

The values then of $\dfrac{m-n}{2}$ are $5\frac{1}{2}$, 2, $\dfrac{1}{2}$.

Let now $5\frac{1}{2}x$, $2x$, $\dfrac{1}{2}x$ be the numbers. Their sum is $12x^2$.

Therefore $\qquad 8x = 12x^2, \quad x = \dfrac{2}{3}$,

and the numbers are $\dfrac{11}{3}, \dfrac{4}{3}, \dfrac{1}{3}$.

36. To find three numbers such that, if the sum of all be subtracted from the square of any one, the result is a square.

$\left(\dfrac{m+n}{2}\right)^2 - mn$ is a square. Take 12 as before, and let $6\frac{1}{2}x$, $4x$, $3\frac{1}{2}x$ be the numbers, their sum being $12x^2$.

Therefore $\qquad x = \dfrac{7}{6}$,

and the numbers are $\dfrac{91}{12}, \dfrac{28}{6}, \dfrac{49}{12}$.

BOOK III.

1. To find three numbers such that, if the square of any one be subtracted from the sum of all, the remainder is a square.

Take two squares x^2, $4x^2$ whose sum $= 5x^2$.

Let the sum of all three numbers be $5x^2$, and two of the numbers x, $2x$. These assumptions satisfy two conditions.

Next divide 5 into the sum of two squares [II. 10] $\dfrac{4}{25}, \dfrac{121}{25}$,

and assume that the third number is $\dfrac{2}{5}x$.

Therefore $x + 2x + \dfrac{2}{5}x = 5x^2$. Therefore $x = \dfrac{17}{25}$,

and the numbers are $\dfrac{17}{25}, \dfrac{34}{25}, \dfrac{34}{125}$.

2. To find three numbers such that, if the square of the sum be added to any one of them, the sum is a square.

Let the square of the sum be x^2, and the numbers $3x^2$, $8x^2$, $15x^2$.

Hence $\qquad\qquad 26x^2 = x,\ x = \dfrac{1}{26}$,

and the numbers are $\dfrac{3}{676}$, $\dfrac{8}{676}$, $\dfrac{15}{676}$.

3.   To find three numbers such that, if any one be subtracted from the square of their sum, the result is a square.

Sum of all $4x$, its square $16x^2$, the numbers $7x^2$, $12x^2$, $15x^2$.

Therefore $\qquad\qquad 34x^2 = 4x,\ x = \dfrac{2}{17}$,

and the numbers are $\dfrac{28}{289}$, $\dfrac{48}{289}$, $\dfrac{60}{289}$.

4.   To find three numbers such that, if the square of their sum be subtracted from any one, the result is a square.

Sum x, the three numbers $2x^2$, $5x^2$, $10x^2$.

Therefore $\qquad\qquad x = \dfrac{1}{17}$,

and the numbers are $\dfrac{2}{289}$, $\dfrac{5}{289}$, $\dfrac{10}{289}$.

5.   To find three numbers such that the sum of any pair exceeds the third by a square, and the sum of all is a square.

Let the sum of the three be $(x+1)^2$; let first + second = third + 1,

so that third $= \dfrac{x^2}{2} + x$; let second + third = first + x^2,

so that first $= x + \dfrac{1}{2}$. Therefore second $= \dfrac{x^2}{2} + \dfrac{1}{2}$.

But first + third = second + square, therefore $2x$ = square = 16, suppose. Therefore $x = 8$, and $(8\frac{1}{2},\ 32\frac{1}{2},\ 40)$ is a solution.

6.   [The same otherwise.]

First find three squares whose sum is a square. Find e.g. what square number $+ 4 + 9$ gives a square, i.e. 36. Therefore $(4,\ 36,\ 9)$ are such squares.

Next find three numbers such that sum of a pair = third + given number, say, first + second − third = 4, second + third − first = 9, third + first − second = 36, by the previous problem.

7.   To find three numbers whose sum is a square, and such that the sum of any pair is a square.

Let the sum be $x^2 + 2x + 1$, sum of first and second x^2, and therefore the third $2x + 1$; let second + third $= (x-1)^2$.
Therefore the first is $4x$, and therefore the second $x^2 - 4x$.
But first + third = square, or $6x + 1 =$ square $= 121$ say.
Therefore $x = 20$,
and the numbers are (80, 320, 41).

8. [The same otherwise.]

9. To find three numbers in A. P. such that the sum of any pair is a square.

First find three square numbers in A. P. any two of which are together > the third. Let x^2, $(x+1)^2$ be two of these; therefore the third is $x^2 + 4x + 2 = (x-8)^2$ say.

Therefore $x = \dfrac{31}{10}$,

or we may take as the squares 961, 1681, 2401.

We have now to find three numbers, the sums of pairs being these numbers.

Sum of the three $= \dfrac{5043}{2} = 2521\frac{1}{2}$,

and we have all the three numbers.

10. Given one number, to find three others such that the sum of any pair of them and the given number is a square, and also the sum of the three and the given number is a square.

Given number 3. Suppose first + second $= x^2 + 4x + 1$, second + third $= x^2 + 6x + 6$, sum of all three $= x^2 + 8x + 13$.
Therefore third $= 4x + 12$, second $= x^2 + 2x - 6$, first $= 2x + 7$.
Also third + first + 3 = square, or $6x + 22 =$ square $= 100$ suppose.
Therefore $x = 13$,
and the numbers are 33, 189, 64.

11. Given one number, to find three others such that, if the given number be subtracted from the sum of any pair of them or from the sum, the results are all squares.

Given number 3. Sum of first two $x^2 + 3$, of next pair $x^2 + 2x + 4$, and sum of the three $x^2 + 4x + 7$. Therefore third $= 4x + 4$, second $= x^2 - 2x$, first $= 2x + 3$. Therefore, lastly, $6x + 4 =$ square $= 64$ say. Therefore $x = 10$, and (23, 80, 44) is a solution.

12. *To find three numbers such that the sum of the product of
any two and a given number is a square.*

Let the given number be 12. Take a square (say 25) and subtract 12. Take the difference (13) for the product of the
first and second numbers, and let these numbers be $13x, \dfrac{1}{x}$.

Again, subtract 12 from another square, say 16, and let the
difference 4 be the product of the second and third
numbers. Therefore the third number $= 4x$.

Hence the third condition gives $52x^2 + 12 =$ square, but
$52 = 4 \cdot 13$, and 13 is not a square, therefore *this equation cannot be solved by our method.*

Thus we must find two numbers to replace 13 and 4 whose
product is a square, and such that either $+ 12 =$ square.
Now the product is a square if both are squares. Hence
we must find two squares such that either $+ 12 =$ square.

The squares 4 and $\dfrac{1}{4}$ satisfy this condition.

Retracing our steps we put $4x, \dfrac{1}{x}, \dfrac{x}{4}$ for the numbers, and we
have to solve the equation
$$x^2 + 12 = \text{square} = (x + 3)^2 \text{ say.}$$

Therefore $x = \dfrac{1}{2}$,

and $\left(2, 2, \dfrac{1}{8}\right)$ is a solution.

13. To find three numbers such that, if a given number is subtracted from the product of any pair, the result is a square.

Given number 10.

Put product of first and second $=$ a square $+ 10 = 4 + 10$ say,
and let first $= 14x$, second $= \dfrac{1}{x}$. Also let product of second
and third $= 19$. Therefore third $= 19x$. Whence $266x^2 - 10$
must be a square; but 266 is not a square.

Hence, as in the preceding problem, we must find two squares
each of which exceeds a square by 10.

Now $\left(\dfrac{10 + 1}{2}\right)^2 - 10 = \left(\dfrac{10 - 1}{2}\right)^2$, therefore $30\frac{1}{4}$ is one such
square. If m^2 be another, $m^2 - 10$ must be a square
$= (m - 2)^2$ say, therefore $m = 3\frac{1}{2}$.

Thus, putting $30\frac{1}{4}x$, $\dfrac{1}{x}$, $12\frac{1}{4}x$ for the numbers, we have, from the third condition, $5929x^2 - 160 = \text{square} = (77x - 2)^2$ say.

Therefore $\qquad x = \dfrac{41}{77}$,

and the numbers are $\dfrac{1240\frac{1}{4}}{77}$, $\dfrac{77}{41}$, $\dfrac{502\frac{1}{4}}{77}$.

14. To find three numbers such that the product of any two added to the third gives a square.

Take a square and subtract part of it for the third number.

Let $x^2 + 6x + 9$ be one of the sums, and let the third number be 9. Therefore product of first and second $= x^2 + 6x$. Let the first $= x$, therefore the second $= x + 6$.

From the two remaining conditions

$$\left.\begin{array}{c} 10x + 54 \\ 10x + 6 \end{array}\right\} \text{ are both squares.}$$

Therefore we have to find two squares differing by 48, which are found to be 16, 64.

and $(1, 7, 9)$ is a solution.

15. To find three numbers such that the product of any two exceeds the third by a square.

First x, second $x + 4$, therefore their product is $x^2 + 4x$, and we suppose the third to be $4x$.

Therefore by the other conditions

$$\left.\begin{array}{c} 4x^2 + 15x \\ 4x^2 - x - 4 \end{array}\right\} \text{ are both squares.}$$

The difference $= 16x + 4 = 4\,(4x + 1)$,

and $\qquad \left(\dfrac{4x + 5}{2}\right)^2 = 4x^2 + 15x.$

Therefore $x = \dfrac{25}{20}$, and the numbers are found.

16. To find three numbers such that the product of any two added to the square of the third gives a square.

Let first be x, second $4x + 4$, third 1. Two conditions are thus satisfied, and the remaining one gives

$$x + (4x + 4)^2 = \text{a square} = (4x - 5)^2 \text{ say}.$$

Therefore $\qquad x = \dfrac{9}{73}$,

and the numbers are 9, 328, 73.

17.   To find three numbers such that the product of any two added to the sum of those two gives a square.

Lemma.   The squares of two consecutive numbers have this property.

Let 4, 9 be two of the numbers, x the third.

Therefore $\left.\begin{array}{c} 10x + 9 \\ 5x + 4 \end{array}\right\}$ must both be squares,

and the difference $= 5x + 5 = 5\,(x + 1)$.

Therefore by Book II.,
$$\left(\frac{x + 6}{2}\right)^2 = 10x + 9 \text{ and } x = 28,$$

and (4, 9, 28) is a solution.

18.   [*Another solution of the foregoing problem.*]

Assume the first to be x, the second 3.

Therefore $4x + 3 = \text{square} = 25$ say, whence $x = 5\frac{1}{2}$, and $5\frac{1}{2}$, 3 satisfy one condition. Let the third be x, $5\frac{1}{2}$ and 3 being the first two.

Therefore $\left.\begin{array}{c} 4x + 3 \\ 6\frac{1}{2}x + 5\frac{1}{2} \end{array}\right\}$ must both be squares,

but, since the coefficients in one expression are both greater than those in the other, but neither of the ratios of corresponding ones is that of a square to a square, our method will not solve them.

Hence (to replace $5\frac{1}{2}$, 3) we must find two numbers such that their product + their sum = square, and the ratio of the numbers each increased by 1 is the ratio of a square to a square.

Let them be y and $4y + 3$, which satisfy the latter condition; and so that product + sum = square we must have $4y^2 + 8y + 3 = \text{square} = (2y - 3)^2$, say.

Therefore $y = \dfrac{3}{10}.$

Assume now $\dfrac{3}{10}$, $4\frac{1}{5}$, x for the numbers.

Therefore $\left.\begin{array}{c} 5\frac{1}{5}x + 4\frac{1}{5} \\[4pt] \dfrac{13x}{10} + \dfrac{3}{10} \end{array}\right\}$ are both squares,

or $\left.\begin{array}{c} 130x + 105 \\ 130x + 30 \end{array}\right\}$ are both squares, the difference = 75, which has two factors 3 and 25,

and $x = \dfrac{7}{10}$ gives a solution,

the numbers being $\dfrac{3}{10}$, $4\frac{1}{5}$, $\dfrac{7}{10}$.

19. To find three numbers such that the product of any two exceeds the sum of those two by a square.

> Put first $= x$, second any number, and we fall into the same difficulty as in the preceding. We have to find two numbers such that their product *minus* their sum = square, and when each is diminished by one they have the ratio of squares. $4y + 1$, $y + 1$ satisfy the latter condition, and $4y^2 - 1 = $ square $= (2y - 2)^2$ say.

> Therefore $y = \dfrac{5}{8}$.

> Assume then as the numbers $\dfrac{13}{8}$, $\dfrac{28}{8}$, x.

> Therefore $\left. \begin{array}{l} 2\frac{1}{2}x - 3\frac{1}{2} \\ \dfrac{5}{8}x - \dfrac{13}{8} \end{array} \right\}$ are both squares,

> or $\left. \begin{array}{l} 10x - 14 \\ 10x - 26 \end{array} \right\}$ are both squares,

> the difference $= 12 = 2.6$, and $x = 3$ is a solution.

> The numbers are $\dfrac{13}{8}$, $3\frac{1}{2}$, 3.

20. To find two numbers such that their product added to both or to either gives a square.

> Assume x, $4x - 1$,

> since $x(4x - 1) + x = 4x^2 = $ square.

> Therefore also $\left. \begin{array}{l} 4x^2 + 3x - 1 \\ 4x^2 + 4x - 1 \end{array} \right\}$ are both squares,

> the difference $= x = 4x \cdot \dfrac{1}{4}$,

> and $x = \dfrac{65}{224}$ gives a solution.

21. To find two numbers such that the product exceeds the sum of both, and also either severally, by a square.

> Assume $x + 1$, $4x$,

> since $4x(x + 1) - 4x = $ square.

Therefore also $\quad \left.\begin{array}{l} 4x^2 + 3x - 1 \\ 4x^2 - x - \ 1 \end{array}\right\}$ are both squares,

the difference $= 4x = 4x \cdot 1$.

Therefore $\qquad\qquad x = 1\frac{1}{4}$,

and $(2\frac{1}{4},\ 5)$ is a solution.

22.   *To find four numbers such that, if we take the square of the*
sum ± any one singly, all the resulting numbers are squares.

  Since in a rational right-angled triangle square on hypotenuse
= squares on sides, square on hypotenuse ± twice product
of sides = square.

  Therefore we must find a square which will admit of division
into two squares in four ways.

  Take the right-angled triangles $(3, 4, 5)$, $(5, 12, 13)$.   Multiply
the sides of the first by the hypotenuse of the second and
vice versâ.

  Therefore we have the triangles $(39, 52, 65)$, $(25, 60, 65)$.
Thus 65^2 is split up into two squares in *two* ways.

Also $\qquad\qquad 65 = 7^2 + 4^2 = 8^2 + 1^2$.

Therefore $65^2 = (7^2 - 4^2)^2 + 4 \cdot 7^2 \cdot 4^2 = (8^2 - 1^2)^2 + 4 \cdot 8^2 \cdot 1^2$.
$$= 33^2 + 56^2 = 63^2 + 16^2,$$

  which gives *two more* ways.

Thus 65^2 is split into two squares in four ways.

Assume now as the sum of the numbers $65x$,

first number $= 2 \cdot 39 \cdot 52x^2 = 4056x^2$
second ,, $= 2\ \ 25 \cdot 60x^2 = 3000x^2$
third   ,, $= 2 \cdot 33 \cdot 56x^2 = 3696x^2$
fourth ,, $= 2 \cdot 16 \cdot 63x^2 = 2016x^2$
$\left.\vphantom{\begin{array}{l}1\\1\\1\\1\end{array}}\right\}$ and the sum $= 12768x^2$.

Therefore $12768x^2 = 65x$ and $x = \dfrac{65}{12768}$,

and the numbers are found, viz.

$$\frac{17136600}{163021824},\quad \frac{12675000}{163021824},\quad \frac{15615600}{163021824},\quad \frac{8517600}{163021824}.$$

23.   To divide a given number into two parts, and to find a
square which exceeds either of the parts by a square.

  Let the given number be 10, and the square $x^2 + 2x + 1$.

  Put one of the parts $2x + 1$, the other $4x$.   Therefore the
conditions are satisfied if $6x + 1 = 10$.

Therefore $$x = \frac{3}{2},$$

and the parts are **6, 4**, the square $6\frac{1}{4}$.

24. To divide a given number into two parts, and to find a square which added to either of the parts produces a square.

Given number 20. Let the square be $x^2 + 2x + 1$.

This is a square if we add $2x + 3$ or $4x + 8$.

Therefore, if these are the parts, the conditions are satisfied when $6x + 11 = 20$, or $x = 1\frac{1}{2}$.

Therefore the numbers into which 20 is divided are (**6, 14**) and the required square is $6\frac{1}{4}$.

BOOK IV.

1. To divide a given number into two cubes, such that the sum of their sides is a given number.

Given number 370, sum of sides 10.

Sides of cubes $5 + x$, $5 - x$. Therefore $30x^2 + 250 = 370$, $x = 2$, and the cubes are 7^3, 3^3.

2. To find two numbers whose difference is given, and also the difference of their cubes.

Difference 6. Difference of cubes 504. Let the numbers be $x + 3$, $x - 3$. Therefore $18x^2 + 54 = 504$.

Therefore $x^2 = 25$, $x = 5$, and the sides of the cubes are **8, 2**.

3. A number multiplied into a square and its side makes the latter product a cube of which the former product is the side; to find the square.

Let the square be x^2. Therefore its side is x, and let the number be $\frac{8}{x}$.

Hence the products are $8x$, 8, and $(8x)^3 = 8$.

Therefore $x^3 = \frac{1}{8^2}$, $x = \frac{1}{4}$.

4. To add the same number to a square and its side and make them the same, [i.e. make the first product a square of which the second product is side][1].

> Square x^2, whose side is x.   Let the number added to x^2 be such as to make a square, say $3x^2$.
>
> Therefore $3x^2 + x =$ side of $4x^2 = 2x$ and $x = \dfrac{1}{3}$.
>
> The square is $\dfrac{1}{9}$ and the number is $\dfrac{1}{3}$.

5. To add the same number to a square and its side and make them the opposite.

> Square x^2, the number $4x^2 - x$.
>
> Hence $5x^2 - x =$ side of $4x^2 = 2x$, and $x = \dfrac{3}{5}$.

6. To add the same square number to a square and a cube and make them the same.

> Let the cube be x^3 and the square any square number of x^2's, say $9x^2$.   Add to the square $16x^2$.   (The 16 is arrived at by taking two factors of 9, say 1 and 9, subtracting them, halving the remainder and squaring.)
>
> Therefore $x^3 + 16x^2 =$ cube $= 8x^3$ suppose and $x = \dfrac{16}{7}$.

Whence the numbers are known.

7. Add to a cube and a square the same square and make them the opposite.

> [Call the cube (1), first square (2), and the added square (3)].
> Now suppose (2) + (3) = (1) [since (2) + (3) = a *cube*].
> Now $a^2 + b^2 \pm 2ab$ is a square.   Suppose then $(1) = a^2 + b^2$, $(3) = 2ab$.   But (3) must be a square.
> Therefore $2ab$ must be a square; hence we put $a = 1, b = 2$.
> Thus suppose $(1) = 5x^2$, $(3) = 4x^2$, $(2) = x^2$.   Now (1) is a cube.
> Therefore $x = 5$,
> and $(1) = 125$, $(2) = 25$, $(3) = 100$.

---

[1] In this and the following enunciations I have kept closely to the Greek, partly for the purpose of showing Diophantos' mode of expression, and partly for the brevity gained thereby.

"To make them the same" means in the case of 4 what I have put in brackets; "to make them the opposite" means to make the first product a side of which the second product is the square.

8. [Another solution of the foregoing.]

Since $(2) + (3) = (1)$, a cube, and $(1) + (3) =$ square, I have to find two squares whose sum + one of them = a square, and whose sum $= (1)$. Let the first square be x^2, the second 4.

Therefore $2x^2 + 4 =$ a square $= (2x - 2)^2$ say. Therefore $x = 4$, and the squares are 16, 4.

Assume now $(2) = 4x^2$, $(3) = 16x^2$.

Therefore $20x^2 =$ a cube, and $x = 20$,

thus $(8000, 1600, 6400)$ is a solution.

9. *To add the same number to a cube and its side, and make them the same.*

Added number x, cube $8x^3$, say. Therefore second sum $= 3x$, and this must be the side of cube $8x^3 + x$, or $8x^3 + x = 27x^3$.

Therefore $19x^3 = x$.

But 19 *is not a square*. Hence we must find a square to replace it. Now the side $3x$ comes from the assumed $2x$. Hence we must find *two consecutive numbers whose cubes differ by a square*. Let them be y, $y + 1$.

Therefore $3y^2 + 3y + 1 =$ square $= (1 - 2y)^2$ say, and $y = 7$. Thus instead of 2 and 3 we must take 7 and 8.

Assuming now added number $= x$, side of cube $= 7x$, side of new cube $= 8x$, we find $343x^3 + x = 512x^3$.

Therefore $x^2 = \dfrac{1}{169}$, $x = \dfrac{1}{13}$.

Therefore $\left(\dfrac{343}{2197}, \dfrac{7}{13}, \dfrac{1}{13}\right)$ is a solution.

10. *To add the same number to a cube and its side and make them the opposite.*

Suppose the cube $8x^3$, its side $2x$, the number $27x^3 - 2x$.

Therefore $35x^3 - 2x =$ side of cube $27x^3$, therefore $35x^2 - 5 = 0$.

This gives no rational value. Now $35 = 27 + 8$, $5 = 3 + 2$.

Therefore we must find two numbers the sum of whose cubes bears to the sum of the numbers the ratio of a square to a square.

Let sum of sides = anything, 2 say, and side of first cube $= z$.

Therefore $8 - 12z + 6z^2 =$ twice a square.

Therefore $4 - 6z + 3z^2 =$ a square $= (2 - 4z)^2$ say, and $z =$ one of the sides $= \dfrac{10}{13}$, and the other side $= \dfrac{16}{13}$. Take for them 5 and 8.

Assuming now as the cube $125x^3$, and as the number $512x^3 - 5x$, we get $637x^3 - 5x = 8x$, and $x = \dfrac{1}{7}$,

and $\left(\dfrac{125}{343}, \dfrac{5}{7}, \dfrac{267}{343}\right)$ is a solution.

11. To find two cubes whose sum equals the sum of their sides.

Let the sides be $2x$, $3x$. This gives $35x^3 = 5x$. This equation gives no rational result. Finding as in the preceding problem an equation to replace it, $637x^3 = 13x$, $x = \dfrac{1}{7}$,

and the cubes are $\dfrac{125}{343}, \dfrac{512}{343}$.

12. To find two cubes whose difference equals the difference of their sides.

Assume as sides $2x$, $3x$. This gives $19x^3 = x$. Irrational; and we have to find two cubes such that $\dfrac{\text{their difference}}{\text{difference of sides}}$ = ratio of squares. Let them be $(z + 1)^3$, z^3.

Therefore $3z^2 + 3z + 1 = \text{square} = (1 - 2z)^2$ say.

Therefore $z = 7$.

Now assume as sides $7x$, $8x$. Therefore $169x^3 = x$, and $x = \dfrac{1}{13}$.

Therefore the two cubes are $\left(\dfrac{7}{13}\right)^3$, $\left(\dfrac{8}{13}\right)^3$.

13. To find two numbers such that the cube of the greater + the less = the cube of the less + the greater.

Assume $2x$, $3x$. Therefore $27x^3 + 2x = 8x^3 + 3x$.

Therefore $19x^3 = x$, which gives an irrational result. Hence, as in 12th problem, we must assume $7x$, $8x$,

and the numbers are as there $\dfrac{7}{13}, \dfrac{8}{13}$.

14. To find two numbers such that either, or their sum, or their difference increased by 1 gives a square.

Take unity from any square for the first number; let it be, say, $9x^2 + 6x$.

But the second $+1 = $ a square. Therefore we must find a square
such that the square found $+ 9x^2 + 6x = $ a square. Take
factors of $9x^2 + 6x$, viz. $(9x + 6, x)$. Square of half difference $= 16x^2 + 24x + 9$.

Therefore, if we put the second number $16x^2 + 24x + 8$, three
conditions are satisfied, and the remaining condition gives
difference $+ 1 = $ square.

Hence $7x^2 + 18x + 9 = $ square $= (3 - 3x)^2$ say.

Therefore $x = 18$,

and (**3024, 5624**) is a solution.

15. To find three square numbers such that their sum equals
the sum of their differences.

Sum of differences $= A - B + B - C + A - C = 2(A - C) = A + B + C$,
by the question.

Let least $(C) = 1$, greatest $= x^2 + 2x + 1$. Therefore sum of the
three squares $= 2x^2 + 4x = x^2 + 2x + 2 + $ the middle one.
Therefore the middle one $(B) = x^2 + 2x - 2$. This is a
square, $= (x - 4)^2$ say. Therefore $x = \dfrac{9}{5}$,

and the squares are $\left(\dfrac{196}{25}, \dfrac{121}{25}, 1\right)$ or (196, 121, 25).

16. *To find three numbers such that the sum of any two multiplied by the third is a given number.*

Let (first + second) . third $= 35$, (second + third) . first $= 27$, and
(third + first) . second $= 32$, and let the third $= x$.

Therefore first + second $= \dfrac{35}{x}$.

Assume first $= \dfrac{10}{x}$, second $= \dfrac{25}{x}$.

Therefore $\left.\begin{array}{l} \dfrac{250}{x^2} + 10 = 27 \\[2mm] \dfrac{250}{x^2} + 25 = 32 \end{array}\right\}$

These equations are inconsistent, but if $25 - 10$ *were equal to*
$32 - 27$ *or 5 they would be right.* Therefore we have to
divide 35 into two parts differing by 5, i.e. 15 and 20.

Thus first number $= \dfrac{15}{x}$, second $= \dfrac{20}{x}$. Therefore $\dfrac{300}{x^2} + 15 = 27$,

$x = 5$, and (**3, 4, 5**) is a solution.

17. *To find three numbers whose sum is a square, and such that the sum of the square of each and the succeeding number is a square.*

Let the middle number be $4x$. Therefore I must find what square $+ 4x$ gives a square. Take two numbers whose product is $4x$, say $2x$ and 2. Therefore $(x-1)^2$ is the square. Thus the first number $= x - 1$.

Again $16x^2 +$ third $=$ square.

Therefore third $=$ a square $- 16x^2 = (4x + 1)^2 - 16x^2$ say, $= 8x + 1$.

Now the three together $=$ square, therefore $13x =$ square $= 169y^2$ say. Therefore $x = 13y^2$. Hence the numbers are $13y^2 - 1$, $52y^2$, $104y^2 + 1$.

Lastly, (third)$^2 +$ first $=$ square.

Therefore $10816y^4 + 221y^2 =$ a square or $10816y^2 + 221 =$ a square $= (104y + 1)^2$ say. Therefore $y = \dfrac{220}{208} = \dfrac{55}{52}$,

and $\left(\dfrac{36621}{2704}, \dfrac{157300}{2704}, \dfrac{317304}{2704}\right)$ is a solution.

18. To find three numbers whose sum is a square, and such that the difference of the square of any one and the succeeding number is a square.

The solution is exactly similar to the last, the numbers being in this case $13y^2 + 1$, $52y^2$, $104y^2 - 1$. The resulting equation is $10816y^2 - 221 =$ square $= (104y - 1)^2$,

whence $y = \dfrac{111}{104}$,

and $\left(\dfrac{170989}{10816}, \dfrac{640692}{10816}, \dfrac{1270568}{10816}\right)$ is a solution.

19. *To find two numbers such that the cube of the first + the second = a cube, the square of the second + the first = a square.*

Let the first be x, the second $8 - x^3$, therefore $x^6 - 16x^3 + 64 + x =$ a square $= (x^3 + 8)^2$ say, whence $32x^3 = x$. This gives an irrational result since 32 is not a square. Now $32 = 4.8$. Therefore we must put in our assumptions $4 . 64$ instead. Then the second number is $64 - x^3$, and we get, as an equation for x,

$256x^3 = 1$. Therefore $x = \dfrac{1}{16}$,

and the numbers are $\dfrac{1}{16}$, $\dfrac{262143}{4096}$.

20. *To find three numbers indefinitely*[1] *such that the product of any two increased by* 1 *is a square.*

Let the product of first and second be $x^2 + 2x$, whence one condition is satisfied, if *second* $= x$, *first* $= x + 2$. Now the product of second and third $+ 1 = $ a square; let this product be $9x^2 + 6x$, so that *third number* $= 9x + 6$. Also the product of third and first $+ 1 = $ square, i.e. $9x^2 + 24x + 13 = $ a square. *Now, if* 13 *were a square, and the coefficient of* x *were* 6 *times the side of this square, the problem would be solved indefinitely as required.*

Now 13 comes from $6 . 2 + 1$, the 6 from $2 . 3$, and the 2 from $2 . 1$. Therefore we want a number to replace $3 . 1$ such that four times it $+ 1 = $ a square; therefore we need only take two numbers whose difference is 1, say 1 and 2 [and $4 . 2 . 1 + (2 - 1)^2 = $ square]. Then, beginning again, we put product of first and second $= x^2 + 2x$, second x, first $x + 2$, product of second and third $= 4x^2 + 4x$, and third $= 4x + 4$. [Then first × third $+ 1 = 4x^2 + 12x + 9$.]

And $(x + 2, x, 4x + 4)$ is a solution.

21. *To find four numbers such that the product of any two, increased by* 1, *becomes a square.*

Assume that the product of first and second $= x^2 + 2x$, first $= x$, second $= x + 2$, and similarly third $= 4x + 4$, fourth $= 9x + 6$, but $(4x + 4)(9x + 6) + 1 = $ square $= 36x^2 + 60x + 25$.

Also for second and fourth,

$9x^2 + 24x + 13 = $ square $= (9x^2 - 24x + 16)$, say.

Therefore $x = \dfrac{1}{16}$.

All the conditions are now satisfied[2],

the solution being $\left(\dfrac{1}{16}, \dfrac{33}{16}, \dfrac{68}{16}, \dfrac{105}{16}\right)$.

22. Find three numbers which are proportional and such that the difference of any two is a square.

Assume x to be the least, $x + 4$ the middle, $x + 13$ the greatest, therefore if 13 were a square we should have an indefinite solution satisfying three of the conditions. We must

---

[1] I.e. in general expressions.

[2] Product of second and third $+ 1 = (x + 2)(4x + 4) + 1 = 4x^2 + 12x + 9$, which is a square.

therefore replace 13 by a square which is the sum of two squares.

Thus if we assume x, $x+9$, $x+25$, three conditions are satisfied, and the fourth gives $x(x+25)=(x+9)^2$, therefore $x=\dfrac{81}{7}$,

and $\left(\dfrac{81}{7}, \dfrac{144}{7}, \dfrac{256}{7}\right)$ is a solution.

23.   *To find three numbers such that the sum of their solid content*[1] *and any one of them is a square.*

Let the product be x^2+2x, and the first number 1, the second $4x+9$; therefore the third $=\dfrac{x^2+2x}{4x+9}$. This cannot be divided out generally unless $x^2:4x=2x:9$ or $x^2:2x=4x:9$, and it could be done if 4 were half of 9.

Now $4x$ comes from $6x-2x$, and 9 from 3^2, therefore we have to find a number m to replace 3 such that $2m-2=\dfrac{m^2}{2}$, therefore $m^2=4m-4$ or $m=2$.[2]

We put therefore for the second number $2x+4$, and the third then becomes $\frac{1}{2}x$.   Therefore also [third condition]

$$x^2+2x+\tfrac{1}{2}x=\text{square}=4x^2 \text{ say, whence } x=\dfrac{5}{6},$$

and $\left(1, \dfrac{34}{6}, \dfrac{2\frac{1}{2}}{6}\right)$ is a solution.

24.   *To find three numbers such that the difference of their solid content and any one of them is a square.*

First x, solid content x^2+x; therefore the product of second and third $=x+1$; let the second $=1$.

Therefore the two remaining conditions give

$$\left.\begin{array}{r}x^2+x-1\\ x^2-1\end{array}\right\} \text{ both squares [Double equation.]}$$

Difference $=x=\frac{1}{2}.2x$, say; therefore $(x+\frac{1}{4})^2=x^2+x-1$, $x=\dfrac{17}{8}$,

and $\left(\dfrac{17}{8}, 1, \dfrac{25}{8}\right)$ is a solution.

---

[1] I.e. the continued product of all three.
[2] Observe the solution of a mixed quadratic.

25. Divide a given number into two parts whose product is a cube *minus* its side.

Given number 6. First part x; therefore second $= 6 - x$, and $6x - x^2 =$ a cube minus its side $= (2x-1)^3 - (2x-1)$ say, so that $8x^3 - 12x^2 + 4x = 6x - x^2$. This would reduce to a simple equation if the coefficient of x were the same on both sides. To make this so, since 6 is fixed, we must put m for 2 in our assumption, where

$$3m - m = 6, \text{ or } m = 3.$$

Therefore, altering the assumption,

$$(3x - 1)^3 - (3x - 1) = 6x - x^2,$$

whence $$x = \frac{26}{27},$$

and the parts are $\dfrac{26}{27}, \dfrac{136}{27}$.

26. *To divide a given number into three parts such that their continued product equals a cube whose side is the sum of their differences.*

Given number 4. Let the product be $8x^3$: now the sum of differences = twice difference between third and first; therefore difference between third and first parts $= x$. Let the first be a multiple of x, say $2x$. Therefore the third $= 3x$.

Hence the second $= \dfrac{4}{3} x$, and, if the second had lain between the first and third, the problem would have been solved.

Now the second came from dividing 8 by $2 . 3$, so that we have to find two consecutive numbers such that $\dfrac{8}{\text{their product}}$ lies between them. Assume m, $m + 1$; therefore $\dfrac{8}{m^2 + m}$ lies between m and $m + 1$.

Therefore $$\frac{8}{m^2 + m} + 1 > m + 1.$$

Therefore $m^2 + m + 8 > m^3 + 2m^2 + m$, or $8 > m^3 + m^2$.

Take $\left(m + \dfrac{1}{3}\right)^3$, which is $> m^3 + m$, and equate it to 8.

Therefore $$m + \frac{1}{3} = 2, \text{ and } m = \frac{5}{3}.$$

Hence we assume for the numbers

$$\frac{5}{3}x, \quad \frac{9}{5}x, \quad \frac{8}{3}x,$$

or $(25x, 27x, 40x)$, multiplying throughout by 15.

Therefore the sum $= 92x = 4$, and $x = \dfrac{1}{23}$,

and $\left(\dfrac{25}{23}, \dfrac{27}{23}, \dfrac{40}{23}\right)$ are the three parts required.

[N.B. The condition $\dfrac{8}{m^2 + m} < m + 1$ is ignored in the work,

and is *incidentally* satisfied.]

27. To find two numbers whose product added to either gives a cube.

Suppose the first number equals a cube number of x's, say $8x$.
Second $x^2 - 1$, (so that $8x^3 - 8x + 8x =$ cube);
also $8x^3 - 8x + x^2 - 1$ must be a cube $= (2x - 1)^3$ say.

Therefore $\qquad 13x^2 = 14x, \quad x = \dfrac{14}{13}$,

and $\left(\dfrac{112}{13}, \dfrac{27}{169}\right)$ is a solution.

28. To find two numbers such that the difference between the product and either is a cube.

Let the first be $8x$, the second $x^2 + 1$ (since $8x^3 + 8x - 8x =$ cube);
also $8x^3 + 8x - x^2 - 1$ must be a cube, which is "impossible" [for to get rid of the third power and the absolute term we can only put this equal to $(2x - 1)^3$, which gives an "irrational" result]. Assume then the first $= 8x + 1$, the second $= x^2$ (since $8x^3 + x^2 - x^2 =$ cube).

Therefore $8x^3 + x^2 - 8x - 1 =$ a cube $= (2x - 1)^3$ say.

Therefore $\qquad\qquad\qquad x = \dfrac{14}{13}$,

and the numbers are $\qquad \dfrac{125}{13}, \dfrac{196}{169}$.

29. *To find two numbers such that their product $\pm$ their sum $= a$ cube.*

Let the first cube be 64, the second 8. Therefore twice the sum of the numbers $= 64 - 8 = 56$, and the sum of the numbers $= 28$, but their product + their sum $= 64$. Therefore their product $= 36$.

Therefore we have to find two numbers whose sum $= 28$, and whose product $= 36$. Assuming $14 + x$, $14 - x$ for these numbers, $196 - x^2 = 36$ and $x^2 = 160$, and if 160 were a a square we could solve it rationally.

Now 160 arises from $14^2 - 36$, and $14 = \frac{1}{2} \cdot 28 = \frac{1}{4} \cdot 56$

$= \frac{1}{4}$ (difference of cubes) ; $36 = \frac{1}{2}$ sum of cubes.

Therefore we have to find two cubes such that

$$\left(\frac{1}{4} \text{ of their difference} \right)^2 - \frac{1}{2} \text{ their sum } = \text{a square.}$$

Let the sides of these cubes be $z + 1$, $z - 1$.

Therefore $\frac{1}{4}$ of their difference $= \frac{3}{2} z^2 + \frac{1}{2}$, and the square of this

$$= \frac{9}{4} z^4 + \frac{3}{2} z^2 + \frac{1}{4}.$$

Hence $\left(\frac{1}{4} \cdot \text{difference} \right)^2 - \frac{1}{2} \cdot \text{sum} = \frac{9}{4} z^4 + \frac{3}{2} z^2 + \frac{1}{4} - \frac{1}{2}(2z^3 + 6z).$

Therefore

$$9z^4 + 6z^2 + 1 - 4z^3 - 12z = \text{a square} = (3z^2 + 1 - 6z)^2 \text{ say,}$$

whence $\qquad 32z^3 = 36z^2$, and $z = \frac{9}{8}$.

Therefore sides of cubes are $\frac{17}{8}$, $\frac{1}{8}$, and the cubes $\frac{4913}{512}$, $\frac{1}{512}$.

Now put product of numbers + their sum $= \dfrac{4913}{512}$

$\qquad\qquad\qquad$ product $-$ sum $= \dfrac{1}{512}$,

therefore their sum $\quad = \dfrac{2456}{512}$,

their product $\qquad = \dfrac{2457}{512}$.

Then let the first number $= x +$ half sum $= x + \dfrac{1228}{512}$,

second $\qquad\qquad = \dfrac{1228}{512} - x.$

Therefore $\qquad \dfrac{1507984}{262144} - x^2 = \dfrac{2457}{512}$.

Therefore $\qquad 262144 x^2 = 250000.$

Hence $\qquad\qquad x = \dfrac{500}{512},$

and $\qquad\qquad \left(\dfrac{1728}{512}, \dfrac{728}{512}\right)$ is a solution.

30. To find two numbers such that their product ± their sum = a cube [same problem as the foregoing].

> *Every square divided into two parts, one of which is its side,*
> *makes the product of these parts + their sum a cube.*

[i.e. $x\,(x^2 - x) + x^2 - x + x =$ a cube.]

Let the square be x^2; the parts are x, $x^2 - x$,

and from the second part of the condition

$$x^3 - x^2 - x^2 = x^3 - 2x^2 = \text{a cube} = \left(\dfrac{x}{2}\right)^3 \text{ say.}$$

Therefore $\qquad \dfrac{7}{8}x^3 = 2x^2, \quad x = \dfrac{16}{7},$

and $\qquad\qquad \left(\dfrac{16}{7}, \dfrac{144}{49}\right)$ is a solution.

31. *To find four square numbers such that their sum + the sum of their sides = a given number.*

Given number 12.   Now $x^2 + x + \dfrac{1}{4} =$ a square.

Therefore the sum of four squares + the sum of their sides + 1 = 13.

Thus we have to divide 13 into 4 squares, and if from each of their sides we subtract $\dfrac{1}{2}$ we shall have the sides of the required squares.

Now $\qquad 13 = 4 + 9 = \dfrac{64}{25} + \dfrac{36}{25} + \dfrac{144}{25} + \dfrac{81}{25},$

and the sides of the required squares are

$$\dfrac{11}{10}, \ \dfrac{7}{10}, \ \dfrac{19}{10}, \ \dfrac{13}{10}.$$

32. To find four squares such that their sum *minus* the sum of their sides equals a given number.

Given number 4.   Then similarly $\left(\text{side of first} - \dfrac{1}{2}\right)^2 + \ldots = 5.$

and 5 is divided into $\dfrac{9}{25}, \dfrac{16}{25}, \dfrac{64}{25}, \dfrac{36}{25},$

and the sides of the squares are $\left(\dfrac{11}{10}, \dfrac{13}{10}, \dfrac{21}{10}, \dfrac{17}{10}\right).$

33. *To divide unity into two parts such that, if given numbers be added to each, the product of the resulting expressions may be a square.*

Let 3, 5 be the numbers to be added, and let the parts be $\left.\begin{array}{c} x \\ 1-x \end{array}\right\}$.

Therefore $(x+3)(6-x) = 18 + 3x - x^2 = $ a square $= 4x^2$ say.

Hence $18 + 3x = 5x^2$; but 5 comes from a square + 1, *and the roots cannot be rational unless*

(this square + 1) $18 + \left(\dfrac{3}{2}\right)^2 = $ a square.

Put $\qquad (m^2 + 1) 18 + \left(\dfrac{3}{2}\right)^2 = $ a square,

or $\qquad 72m^2 + 81 = $ a square $= (8m + 9)^2$ say.

Therefore $\qquad\qquad m = 18.$

Hence we must put

$$(x+3)(6-x) = 18 + 3x - x^2 = 324x^2.$$

Therefore $\qquad 325x^2 - 3x - 18 = 0.$

Therefore $\qquad x = \dfrac{78}{325} = \dfrac{6}{25},$

and $\qquad \left(\dfrac{6}{25}, \dfrac{19}{25}\right)$ is a solution.

34. [*Another solution of the foregoing.*]

Suppose the first $x - 3$, the second $4 - x$; therefore

$$x(9 - x) = \text{square} = 4x^2 \text{ say,}$$

and $5x^2 = 9x$, whence $x = \dfrac{9}{5}$, *but I cannot take 3 from* $\dfrac{9}{5}$, and x must be $> 3 < 4$.

Now the value of x comes from $\dfrac{9}{\text{a square} + 1}$. Therefore, since $x > 3$, this square $+ 1 < 3$, therefore the square < 2. It is also $> \dfrac{5}{4}$.

Therefore I must find a square between $\dfrac{5}{4}$ and 2, or $\dfrac{80}{64}$ and $\dfrac{128}{64}$.

And $\dfrac{100}{64}$ or $\dfrac{25}{16}$ will satisfy the conditions.

Put now $\qquad\qquad x(9 - x) = \dfrac{25}{16}x^2.$

Therefore $\qquad\qquad x = \dfrac{144}{41}$,

and $\qquad\qquad \left(\dfrac{21}{41},\ \dfrac{20}{41}\right)$ is a solution.

35. *To divide a given number into three parts such that the product of the first and second, with the third added or subtracted, may be a square.*

> Given number 6, the third part x, the second any number less than 6, say 2.   Therefore the first $= 4 - x$.
>
> Hence $8 - 2x \pm x = $ a square. [*Double-equation.*] *And it cannot be solved by our method* since the ratio of the coefficients of x is not a ratio of squares.   Therefore we must find a number y to replace 2, such that
>
> $$\frac{y+1}{y-1} = \text{a square} = 4 \text{ say.}$$
>
> Therefore $\qquad y + 1 = 4y - 4$, and $y = \dfrac{5}{3}$.
>
> Put now the second part $= \dfrac{5}{3}$, therefore the first $= \dfrac{13}{3} - x.$
>
> Therefore $\qquad \dfrac{65}{9} - \dfrac{5}{3}\,x \pm x = $ a square.
>
> Thus $\qquad \left.\begin{array}{l} 65 - \ 6x \\ 65 - 24x \end{array}\right\}$ are both squares,
>
> or $\left.\begin{array}{l} \ 65 - 24x \\ 260 - 24x \end{array}\right\}$ are both squares : difference $= 195 = 15.\ 13.$
>
> Hence $\qquad \left(\dfrac{15-13}{2}\right)^2 = 65 - 24x$, and $24x = 64$, $x = \dfrac{8}{3}$.
>
> Therefore the parts are $\qquad \left(\dfrac{5}{3},\ \dfrac{5}{3},\ \dfrac{8}{3}\right).$

36. *To find two numbers such that the first with a certain fraction of the second is to the remainder of the second, and the second with the same fraction of the first is to the remainder of the first, each in given ratios.*

> Let the first with the fraction of the second $= 3$ times the remainder of the second, and the second with the same fraction of the first $= 5$ times the remainder of the first.
>
> Let the second $= x + 1$, and let the part of it received by the first be 1.   Therefore the first $= 3x - 1$ [for $3x - 1 + 1 = 3x$].

Also first + second = $4x$, and first + second = sum of the numbers

after interchange, therefore $\dfrac{\text{first} + \text{second}}{\text{remainder of first}} = 6.$

Therefore *the remainder of the first* $= \dfrac{2}{3}x$, *and hence the second*

receives from the first $3x - 1 - \dfrac{2}{3}x = \dfrac{7}{3}x - 1.$

Hence $\dfrac{\frac{7}{3}x - 1}{3x - 1} = \dfrac{1}{x + 1}$, therefore $\dfrac{7}{3}x^2 + \dfrac{4}{3}x - 1 = 3x - 1,$

and $x = \dfrac{5}{7}.$

Therefore the first number $= \dfrac{8}{7}$, and the second $= \dfrac{12}{7}$; and 1 is

$\dfrac{7}{12}$ of the second.

Multiply by 7 and the numbers are 8, 12; and the fraction is

$\dfrac{7}{12}$; but 8 is not divisible by 12, so multiply by 3,

and (**24, 36**) is a solution.

37.　To find two numbers indefinitely such their product + their sum = a given number.

Given number 8.　Assume the first to be x, the second 3.

Therefore $3x + x + 3 = $ given number $= 8.$

Therefore $x = \dfrac{5}{4}$, and the numbers are $\left(\dfrac{5}{4},\, 3\right).$

Now $\dfrac{5}{4}$ arises from $\dfrac{8 - 3}{3 + 1}.$　Therefore we may put $mx + n$ for

the second number, and the first $= \dfrac{8 - (mx + n)}{mx + n + 1}.$

38.　To find three numbers such that (the product + the sum) of any two equals a given number.

Condition.　Each number must be 1 less than some square.

Let product + sum of first and second = 8, of second and third = 15, of third and first = 24.

Then $\dfrac{8 - \text{second}}{\text{second} + 1} = $ the first: let the second $= x - 1.$

Therefore $\dfrac{9 - x}{x} = $ first $= \dfrac{9}{x} - 1.$　Similarly third $= \dfrac{16}{x} - 1.$

Therefore $\left(\dfrac{9}{x}-1\right)\left(\dfrac{16}{x}-1\right)+\dfrac{25}{x}-2=24$, and $\dfrac{144}{x^2}-1=24$,

therefore $x=\dfrac{12}{5}$,

and $\left(\dfrac{33}{12},\dfrac{7}{5},\dfrac{68}{12}\right)$ is a solution.

39.   To find two numbers indefinitely such that their product exceeds their sum by a given number.

Let the first number be x, the second 3. Therefore product

$-\text{sum}=3x-x-3=2x-3=8$ (say).   Therefore $x=\dfrac{11}{2}$.

Thus the first $=\dfrac{11}{2}$, the second $=3$.   But $\dfrac{11}{2}=\dfrac{8+3}{3-1}$.

Hence, putting the second $=x+1$, the first $=\dfrac{x+9}{x}$.

40.   To find three numbers such that the product of any two exceeds their sum by a given number.

Condition.   Each of the given numbers must be 1 less than some square.

Let them be 8, 15, 24.

Therefore first number $=\dfrac{8+\text{second}}{\text{second}-1}=\dfrac{x+9}{x}$, say.   Therefore

the first $=\dfrac{9}{x}+1$, the second $=x+1$, and the third $=\dfrac{16}{x}+1$.

Therefore $\left(\dfrac{9}{x}+1\right)\left(\dfrac{16}{x}+1\right)-\dfrac{25}{x}-2=24$.

Or $\dfrac{144}{x^2}-1=24$, $x=\dfrac{12}{5}$,

and $\left(\dfrac{57}{12},\dfrac{17}{5},\dfrac{92}{12}\right)$ is a solution.

41.   To find two numbers indefinitely whose product has to their sum a given ratio.

Let the ratio be $3:1$, the first number x, the second 5.

Therefore $5x=3(5+x)$, and $x=\dfrac{15}{2}$.

But $\dfrac{15}{2}=\dfrac{5\cdot3}{5-3}$, and, putting x for 5,

·the indefinite solution is: first $=\dfrac{3x}{x-3}$, second $=x$.

42.   To find three numbers such that for any two their product bears to their sum a given ratio.

Let $\dfrac{\text{first and second multiplied}}{\text{first} + \text{second}} = 3$, and let the other ratios be

4 and 5, the second number x.   Therefore first $= \dfrac{3x}{x-3}$, third

$= \dfrac{4x}{x-4}$.

Also $\dfrac{3x}{x-3} \cdot \dfrac{4x}{x-4} = 5 \left(\dfrac{3x}{x-3} + \dfrac{4x}{x-4} \right)$ or $12x^2 = 35x^2 - 120x$.

Therefore $x = \dfrac{120}{23}$,

and $\left(\dfrac{360}{51}, \dfrac{120}{23}, \dfrac{480}{28} \right)$ is the solution.

43.   *To find three numbers such that the product of any two has to the sum of the three a given ratio.*

Let the ratios be 3, 4, 5.   First seek three numbers such that the product of any two has to an arbitrary number (say 5) the given ratio.   Of these, let the product of the first and the second $= 15$.

Therefore if $x =$ the second, the first $= \dfrac{15}{x}$.

But the second multiplied by the third $= 20$.

Therefore the third $= \dfrac{20}{x}$, and $\dfrac{20 \cdot 15}{x^2} = 25$.

Therefore $\quad\quad\quad 25x^2 = 20 \cdot 15$.

And, if $20 \cdot 15$ were a square, what is required would be done.

Now $15 = 3 \cdot 5$ and $20 = 4 \cdot 5$, and 15 is made up of the ratio $3 : 1$ and the *arbitrary* number 5.

Therefore we must find a number m such that $\dfrac{12m^2}{5m} =$ ratio of a square to a square.

Thus $12m^2 \cdot 5m = 60m^3 =$ square $= 900m^2$, say.   Therefore $m = 15$.

Let then the sum of the three $= 15$,

and the product of the first and second $= 45$, therefore the first $= \dfrac{45}{x}$.

Similarly the third $= \dfrac{60}{x}$; therefore $\dfrac{45 \cdot 60}{x^2} = 75$ and $x = 6$.

Therefore the first number $= \dfrac{45}{6}$, the third $= 10$,

and the sum of the three $= 23\frac{1}{2} = \dfrac{47}{2}$. *Now, if this were* 15, *the problem would be solved.*

Put therefore $15x^2$ for the sum of the three, and for the numbers $7\frac{1}{2}x$, $6x$, $10x$.

Therefore $23\frac{1}{2}x = 15x^2$, and $x = \dfrac{47}{30}$,

whence $\left(\dfrac{705}{60}, \dfrac{282}{30}, \dfrac{470}{30} \right)$ is a solution.

44. *To find three numbers such that the product of their sum and the first is a triangular number, that of their sum and the second a square, and that of their sum and the third a cube.*

Let the sum be x^2, and the first $\dfrac{6}{x^2}$, the second $\dfrac{4}{x^2}$, the third $\dfrac{8}{x^2}$, which will satisfy the three conditions.

But the sum $= \dfrac{18}{x^2} = x^2$ or $18 = x^4$.

Therefore *we must replace* 18 *by a fourth power.*

But $18 = $ sum of a triangular number, a square and a cube; let the fourth power be x^4, which must be made up in the same way, and let the square be $x^4 - 2x^2 + 1$. Therefore the triangular number + the cube $= 2x^2 - 1$; let the cube be 8, therefore the triangular number $= 2x^2 - 9$. *But* 8 *times a triangular number* $+ 1 = a$ *square.*

Therefore $16x^2 - 71 = $ a square $= (4x - 1)^2$ say; therefore $x = 9$, and the triangular number $= 153$, the square $= 6400$ and the cube $= 8$.

Assume then as the first number $\dfrac{153}{x^2}$, as the second $\dfrac{6400}{x^2}$, as the third $\dfrac{8}{x^2}$.

Therefore $\dfrac{6561}{x^2} = x^2$ and $x = 9$.

Thus $\left(\dfrac{153}{81}, \dfrac{6400}{81}, \dfrac{8}{81} \right)$ is a solution.

45. *To find three numbers such that the difference of the greatest and the middle has to the difference of the middle and the least a given ratio, and also the sum of any pair is a square.*

Ratio 3. Since middle number + least = a square, let them = 4.

Therefore middle > 2 ; let it be $x + 2$, so that least = $2 - x$.

Therefore the interval of the greatest and the middle = $6x$, whence the greatest = $7x + 2$.

Therefore $\left.\begin{matrix} 8x + 4 \\ 6x + 4 \end{matrix}\right\}$ are both squares [*Double equation*] : take two numbers whose product = $2x$, say $\dfrac{x}{2}$ and 4, and proceed by the rule. Therefore $x = 112$, *but I cannot take* 112 *from* 2 ; therefore x must be found to be < 2, so that $6x + 4 < 16$.

Thus there are to be three squares $8x + 4$, $6x + 4$, 4; and difference of greatest and middle = $\frac{1}{3}$ of difference between middle and least.

Therefore we must find three squares having this property, such that the least = 4 and the middle one < 16.

Let side of middle one be $z + 2$, whence the greatest is equal to

$$\frac{z^2 + 4z}{3} + z^2 + 4z + 4 = \frac{4}{3}z^2 + \frac{16}{3}z^2 + 4.$$

Therefore this is a square, or $3z^2 + 12z + 9 = $ a square; but the middle of the required squares < 16, therefore $z < 2$.

Put now $3z^2 + 12z + 9 = (mz - 3)^2 = m^2z^2 - 6mz + 9$.

Therefore $z = \dfrac{6m + 12}{m^2 - 3}$, which must be < 2.

Hence $6m + 12 < 2m^2 - 6$, or $2m^2 > 6m + 18$,

and $18 . 2 + 3^2 = 45$; therefore we may put $m = \dfrac{3}{2} + \dfrac{7}{2}$.

Thus we have $3z^2 + 12z + 9 = (3 - 5z)^2$.

Hence $z = \dfrac{21}{11}$, and the side of the middle square = $\dfrac{43}{11}$, and the square itself = $\dfrac{1849}{121}$.

Turning to the original problem, we put $\dfrac{1849}{121} = 6x + 4$.

Therefore $x = \dfrac{1365}{726}$, which *is* < 2.

Hence the greatest of the required numbers

$$= 7x + 2 = \frac{11007}{726},$$

and the second of them $= x + 2 = \dfrac{2817}{726}$,

and the third $= 2 - x = \dfrac{87}{726}$.

46.   *To find three numbers such that the difference of the squares of the greatest and the middle numbers has to the difference of the middle and the least a given ratio, and the sums of all pairs are severally squares.*

Ratio 3.   Let greatest + middle = the square $16x^2$. Therefore greatest is $> 8x^2$, say $8x^2 + 2$. Hence middle $= 8x^2 - 2$, and greatest + middle $>$ greatest + least, therefore greatest + least $< 16x^2 > 8x^2 = 9x^2$, say ; therefore the least number $= x^2 - 2$.

Now difference of squares of greatest and middle $= 64x^2$, and difference of middle and least $= 7x^2$, but $64 \neq 21$.

Now 64 comes from $32 \cdot 2$, so that I must find a number m such that $32m = 21$.   Therefore $m = \dfrac{21}{32}$.

Assume now that the greatest of the numbers sought $= 8x^2 + \dfrac{21}{32}$, the middle $= 8x^2 - \dfrac{21}{32}$, the least $= x^2 - \dfrac{21}{32}$.

[Therefore difference of squares of greatest and middle $= 21x^2 = 3 \cdot 7x^2$.]

The only condition left is

$$8x^2 - \frac{21}{32} + x^2 - \frac{21}{32} = \text{a square,}$$

or $9x^2 - \dfrac{21}{16} = \text{a square} = (3x - 6)^2$ say.

Therefore $x = \dfrac{597}{576}$.

Hence $\left(\dfrac{3069000}{331776}, \ \dfrac{2633544}{331776}, \ \dfrac{138681}{331776} \right)$ is a solution.

BOOK V.

1. To find three numbers in G. P. such that each exceeds a given number by a square.

Given number 12. Find a *square* which exceeds 12 by a square [by II. 11], say $42\frac{1}{4}$. Let the first number be $42\frac{1}{4}$, the third x^2, so that the middle one $= 6\frac{1}{2}x$.

Therefore $\left.\begin{array}{c} x^2 - 12 \\ 6\frac{1}{2}x - 12 \end{array}\right\}$ are both squares : their difference

$$= x^2 - 6\frac{1}{2}\,x = x\left(x - 6\frac{1}{2}\right),$$

therefore as usual we find the value of x, viz. $\dfrac{361}{104}$,

and $\qquad \left(42\frac{1}{4},\ \dfrac{2346\frac{1}{2}}{104},\ \dfrac{130321}{10816}\right)$ is a solution.

2. *To find three numbers in G. P. such that each together with the same given number equals a square.*

Given number 20. Take a square which exceeds 20 by a square, say 36, so that $16 + 20 = 36 =$ a square.

Put then one of the extremes 16, the other x^2, so that the middle term $= 4x$.

Therefore $\left.\begin{array}{c} x^2 + 20 \\ 4x + 20 \end{array}\right\}$ are both squares : their difference

$$= x^2 - 4x = x\left(x - 4\right),$$

whence we have $4x + 20 = 4$, *which gives an irrational result,*

but the $4 = \frac{1}{4}(16)$, and we should have in place of 4 some number > 20. Therefore to replace 16 we must find some square $> 4 \cdot 20$, and such that with the addition of 20 it becomes a square.

Now $81 > 80$; therefore, putting for the required square $(m + 9)^2$, $(m + 9)^2 + 20 =$ square $= (m - 11)^2$ say. Therefore $m = \frac{1}{2}$, and the square $= \left(9\frac{1}{2}\right)^2 = 90\frac{1}{4}$.

H. D.   14

Assuming now for the numbers $90\frac{1}{4}$, $9\frac{1}{2}x$, x^2, we **have**,

$$\left.\begin{array}{l} x^2 + 20 \\ 9\frac{1}{2}x + 20 \end{array}\right\} \text{ are both squares: and the difference } = x(x-9\frac{1}{2}),$$

whence we derive $\quad x = \dfrac{41}{152}$,

and $\quad \left(90\frac{1}{4},\ \dfrac{389\frac{1}{2}}{152},\ \dfrac{1681}{23104}\right)$ is a solution.

3. *Given one number, to find three others such that any one of them or the product of any two, when added to the given number, produces a square.*

Given number 5. *Porism.* If of two numbers each and their product together with the same number make squares, the two numbers arise from two consecutive squares.

Assume then $(x+3)^2$, $(x+4)^2$, and put for the first number $x^2 + 6x + 4$, and for the second $x^2 + 8x + 11$, and let the third equal twice their sum *minus* 1, or $4x^2 + 28x + 29$.

Therefore $\quad 4x^2 + 28x + 34 = $ a square $= (2x - 6)^2$ say.

Hence $\qquad\qquad x = \dfrac{1}{26}$,

and $\quad \left(\dfrac{2861}{676},\ \dfrac{7645}{676},\ \dfrac{20336}{676}\right)$ is a solution.

4. Given one number, to find three others such that each, and the product of any two exceed the given number by some square.

Given number 6. Take two consecutive squares x^2, $x^2 + 2x + 1$, add 6 to each, and let the first number $= x^2 + 6$, the second number $= x^2 + 2x + 7$, the third being equal to **twice** the sum of first and second *minus* 1, or $4x^2 + 4x + 25$.

Therefore third *minus* $6 = 4x^2 + 4x + 19 = $ square $= (2x - 6)^2$ say.

Therefore $\qquad\qquad x = \dfrac{17}{28}$,

and $\quad \left(\dfrac{4993}{784},\ \dfrac{6729}{784},\ \dfrac{22660}{784}\right)$ is a solution.

[Observe in this problem the assumption of the *Porism* numbered (1) above (pp. 122, 123).]

5. *To find three squares such that the product of any two, added to the sum of those two, or to the remaining one, gives a square.*

Porism. If any two consecutive squares be taken, and a **third** number which exceeds twice their sum by 2, these three numbers have the property of the numbers required by the problem.

Assume as the first $x^2 + 2x + 1$, and as the second $x^2 + 4x + 4$.

Therefore the third $= 4x^2 + 12x + 12$.

Hence $x^2 + 3x + 3 =$ a square $= (x - 3)^2$ say, and $x = \dfrac{2}{3}$.

Therefore $\left(\dfrac{25}{9}, \dfrac{64}{9}, \dfrac{196}{9}\right)$ is a solution.

6. To find three numbers such that each exceeds 2 by a square, and the product of any two *minus* both, or *minus* the remaining one = a square.

Add 2 to numbers found as in 5th problem. Let the first be $x^2 + 2$, the second $x^2 + 2x + 3$, the third $4x^2 + 4x + 6$, and all the conditions are satisfied, except

$$4x^2 + 4x + 6 - 2 = \text{a square} = 4\,(x - 2)^2 \text{ say.}$$

Therefore $x = \dfrac{3}{5}$,

and $\left(\dfrac{59}{25}, \dfrac{114}{25}, \dfrac{246}{25}\right)$ is a solution.

7. To find two numbers such that the sum of their product and the squares of both is a square. [*Lemma to the following problem.*]

First number x, second any number (m), say 1.

Hence $x^2 + x + 1 =$ a square $= (x - 2)^2$ say, and $x = \dfrac{3}{5}$.

Therefore $\left(\dfrac{3}{5}, 1\right)$ is a solution, or $(3, 5)$.

8. *To find three right-angled triangles* [1] *whose areas are equal.*

First find two numbers such that their product + sum of their squares = a square. i.e. 3, 5, as in the preceding problem
$$[15 + 3^2 + 5^2 = 7^2].$$

Now form three right-angled triangles from
$$(7, \ 3), \ (7, \ 5), \ (7, \ 3 + 5),$$
respectively, i.e. the triangles
$$(7^2 + 3^2, \ 7^2 - 3^2, \ 2 \cdot 7 \cdot 3), \ \&\text{c.}$$

---

[1] I.e. rational right-angled triangles. *As all the triangles which Diophantos treats of are of this kind, I shall sometimes use simply the word "triangle" to represent "rational right-angled triangle," for the purposes of brevity*, where the latter expression is of very frequent occurrence.

and we have the triangles

(40, 42, 58), (24, 70, 74), (15, 112, 113)

and the area of each = 840.

$$[(7^2 - 3^2)\, 7 \cdot 3 = (7^2 - 5^2)\, 7 \cdot 5 = (8^2 - 7^2)\, 8 \cdot 7].$$

[¹ For if $\qquad ab + a^2 + b^2 = c^2,$

$(c^2 - a^2)\, ca = (c^2 - b^2)\, cb = \{(a+b)^2 - c^2\}\, (a+b)\, c,$

since each $\qquad\qquad = abc\, (a+b)].$

9. To find three numbers such that the square of any one ± the sum of the three = a square.

Since, in a right-angled triangle, (hypotenuse)² ± twice product of sides = a square, we make the three numbers hypotenuses, and the sum of the three four times the area.

Therefore I must find three triangles having the same area, i.e. as in the preceding problem,

(40, 42, 58), (24, 70, 74), (15, 112, 113).

Therefore, putting for the numbers $58x$, $74x$, $113x$, their sum $= 245x =$ four times the area of any one of the triangles $= 3360x^2$, and $x = \dfrac{7}{96}$.

Therefore $\qquad \left(\dfrac{406}{96},\ \dfrac{518}{96},\ \dfrac{791}{96}\right)$ is a solution.

10. Given three squares, it is possible to find three numbers such that the products of the three pairs are respectively equal to those squares.

Squares 4, 9, 16. One number x, the second $\dfrac{4}{x}$, the third $\dfrac{9}{x}$,

and $\qquad \dfrac{36}{x^2} = 16$, and $x = 1\frac{1}{2}$.

---

¹ Nesselmann suggests that Diophantos discovered this as follows. Let the triangles formed from $(n\ m)$, $(q\ m)$, $(r\ m)$ have their areas equal,

therefore $n\,(m^2 - n^2) = q\,(m^2 - q^2) = r\,(r^2 - m^2)$, therefore $m^2 n - n^3 = m^2 q - q^3$,

$$m^2 = \frac{n^3 - q^3}{n - q} = n^2 + nq + q^2.$$

Again, given $(q\ m\ n)$, to find r;

$\qquad q\,(m^2 - q^2) = r\,(r^2 - m^2)$, and $m^2 - q^2 = n^2 + nq$

from above, therefore $\quad q\,(n^2 + nq) = r\,(r^2 - n^2 - nq - q^2),$

or $\qquad\qquad q\,(n^2 + nr) + q^2\,(n + r) = r\,(r^2 - n^2).$

Dividing by $r + n$, $\qquad qn + q^2 = r^2 - rn,$

therefore $\qquad\qquad (q + r)n = r^2 - q^2,$

and $\qquad\qquad\qquad r = q + n.$

Therefore the numbers are $\left(1\frac{1}{2},\ \frac{8}{3},\ 6\right)$.

We observe that $x=\frac{6}{4}$, where $6=$ product of 2, 3, and $4=$ side of 16.

Hence *rule.* Take the product of the sides, 2, 3, divide by the side of the third square, and divide 4, 9 again by the result.

11. To find three numbers such that the product of any two $\pm$ the sum of the three $=$ a square.

As in 9th problem, find three right-angled triangles having equal areas: the squares of the hypotenuses are 3364, 5476, 12769. Now find as in 10th problem three numbers, the products of pairs of which equal these squares, which we take because each $\pm$ (4. area) or $3360=$ a square; the three numbers then are

$$\frac{4292}{113}\,x,\ \frac{3277}{37}\,x,\ \frac{4181}{29}\,x.$$

It only remains that the sum $=3360x^2$.

Therefore $\qquad \dfrac{32824806}{121249}\,x=3360x^2.$

Therefore $\qquad x=\dfrac{32824806}{407396640};$

whence the numbers are known.

12. *To divide unity into two parts such that if the same given number be added to either part the result will be a square.*

Condition. The added number must not be odd......[the text of this condition is discussed on p. 129 and note.]

Given number 6. Therefore 13 must be divided into two two squares so that each >6. Thus if I divide 13 into squares whose difference <1, this condition is satisfied.

Take $\dfrac{13}{2}=6\frac{1}{2}$, and I wish to add to $6\frac{1}{2}$ a small fraction which will make it a square,

or, multiplying by 4, I wish to make $\dfrac{1}{x^2}+26$ a square, or

$$26x^2+1=\text{a square}=(5x+1)^2\text{ say,}$$
whence $\qquad\qquad\qquad x=10.$

Therefore to make 26 into a square I must add $\dfrac{1}{100}$,

or to make $6\frac{1}{2}$ into a square I must add $\dfrac{1}{400}$,

and $\dfrac{1}{400} + \dfrac{13}{2} = \left(\dfrac{51}{20}\right)^2$.

Therefore I must divide 13 *into two squares such that their sides may be as nearly as possible equal to* $\dfrac{51}{20}$. [παρισότητος ἀγωγή, above described, pp. 117—120.]

Now $13 = 2^2 + 3^2$. Therefore I seek two numbers such that 3 *minus* the first $= \dfrac{51}{20}$, or the first $= \dfrac{9}{20}$, and 2 *plus* the second $= \dfrac{51}{20}$, so that the second $= \dfrac{11}{20}$.

I write accordingly $(11x + 2)^2$, $(3 - 9x)^2$ for the required squares $\left[\text{substituting } x \text{ for } \dfrac{1}{20}\right]$.

Therefore the sum $= 202x^2 - 10x + 13 = 13$.

Hence $x = \dfrac{5}{101}$, and the sides are $\dfrac{257}{101}$, $\dfrac{258}{101}$,

and, subtracting 6 from the squares of each, we find as the parts of unity

$$\left(\dfrac{4843}{10201}, \dfrac{5358}{10201}\right).$$

13.   *To divide unity into two parts such that, if we add given numbers to each, the results are both squares.*

Let the numbers be 2, 6, and let them be represented in the figure. Suppose $DA = 2$, $AB = 1$, $BE = 6$, G a point in AB so chosen that DG, GE may both be squares. Now $DE = 9$.

Therefore I have to divide 9 *into two squares such that one of them lies between* 2 *and* 3.

Let the latter square be x^2. Therefore the second square $= 9 - x^2$, where $x^2 > 2 < 3$.

Take two squares, one > 2, the other < 3, [the former square being the smaller], say $\dfrac{289}{144}$, $\dfrac{361}{144}$. Therefore, if we can make x^2 lie between these, what was required is done.

We must have $\qquad x > \dfrac{17}{12} < \dfrac{19}{12}$.

Hence, in making $9 - x^2$ a square, we must find
$$x > \dfrac{17}{12} < \dfrac{19}{12} .$$

Put $9 - x^2 = (3 - mx)^2$. Therefore $x = \dfrac{6m}{m^2 + 1}$, which must be
$$> \dfrac{17}{12} < \dfrac{19}{12} .$$

Thus $72m > 17m^2 + 17$, and $36^2 - 17.\ 17 = 1007$ which[1] is $\not> 31^2$, hence m is $\not> \dfrac{67}{17}$. Similarly m is $\not< \dfrac{66}{19}$.

Let $m = 3\frac{1}{2}$. Therefore $9 - x^2 = \left(3 - \dfrac{7}{2} x\right)^2$,

and $\qquad\qquad\qquad x = \dfrac{84}{53}$.

Hence $x^2 = \dfrac{7056}{2809}$, and the segments of 1 are $\left(\dfrac{1438}{2809},\ \dfrac{1371}{2809}\right)$.

14. *To divide unity into three parts such that, if we add the same number to the three parts severally, the results are all squares.*

Condition. Given number must not be 2......[Condition remarked upon above, pp. 130, 131.]

Given number 3. Thus 10 is to be divided into three squares such that each > 3.

Take $\dfrac{1}{3}$ of 10, or $3\frac{1}{3}$, and find x so that $\dfrac{1}{9x^2} + 3\frac{1}{3}$ may be a square, or $30x^2 + 1 = $ a square $= (5x + 1)^2$ say.

Therefore $\qquad\qquad\qquad x = 2$,

and $\qquad\qquad \dfrac{1}{36} + 3\frac{1}{3} = \dfrac{121}{36} = $ a square.

Therefore we have to divide 10 into three squares each near to $\dfrac{121}{36}$, [παρισότητος ἀγωγή].

---

[1] I.e. the integral part of the root is $\not> 31$. The limits taken are *a fortiori* limits as explained on p. 93, n. 3 and 4. Strictly speaking, we could only say, taking integral limits, that $\sqrt{1007} < 32$, but this limit is not narrow enough to secure a correct result in the work which follows.

Now $10 = 3^2 + 1^2 =$ the sum of the three squares $9, \dfrac{9}{25}, \dfrac{16}{25}$.

Comparing the sides $3, \dfrac{3}{5}, \dfrac{4}{5}$ with $\dfrac{11}{6}$, or (multiplying by 30)

$90, 18, 24$ with 55, we must make each side approach 55.

Put therefore for the sides

$$3 - 35x, \ 31x + \dfrac{4}{5}, \ 37x + \dfrac{3}{5}$$

$[35 = 90 - 55, \ 31 = 55 - 24, \ 37 = 55 - 18]$,

we have the sum of the squares

$$= 3555x^2 - 116x + 10 = 10.$$

Therefore $\qquad\qquad x = \dfrac{116}{3555}$,

and this solves the problem.

15. To divide unity into three parts such that, if three given numbers be added, each to one of the parts, the results are all squares.

Given numbers 2, 3, 4. Then I have to divide 10 into three squares such that the first > 2, the second > 3, the third > 4. Let us add $\dfrac{1}{2}$ unity to each, and find three squares whose sum is 10, the first lying between 2, $2\frac{1}{2}$, the second between 3, $3\frac{1}{2}$, and the third between 4, $4\frac{1}{2}$.

Divide 10 into two squares, one of which lies between 2 and $2\frac{1}{2}$. Then this square *minus* 1 will give one of the parts of unity.

Next divide the other square into two, one lying between 3, $3\frac{1}{2}$; this gives the second part, and therefore the third.

16. To divide a given number into three parts such that the sums of all pairs are squares.

Number 10. Then since the greatest + the middle part $=$ a square, &c., the sum of any pair is a square < 10, but twice the sum of the three $= 20$. *Therefore 20 is to be divided into three squares each of which < 10.* Now $20 = 16 + 4$. Therefore we must divide 16 into two squares, one of which lies between 6 and 10; we then have three squares each of which is < 10, and whose sum $= 20$, and by subtracting each of these squares from 10 we get the parts required.

[16 must be divided into the two squares by v. 13.]

17. To divide a given number into four parts such that the sum of any three is a square.

> Number 10. Then three times the sum = the sum of four squares.
>
> Hence 30 must be divided into four squares, each of which < 10. If we use the method of παρισότης and make each near $7\frac{1}{2}$, and then subtract each square found from 10, we have the required parts.
>
> But, observing that $30 = 16 + 9 + 4 + 1$, I take 4, 9 and divide 17 into two squares each of which < 10 > 7. Then subtract each of the four squares from 10 and we have the required parts.

18. *To find three numbers such that, if we add any one of them to the cube of their sum, the result is a cube.*

> Let the sum be x, the numbers $7x^3$, $26x^3$, $63x^3$. Hence, for the last condition, $96x^3 = x$. *But* 96 *is not a square.* Therefore it must be replaced. Now it arises from $7 + 26 + 63$.
>
> Therefore I have to find three numbers, each 1 less than a cube, whose sum is a square. Let the sides of the cubes be $m + 1$, $2 - m$, 2, whence the numbers are
> $$m^3 + 3m^2 + 3m, \quad 7 - 12m + 6m^2 - m^3, \quad 7,$$
> and the sum $= 9m^2 - 9m + 14 =$ a square $= (3m - 4)^2$.
>
> Therefore $$m = \frac{2}{15},$$
> and the numbers are $$\frac{1538}{3375}, \quad \frac{18577}{3375}, \quad 7.$$
> Therefore, putting the sum $= x$, and the numbers of the problem
> $$\frac{1538}{3375} x^3, \quad \frac{18577}{3375} x^3, \quad 7x^3,$$
> we find $$x = \frac{15}{54};$$ therefore, &c.

19. *To find three numbers such that, if we subtract any one of them from the cube of the sum, the result is a cube.*

> Let the sum be x, the numbers $\frac{7}{8} x^3$, $\frac{26}{27} x^3$, $\frac{63}{64} x^3$.
>
> Therefore $$\frac{4877}{1728} x^3 = x;$$
> but $\frac{4877}{1728} = 3 -$ the sum of three cubes.

Therefore we must find three cubes, each <1, such that $(3-\text{their sum}) = \text{a square} = 2\frac{1}{4}$ say. *Therefore we have to find three cubes whose sum is* $\dfrac{3}{4} = \dfrac{162}{216}$, or we have to divide 162 into three cubes. But $162 = 125 + 64 - 27$.

Now (Porism) *the difference of two cubes can be transformed into the sum of two cubes.* Having then found the three cubes we start again,

and $x = 2\frac{1}{4}x^3$, so that $x = \dfrac{2}{3}$, which, with the three cubes, determines the result.

20. *To find three numbers such that, if we subtract the cube of their sum from any one of them, the result is a cube.*

Sum $= x$, and let the numbers be $2x^3$, $9x^3$, $28x^3$. Therefore $39x^2 = 1$, and we must replace 39, which $=$ sum of three cubes $+ 3$.

Therefore we must find three cubes whose sum $+ 3 = $ a square.

Let their sides be m, $3 - m$, and any number, say 1.

Therefore $9m^2 + 31 - 27m = \text{square} = (3m - 7)^2$ say, so that $m = \dfrac{6}{5}$, and the sides of the cubes are $\dfrac{6}{5}$, $\dfrac{9}{5}$, 1.

Starting again, let the sum be x, and the numbers

$$\frac{341}{125}x^3, \quad \frac{854}{125}x^3, \quad \frac{250}{125}x^3,$$

so that $\quad 1445x^2 = 125, \quad x^2 = \dfrac{25}{289}, \quad x = \dfrac{5}{17}$;

thus the numbers are known.

21. To find three numbers, whose sum is a square, such that the cube of their sum added to any one of them gives a square.

Let the sum be x^2, the numbers $3x^6$, $8x^6$, $15x^6$. Therefore $26x^4 = 1$; and, if 26 were a fourth power, this would give the result.

To replace it by a fourth power, we must find three squares whose sum diminished by $3 = $ a fourth power, or three numbers such that each increased by $1 = $ a square, and the sum of the three $= $ a fourth power. *Let these be*

$m^4 - 2m^2$, $m^2 + 2m$, $m^2 - 2m$ [sum $= m^4$]; then if we put m anything, say 3,

the numbers are   63, 15, 3.

Thus, putting for the sum x^2, and for the numbers $3x^6$, $15x^6$, $63x^6$, $x = \dfrac{1}{3}$, and the problem is solved.

22. To find three numbers whose sum equals a square, and such that the cube of the sum exceeds any one of them by a square.

[Incomplete in the text.]

23. To divide a given fraction into three parts, such that each exceeds the cube of the sum by a square.

Given fraction $\dfrac{1}{4}$. Therefore each $= \dfrac{1}{64} +$ a square. Therefore the sum of the three $=$ sum of three squares $+ \dfrac{3}{64}$. Therefore we have simply to divide $\dfrac{13}{64}$ into three squares.

24. *To find three squares such that their continued product added to any one of them gives a square.*

Let the "solid content" $= x^2$, and we want three squares such that each increased by 1 gives a square. They can be got from right-angled triangles by dividing the square of one of the sides about the right angle by the square of the other. Let the squares then be

$$\frac{9}{16}\,x^2, \quad \frac{25}{144}\,x^2, \quad \frac{64}{225}\,x^2.$$

Therefore the solid content $= \dfrac{14400}{518400}\,x^6$. This $= x^2$.

Therefore $\dfrac{120}{729}\,x^2 = 1$,

but $\dfrac{120}{720}$ is not a square.

Thus we must find three right-angled triangles such that, if b's are their bases, p's are their perpendiculars, $p_1 p_2 p_3 b_1 b_2 b_3 =$ square, or assuming one triangle arbitrarily (3, 4, 5), we have to make $12 p_1 p_2 b_1 b_2$ a square, or $\dfrac{3 p_1 b_1}{p_2 b_2}$

a square. "This is easy" (Diophantos [1]) and the triangles

(3, 4, 5), (8, 15, 17), (9, 40, 41),

satisfy the condition,

and $\qquad x = \dfrac{10}{3}$;

the squares then are $\left(\dfrac{25}{4}, \; \dfrac{256}{81}, \; \dfrac{9}{16}\right)$.

25. *To find three squares such that their continued product exceeds any one of them by a square.*

Let the "solid content" $= x^2$, and let the numbers be got from right-angled triangles, being namely

$$\frac{16}{25} x^2, \; \frac{25}{169} x^2, \; \frac{64}{289} x^2.$$

Therefore $\qquad \dfrac{4.5.8}{5.13.17} x^2 = 1,$

and the first side ought to be a square.

As before, find three triangles, assuming one (3, 4, 5) such that $h_1 h_2 h_3 p_1 p_2 p_3 = $ a square [2], [letters denoting hypotenuses and bases], or such that $20 \dfrac{p_2 h_2}{h_1 p_1} = $ a square.

[For the rest the text is in a very unsatisfactory state.]

---

[1] Diophantos does not give the work here, but merely the results. Moreover there is a mistake in the text of (5, 12, 13) for (8, 15, 17), and the problem is not finished.

Schulz works out this part of the problem thus:

Find two right-angled triangles whose areas are in the ratio $m:1$. Let the sides of the first be formed from $(2m+1, m-1)$, and of the second from $(m+2, m-1)$, so that two sides of the first are $4m^2 - 2m - 2$, $3m^2 + 6m$ and the area $= 6m^4 + 9m^3 - 9m^2 - 6m$.

Two sides of the second are $2m^2 + 2m - 4$, $6m + 3$, and m times the area $= 6m^4 + 9m^3 - 9m^2 - 6m$. Now put e.g. $m = 3$, therefore the first triangle is formed from 7, 2, viz. (28, 45, 53); second from 5, 2, viz. (20, 21, 29).

[2] Cossali remarks: "Construct the triangles (i, b, p) [$i = $ ipotenusa],

$$\left(\frac{b^2 + 4p^2}{b}, \; \frac{b^2 - 4p^2}{b}, \; \frac{4bp}{b} = 4p\right),$$

and $\left(\dfrac{ib^2 + 4ip^2}{b}, \; \dfrac{b.4bp - p(b^2 - 4p^2)}{b}, \; \dfrac{p.4bp + b(b^2 - 4p^2)}{b} = b^2\right),$

then $\dfrac{i(b^2 + 4p^2)(ib^2 + 4ip^2)}{b^2} : p.4p.b^2 = \dfrac{i^2(b^2 + 4p^2)^2}{b^2} : 4p^2 b^2,$

26.   To find three squares such that each exceeds their continued product by a square.

Let the "solid content" $= x^2$, and the squares have to be found by means of the same triangles as before.   We put $25x^2$, $625x^2$, $14784x^2$ for them, &c.

[Text again corrupt.]

27.   To find three squares such that the product of any two increased by 1 is a square.

Product of first and second + 1 = a square, and the third is a square.

Therefore solid content + each = a square ; and the problem reduces to the 24th above.

28.   To find three squares such that the product of any two diminished by 1 is a square.

[Same as 25th problem.]

or the solid content of the three hypotenuses has to that of the three perpendiculars the ratio of a square to a square.

It is in his note on this imperfect problem that Fermat makes the error which I referred to above. He says on the problem of *finding two triangles such that the products of hypotenuse and one side of each have a given ratio* "This question troubled me for a long time, and any one on trying it will find it very difficult: but I have at last discovered a general method of solving it.

"Let e. g. ratio be 2. Form triangles from $(a\,b)$ and $(a\,d)$. The rectangles under the hypotenuses and the perpendiculars are respectively $2ba^3 + 2b^3a$, $2da^3 + d^3a$, therefore since the ratio is 2, $ba^3 + b^3a = 2\,(da^3 + d^3a)$, therefore by transposition $2d^3 - b^3 = ba^2 - 2da^2$; therefore, if $\dfrac{2d^3 - b^3}{b - 2d}$ be made a square, the problem will be solved. Therefore I have to find two cubes d^3, b^3 such that $2d^3 - b^3$ divided or *multiplied* by $b - 2d =$ a square. Let $x + 1$, 1 be the sides, therefore

$$2d^3 - b^3 = 2x^3 + 6x^2 + 6x + 1,\; 2b - d = 1 - x,$$

therefore

$$(1 - x)\,(1 + 6x + 6x^2 + 2x^3) = 1 + 5x - 4x^3 - 2x^4 = \text{square} = \left(\frac{5}{2}x + 1 - \frac{25}{8}x^2\right)^2,$$

and everything is clear."

[Now Fermat makes the mistake of taking $2b - d$ instead of $b - 2d$, and thus he fails to solve the problem. Brassinne (author of a Précis of Diophantos and Fermat) thinks to mend the matter by making $(1 + 6x + 6x^2 + 2x^3)(1 + 2x)$ a square, whereas, the quantity to be made a square is $(1 + 6x + 6x^2 + 2x^3)(-1 - 2x)$. The solution is thus incurably wrong.]

Fermat seems afterwards to have discovered that his solution did not help to solve this particular problem of Diophantos, but does not seem to have seen that the solution is inconsistent with his own problem itself.

29. To find three squares such that unity diminished by the product of any two = a square.

[Same as (26).]

30. *Given a number, find three squares such that the sum of any two together with the given number produces a square.*

Given number 15. Let one of the required squares = 9. Therefore I must find two other squares, such that each + 24 = a square, and their sum + 15 = a square. Take two pairs of numbers whose product = 24, and let them be the sides of a right-angled triangle[1] which contain the right angle, say $\frac{4}{x}$, $6x$; let the side of one square be half the difference, or $\frac{2}{x} - 3x$.

Again, take other factors $\frac{3}{x}$, $8x$, and half the difference

$= \frac{3}{2x} - 4x =$ side of the other square, say.

Therefore $\left(\frac{3}{2x} - 4x\right)^2 + \left(\frac{2}{x} - 3x\right)^2 + 15 =$ a square,

or $\qquad \frac{6\frac{1}{4}}{x^2} + 25x^2 - 9 =$ a square $= 25x^2$ say.

Therefore $x = \frac{5}{6}$, and the problem is solved.

31. *Given a number, to find three squares such that the sum of any pair exceeds the given number by a square.*

Given number 13. Let one of the squares be 25. Therefore we must seek two more such that each + 12 = a square, and (sum of both) − 13 = a square. Divide 12 into products $\left(3x, \frac{4}{x}\right)$ and $\left(4x, \frac{3}{x}\right)$, and let the squares be

$$\left(\frac{3}{2}x - \frac{2}{x}\right)^2, \quad \left(2x - \frac{3}{2x}\right)^2.$$

Therefore $\left(\frac{3}{2}x - \frac{2}{x}\right)^2 + \left(2x - \frac{3}{2x}\right)^2 - 13 =$ a square,

or $\qquad \frac{6\frac{1}{4}}{x^2} + 6\frac{1}{4}x^2 - 25 =$ a square $= \frac{6\frac{1}{4}}{x^2}$ say.

Therefore $x = 2$, and the problem is solved.

[1] I.e. corresponding factors in the two pairs, in this case $6x$, $8x$.

32. *To find three squares such that the sum of their squares is a square.*

Let one be x^2, the second 4, the third 9. Therefore

$$x^4 + 97 = \text{a square} = (x^2 - 10)^2 \text{ say.}$$

Therefore $x^2 = \dfrac{3}{20}$, but 3.20 is not a square and must be replaced.

Hence I have to find p^2, q^2 *and* m *such that* $\dfrac{m^2 - p^4 - q^4}{2m} = a$

square. Let $p^2 = z^2$, $q^2 = 4$, and $m = z^2 + 4$. Therefore $m^2 - p^4 - q^4 = (z^2 + 4)^2 - z^4 - 16 = 8z^2$. Hence we must

have, $\dfrac{8z^2}{2z^2 + 8} = \text{a square, or } \dfrac{4z^2}{z^2 + 4} = \text{a square.}$

Put $\qquad z^2 + 4 = (z + 1)^2$ say.

Therefore $z = \dfrac{3}{2}$, and the squares are $p^2 = \dfrac{9}{4}$, $q^2 = 4$, and

$m = \dfrac{25}{4}$, or, taking 4 times each, $p^2 = 9$, $q^2 = 16$, $m = 25$.

Starting again, put the first square $= x^2$, the second $= 9$, the third $= 16$, whence the sum of the squares $= x^4 + 337$ $= (x^2 - 25)^2$.

Therefore $\qquad x = \dfrac{12}{5}$,

and $\left(\dfrac{144}{25}, 9, 16\right)$ is a solution.

33. [*Epigram-problem*].

'Οκταδράχμους καὶ πενταδράχμους χόεας τὶς ἔμιξε,
  Τοῖς προπολοῖσι πιεῖν χρῆστ' ἀποταξάμενος.
Καὶ τιμὴν ἀπέδωκεν ὑπὲρ πάντων τετράγωνον,
  Τὰς ἐπιταχθείσας δεξάμενον μονάδας,
Καὶ ποιοῦντα πάλιν ἕτερόν σε φέρειν τετράγωνον
  Κτησάμενον πλευρὰν σύνθεμα τῶν χοέων.
Ὥστε διάστειλον τοὺς ὀκταδράχμους πόσοι ἦσαν,
  Καὶ πάλι τοὺς ἑτέρους παῖ λέγε πεντεδράχμους.

Let the given number (ἐπιταχθεῖσαι μονάδες) be 60. The meaning is: A man buys a certain number of χόες of wine, some at 8 drachmas, the rest at 5 each. He pays for them a *square* number of drachmas. And if we add 60 to this number the result is a square whose side =the whole number of χόες. Required how many he bought at each price.

Let $x =$ the whole number of χόες. Therefore $x^2 - 60 =$ the price paid, which is a square, $(x - m)^2$ say. Now $\frac{1}{5}$ of the price of the five-drachma χόες $+ \frac{1}{8}$ of the price of the eight-drachma χόες $= x$. We cannot have a rational solution unless $x > \frac{1}{8}(x^2 - 60) < \frac{1}{5}(x^2 - 60)$.

Therefore $x^2 > 5x + 60 < 8x + 60$.

Hence $x^2 = 5x +$ a number > 60, or x is[1] $\not< 11$.

Also $x^2 \not< 8x + 60$.

Therefore x is $\not> 12$, so that x *must lie between* 11 *and* 12.

But $x^2 - 60 = (x - m)^2$,

therefore $x = \dfrac{m^2 + 60}{2m}$, which $> 11, < 12$,

whence $m^2 + 60 > 22m < 24m$.

From these we find, m is not > 21, and not < 19.

Hence we put $x^2 - 60 = (x - 20)^2$,

and $x = 11\frac{1}{2}$.

Thus $x^2 = 132\frac{1}{4}$, $x^2 - 60 = 72\frac{1}{4}$,

and $72\frac{1}{4}$ has to be divided into two numbers such that $\frac{1}{5}$ of the first $+ \frac{1}{8}$ of the second $= 11\frac{1}{2}$. Let the first $= z$.

Therefore $\dfrac{z}{5} + \dfrac{1}{8}\left(72\frac{1}{4} - z\right) = 11\frac{1}{2}$,

or $\dfrac{3z}{40} = 11\frac{1}{2} - 9\frac{1}{32} = \dfrac{79}{32}$,

and $z = \dfrac{5 \cdot 79}{12}$.

Therefore the number of χόες at five-drachmas $= \dfrac{79}{12}$.

     ,,   ,,   ,,   eight   ,, $= \dfrac{59}{12}$.

[At the end of Book v. Bachet adds 45 Greek arithmetical epigrams collected by Salmasius, which however have nothing to do with Diophantos.]

---

[1] See pp. 90, 91 for an explanation of these limits.

BOOK VI.

1. *To find a rational right-angled triangle such that the hypotenuse exceeds each side by a cube.*

Suppose a triangle formed from the two numbers x, 3.

Therefore hypotenuse $= x^2 + 9$, perpendicular $= 6x$, base $= x^2 - 9$.

Therefore by the question $x^2 + 9 - (x^2 - 9)$ should be a cube, or 18 should be a cube, which it is not. Now $18 = 2 \cdot 3^2$, therefore we must replace the number 3 by m, where $2m^2 = $ a cube; i. e. $m = 2$.

Thus, forming the triangle from x, 2, viz. $(x^2 + 4,\ 4x,\ x^2 - 4)$, we must have $x^2 - 4x + 4$ a cube.

Therefore $(x - 2)^2 = $ a cube, or $x - 2 = $ a cube $= 8$ say.

Hence $\qquad\qquad x = 10$,

and the triangle is **(40, 96, 104)**.

2. To find a right-angled triangle such that the sum of the hypotenuse and either side is a cube.

Form a triangle as before from two numbers, and one of them must be a number twice whose square $=$ a cube, i. e. 2.

Therefore, forming a triangle from x, 2, or $(x^2 + 4,\ 4x,\ 4 - x^2)$ we must have $x^2 + 4x + 4$ a cube, and $x^2 < 4$.

Hence $x + 2 = $ a cube, which must be $< 4 > 2 = \dfrac{27}{8}$ say.

Therefore $\qquad\qquad x = \dfrac{11}{8}$,

and the triangle is $\left(\dfrac{135}{64},\ \dfrac{352}{64},\ \dfrac{377}{64} \right)$.

3. *To find a right-angled triangle such that the sum of the area and a given number is a square.*

Let 5 be the given number, $(3x,\ 4x,\ 5x)$ the triangle.

Therefore $\qquad 6x^2 + 5 = $ square $= 9x^2$ say.

Hence $3x^2 = 5$, and $\dfrac{5}{3}$ *is not a square ratio.*

Hence I must find a triangle and a number such that the difference of the square of the number and the area of the triangle has to 5 a square ratio, i. e. $= \dfrac{1}{5}$ of a square.

H. D. $\qquad\qquad\qquad\qquad\qquad\qquad\qquad\qquad$ **15**

Form a triangle from x, $\dfrac{1}{x}$; then the area $= x^2 - \dfrac{1}{x^2}$, and let the

number $= x + \dfrac{2.5}{x}$, so that $4.5 + \dfrac{101}{x^2} = \dfrac{1}{5}$ of a square,

or, $4.25 + \dfrac{505}{x^2} =$ a square $= \left(10 + \dfrac{5}{x}\right)^2$ say.

Whence $\qquad\qquad\qquad x = \dfrac{24}{5}$.

The triangle must therefore be formed from $\dfrac{24}{5}$, $\dfrac{5}{24}$,

and the number is $\dfrac{413}{60}$.

Put now for the original triangle $(hx,\ px,\ bx)$, where (hpb) is

the triangle formed from $\dfrac{24}{5}$, $\dfrac{5}{24}$, and $\dfrac{pbx^2}{2} + 5 = \dfrac{170569}{3600}\,x^2$,

and we have the solution.

4.   To find a right-angled triangle such that its area exceeds a given number by a square.

Number 6, triangle $(3x,\ 4x,\ 5x)$.

Therefore $\qquad 6x^2 - 6 =$ square $= 4x^2$ say.

Hence, as before, we must find a triangle and a number such

that the area of the triangle $-$ (number)$^2 = \dfrac{1}{6}$ of a square.

Form the triangle from m, $\dfrac{1}{m}$.

Therefore its area $= m^2 - \dfrac{1}{m^2}$, and let the number be $m - \dfrac{6}{2} \cdot \dfrac{1}{m}$.

Hence $\qquad 6\left(6 - \dfrac{10}{m^2}\right) =$ a square,

or, $\qquad 36m^2 - 60 =$ a square $= (6m - 2)^2$.

Therefore $m = \dfrac{8}{3}$, and the triangle must be formed from $\left(\dfrac{8}{3}, \dfrac{3}{8}\right)$,

the number being $\dfrac{37}{24}$.

We now start again, and the rest is obvious.

5.   To find a right-angled triangle such that a given number exceeds the area by a square.

Number 10, triangle $(3x,\ 4x,\ 5x)$.   Therefore $10 - 6x^2 =$ a square, and a triangle and a number must be found such that $(\text{number})^2$ + area of triangle $= \dfrac{1}{10}$ of a square.   Form a triangle from $m, \dfrac{1}{m}$, and let the number, be $\dfrac{1}{m} + 5m$.

Therefore $\qquad 260m^2 + 100 = $ a square,

or $\qquad 65m^2 + 25 = $ a square $= (8m + 5)^2$ say.

Therefore $\qquad\qquad m = 80$.

The rest is obvious.

6.   *To find a right-angled triangle such that the sum of the area and one side*[1] *about the right angle is a given number.*

Given number 7.   Triangle $(3x, 4x, 5x)$,

therefore $\qquad\qquad 6x^2 + 3x = 7$.

To solve this, $\left(\dfrac{3}{2}\right)^2 + 6 \cdot 7$ *not being a square, is not possible.*

Hence we must substitute for $(3, 4, 5)$ a right-angled triangle such that $\left(\dfrac{\text{one side}}{2}\right)^2 + 7$ times the area $=$ a square.   Let one side be x, the other 1.

Therefore $\qquad \dfrac{7}{2}x + \dfrac{1}{4} = $ a square,

or $\qquad\qquad\qquad 14x + 1 = $ a square $\Big\}$.

Also, since the triangle is rational, $x^2 + 1 = $ a square $\Big\}$.

Now the difference $= x^2 - 14x = x(x - 14)$.   Therefore, putting $7^2 = 14x + 1$, we have $x = \dfrac{24}{7}$.   Therefore the triangle is $\left(\dfrac{24}{7}, 1, \dfrac{25}{7}\right)$, or we may make it $(24, 7, 25)$.

Going back, we take as the triangle $(24x, 7x, 25x)$.

Therefore $84x^2 + 7x = 7$, and $x = \dfrac{1}{4}$.

Hence the triangle is $\left(6, \dfrac{7}{4}, \dfrac{25}{4}\right)$.

7.   To find a right-angled triangle such that its area exceeds one of its sides by a given number.

[1] N.B.   For brevity and distinctness I shall in future call the sides about the right angle simply "sides," and not apply the term to the hypotenuse, which will always be called "hypotenuse."

Given number 7. Therefore, as before, we have to find a right-angled triangle such that $\left(\dfrac{\text{one side}}{2}\right)^2 + 7$ times area = a square, i.e. the triangle (7, 24, 25).

Let the triangle of the problem be $(7x, 24x, 25x)$.

Therefore $84x^2 - 7x = 7$, and $x = \dfrac{1}{3}$.

8. *To find a right-angled triangle such that the sum of its area and both sides = a given number.*

Number 6. Again I have to find a right-angled triangle such that $\left(\dfrac{\text{sum of sides}}{2}\right)^2 + 6$ times area = a square. Let m, 1 be the sides; therefore $\left(\dfrac{m+1}{2}\right)^2 + 3m = \dfrac{m^2}{4} + \dfrac{7m}{2} + \dfrac{1}{4} = $ a square, and $m^2 + 1 = $ a square.

Therefore $\left.\begin{array}{r} m^2 + 14m + 1 \\ m^2 + 1 \end{array}\right\}$ are both squares,

and the difference $= 2m \cdot 7$.

Therefore $m = \dfrac{45}{28}$,

and the subsidiary triangle is $\left(\dfrac{45}{28}, 1, \dfrac{53}{28}\right)$ or (45, 28, 53).

Assume now for the triangle of the problem $(45x, 28x, 53x)$.

Therefore $630x^2 + 73x = 6$,

and x is rational.

9. To find a right-angled triangle such that its area exceeds the sum of both sides by a given number.

Number 6. As before we find subsidiary triangle (28, 45, 53).

Therefore, taking for the required triangle $(28x, 45x, 53x)$, we find $630x^2 - 73x = 6$,

and $x = \dfrac{6}{35}$.

10. *To find a right-angled triangle such that the sum of its area, hypotenuse, and one side is a given number.*

Given number 4. Assuming hx, px, bx, $\dfrac{pbx^2}{2} + hx + bx = 4$, and in order that this equation may have a rational solution I must find a triangle such that

$\left(\dfrac{\text{hypotenuse + one side}}{2}\right)^2 + 4$ times area = a square.

Make a right-angled triangle from m, $m + 1$. Therefore

$$\left(\frac{\text{hypotenuse} + \text{one side}}{2}\right)^2 = \left(\frac{2m^2 + 2m + 1 + 2m + 1}{2}\right)^2$$
$$= m^4 + 4m^3 + 6m^2 + 4m + 1$$

and 4 times area $= 4m \, (m + 1) \, (2m + 1)$

which $= 8m^3 + 12m^2 + 4m$.

Therefore

$$m^4 + 12m^3 + 18m^2 + 8m + 1 = \text{a square} = (m^2 + 6m - 1)^2 \text{ say.}$$

Hence
$$m = \frac{5}{4},$$

and the triangle must be formed from $\left(\dfrac{5}{4}, \ \dfrac{9}{4}\right)$, or $(5, 9)$.

Thus we must assume for the triangle of the problem the similar triangle $(28x, 45x, 53x)$, and $630x^2 + 81x = 4$.

Therefore
$$x = \frac{4}{105}.$$

11. To find a right-angled triangle such that its area exceeds the sum of the hypotenuse and one side by a given number.

Number 4. As before, by means of the triangle $(28, 45, 53)$
we get $630x^2 - 81x = 4$.

Therefore
$$x = \frac{1}{6}.$$

12. To find a right-angled triangle such that the difference of its sides is a square, and also the greater alone is a square, and, thirdly, its area + the less side = a square.

Let the triangle be formed from two numbers, the greater side being twice their product. Hence I must find two numbers such that twice their product is a square and also exceeds the difference of their squares by a square. This is true for any two numbers of which the greater = twice the less.

Form then the triangle from x, $2x$, and two conditions are fulfilled. The third condition gives $6x^4 + 3x^2 =$ a square, or $6x^2 + 3 =$ a square. Therefore we must seek a number such that six times its square with 3 produces a square, i.e. 1, and an infinite number of others.

Hence the triangle required is formed from 1, 2.

Lemma. Given two numbers whose sum is a square, an infinite number of squares can be found which by multiplication with one of the given ones and the addition of the other to this product give squares.

Given numbers 3, 6.   Let $x^2 + 2x + 1$ be the square required, which will satisfy

$3(x^2 + 2x + 1) + 6 =$ a square, or $3x^2 + 6x + 9 =$ a square.

This indeterminate equation has an infinite number of solutions.

13.   *To find a right-angled triangle such that the sum of its area and either of its sides = a square.*

Let the triangle be $(5x, 12x, 13x)$.

Therefore $30x^2 + 12x =$ a square $= 36x^2$ say.

Therefore $6x = 12$, and $x = 2$.

But $30x^2 + 5x$ is not a square when $x = 2$.   Therefore I must find a square m^2x^2 to replace $36x^2$ such that the value

$$\frac{12}{m^2 - 30}$$ *of x is real and satisfies $30x^2 + 5x =$ a square.*

This gives by substitution $\dfrac{60m^2 + 2520}{m^4 - 60m + 900} =$ a square.

Therefore $60m^2 + 2520 =$ a square.   *If then [by Lemma] we had $60\,m^2 + 2520$ equal to a square, the equation could be solved.*

Now 60 arises from 5, 12, i.e. from the product of the sides of $(5, 12, 13)$; 2520 is the continued product of the area, the greater side and the difference of the sides $[30.12.\overline{12-5}]$.

Hence we must find a subsidiary triangle such that the product of the sides + the continued product of greater side, difference of sides and area = a square.

Or, *if we make the greater side a square*, we must have [dividing by it], less side + product of difference of sides and area = a square.   Therefore we must, given two numbers (area and less side), find some square such that if we multiply it by the area and add the less side, the result is a square.   *This is done by the Lemmas*[1] and the auxiliary triangle is $(3, 4, 5)$.

---

[1] Diophantos has expressed this rather curtly. If $(h\ p\ b)$ be the triangle $(b > p)$, we have to make $bp + \frac{1}{2}bp \cdot (b - p)\,b$

a square, or if b is a square, $p + \frac{1}{2}\,bp\,(b - p)$ must be a square.

Thus, if the original triangle is $(3x, 4x, 5x)$,

we have $\left.\begin{array}{c} 6x^2 + 4x \\ 6x^2 + 3x \end{array}\right\}$ are both squares.

Let $x = \dfrac{4}{m^2 - 6}$ be the solution of the first equation.

Therefore the second gives $\dfrac{96}{m^4 - 12m^2 + 36} + \dfrac{12}{m^2 - 6} =$ a square.

Hence $12m^2 + 24 =$ a square,

and we must find a square such that twelve times it $+ 24 =$ a square [as in *Lemma*].

Therefore $m^2 = 25$,

and $x = \dfrac{4}{19}$.

Therefore the triangle required is $\left(\dfrac{12}{19}, \dfrac{16}{19}, \dfrac{20}{19}\right)$.

14. To find a right-angled triangle such that its area exceeds either side by a square.

The triangle found as before to be similar to $(3, 4, 5)$, i.e. $(3x, 4x, 5x)$.

Therefore $6x^2 - 4x =$ square $= m^2 (< 6)$.

Hence $x = \dfrac{4}{6 - m^2}$,

and $\dfrac{96}{(6 - m^2)^2} - \dfrac{12}{6 - m^2} =$ a square, or $24 + 12m^2 =$ a square.

Let $m = 1$ say.

Therefore $x = \dfrac{4}{5}$,

and the triangle is $\left(\dfrac{12}{5}, \dfrac{16}{5}, 4\right)$.

Or, putting $m = z + 1$, we find $3z^2 + 6z + 9 =$ a square, and $z \not= \dfrac{13}{9}$, $z + 1 \not= \dfrac{22}{9}$, so that x is rational.

This relation can be satisfied in an infinite number of ways if $b - p$ is a square, and also $p + \frac{1}{2} bp$.

Therefore we have to find a triangle such that greater side = square, difference of sides = square, less side + area = square.

Form the triangle from (a, b), therefore greater side $= 2ab$, which is a square, if $a = 2b$, difference of sides $= 4b^2 - 3b^2 =$ a square, less side + area $= 3b^2 + 6b^2 =$ a square.

15.   To find a right-angled triangle such that its area exceeds either the hypotenuse or one side by a square.

Let the triangle be $(3x,\ 4x,\ 5x)$.

Therefore $\left.\begin{array}{l} 6x^2 - 5x \\ 6x^2 - 3x \end{array}\right\}$ are both squares.

Making the latter a square, we find $x = \dfrac{3}{6 - m^2}$, $(m^2 < 6)$.

Therefore   from   the   first $\dfrac{54}{(6 - m^2)^2} - \dfrac{15}{6 - m^2} = $ a   square,   or

$15m^2 - 36 = $ a square.

This equation we cannot solve, since 15 is not the sum of two squares.

Now $15m^2 = $ the product of a square less than the area, the hypotenuse, and one side ; $36 = $ the continued product of the area, one side, and the difference between the hypotenuse and that side.

Hence we must find a right-angled triangle and a square such that the square is < 6, and the continued product of the square, the hypotenuse of the triangle, and one side of it exceeds the continued product of the area, the said side and the difference between the hypotenuse and that side by a square.

[Lacuna and corruption in text[1]].

Form the triangle from two "similar plane numbers" [numbers of the form ab, abc^2], say 4, 1.   This will satisfy the conditions, and let the square be 36.   (< area.)

The triangle is then $(8x,\ 15x,\ 17x)$.

Therefore $60x^2 - 8x = 36x^2$ say.

Thus $x = \dfrac{1}{3}$,

and the triangle is $\left(\dfrac{8}{3},\ 5,\ \dfrac{17}{3}\right)$.

---

[1] Schulz works out the subsidiary part of this problem thus, or rather only proves the result given by Diophantos that the triangle must be formed from two "similar plane numbers" a, ab^2 [i.e. a. 1 and ab. b.] ; and hyp. $h = a^2b^4 + a^2$, greater side $g = a^2b^4 - a^2$, less side $k = 2a^2b^2$, area $f = \frac{1}{2}kg$.   Now

$$h - k = a^2b^4 - 2a^2b^2 + a^2 = (ab^2 - a)^2,$$

a square ; and $hkz^2 - kf(h - k)$ is a square if $z^2 = \frac{1}{2}(h - k)k$, for, if we then divide by the square $h - k$ and twice by the square $\frac{1}{2}k$, we get $2(h - g) = 4a^4$, which is a square.

16. Given two numbers, if some square be multiplied by one of them, and the other be subtracted, the result being a square, then another square can be found greater than the first square which has the same property. [*Lemma* to the following problem.]

Numbers 3, 11, side of square 5, so that $3 \cdot 25 - 11 = 64 = a$ square. Let the required square be $(x + 5)^2$.

Therefore

$3 (x + 5)^2 - 11 = 3x^2 + 30x + 64 = a$ square $= (8 - 2x)^2$ say.

Hence $x = 62$.

The side of the square $= 67$, and the square itself $= 4489$.

17. *To find a right-angled triangle such that the sum of the area and either the hypotenuse or one side = a square.*

We must first seek a triangle (h, k, g) and a square z^2 such that $hkz^2 - ka (h - k) = a$ square, and $z^2 > a$, the area.

Let the triangle be formed from 4, 1, and the square be 36, but, the triangle being (8, 15, 17), the square is not $>$ area.

Therefore we must find another square to replace 36 by the *Lemma* in the preceding. But

$hk = 136, ka (h - k) = 480 \cdot 9 = 4320.$

Thus $36 \cdot 136 - 4320 = a$ square, and we want to find a larger square (m^2) than 36 such that $136m^2 - 4320 = a$ square.

Putting $m = z + 6$, $(z^2 + 12z + 36) 136 - 4320 =$ square,

or, $136z^2 + 1632z + 576 = a$ square $= (nz - 24)^2$ say.

This equation has any number of solutions, of which one gives 676 for the value of $(z + 6)^2$ [putting $n = 16$].

Hence, putting for the triangle (8x, 15x, 17x), we get

$60x^2 + 8x = 676x^2.$

Therefore $x = \dfrac{1}{77}$.

18. *To find a right-angled triangle such that the line bisecting an acute angle is rational.*

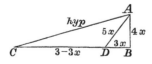

Let the bisector $(AD) = 5x$ and one section of the base (DB) $3x$, so that the perpendicular $= 4x$.

Let the whole base be some multiple of 3, say 3. Then
$$CD = 3 - 3x.$$
But, since AD bisects the $\angle\, BAC$, the hypotenuse $= \dfrac{4}{3}(3 - 3x)$,

therefore the hypotenuse $= 4 - 4x$.

Hence $16x^2 - 32x + 16 = 16x^2 + 9$, and $x = \dfrac{7}{32}$.

Multiplying throughout by 32, the perpendicular $= 28$, the base $= 96$, the hypotenuse $= 100$, the bisector $= 35$.

19.   *To find a right-angled triangle such that the sum of its area and hypotenuse = a square, and its perimeter = a cube.*

Let the area $= x$, the hypotenuse $=$ some square *minus x*, say $16 - x$; the product of the sides $= 2x$. Therefore, if one of the sides be 2, the other is x, and the perimeter $= 18$, *which is not a cube.*

Therefore we must find a square which by the addition of 2 becomes a cube.

Let the side of the square be $(x + 1)$, and the side of the cube $(x - 1)$.

Therefore $x^3 - 3x^2 + 3x - 1 = x^2 + 2x + 3$, from which $x = 4$.

Hence the side of the square is 5, and of the cube 3.

Again, assuming area $= x$, hypotenuse $= 25 - x$, we find that the perimeter $=$ a cube (sides of triangle being x, 2).

But (hypotenuse)$^2 =$ sum of squares of sides.

Therefore $x^2 - 50x + 625 = x^2 + 4,$

and $x = \dfrac{621}{50}$.

20.   *To find a right-angled triangle such that the sum of its area and hypotenuse = a cube, and the perimeter = a square.*

Area x, hypotenuse some cube *minus x*, sides x, 2.

Therefore we have to find a cube which by the addition of 2 becomes a square. Let the side of the cube $= m - 1$.

Therefore $m^3 - 3m^2 + 3m + 1 =$ a square $= \left(\dfrac{3}{2}\,m + 1\right)^2$ say.

Thus $m = \dfrac{21}{4}$, and the cube $= \left(\dfrac{17}{4}\right)^3$.

Put then the area x, the sides x and 2, the hypotenuse $\dfrac{4913}{64} - x$.

Therefore $\left(\dfrac{4913}{64} - x\right)^2 = x^2 + 4$ gives x.

21. *To find a right-angled triangle such that the sum of its area and one side is a square and its perimeter is a cube.*

Make a right-angled triangle from x, $x + 1$.

Therefore the perpendicular $= 2x + 1$, the base $= 2x^2 + 2x$, the hypotenuse $= 2x^2 + 2x + 1$.

First, $4x^2 + 6x + 2 =$ a cube, or $(4x + 2)(x + 1) =$ a cube. If we divide all the sides by $x + 1$ we have to make $4x + 2$ a cube.

Secondly, area $+$ perpendicular $=$ a square.

Therefore $\dfrac{2x^3 + 3x^2 + x}{(x + 1)^2} + \dfrac{2x + 1}{x + 1} =$ a square.

Hence $\dfrac{2x^3 + 5x^2 + 4x + 1}{x^2 + 2x + 1} = 2x + 1 =$ a square.

But $4x + 2 =$ a cube. Therefore we must find a cube which is double of a square.

Therefore $\qquad 2x + 1 = 4$, $x = \dfrac{3}{2}$,

and the triangle is $\left(\dfrac{8}{5}, \dfrac{15}{5}, \dfrac{17}{5} \right)$.

22. To find a right-angled triangle such that the sum of its area and one side is a cube, while its perimeter is a square.

Proceeding as before, we have to make

$$\left. \begin{array}{l} 4x + 2 \text{ a square} \\ 2x + 1 \text{ a cube} \end{array} \right\}.$$

Therefore the cube $= 8$, the square $= 16$, $x = \dfrac{7}{2}$,

and the triangle is $\left(\dfrac{16}{9}, \dfrac{63}{9}, \dfrac{65}{9} \right)$.

23. *To find a right-angled triangle such that its perimeter is a square, and the sum of its perimeter and area is a cube.*

Form a right-angled triangle from x, 1.

Therefore the sides are $2x$, $x^2 - 1$, and the hypotenuse $x^2 + 1$.

Hence $2x^2 + 2x$ should be a square, and $x^3 + 2x^2 + x$ a cube.

It is easy to make $2x^2 + 2x$ a square : let it $= m^2 x^2$.

Therefore $x = \dfrac{2}{m^2 - 2}$, and from the second condition

$$\dfrac{8}{(m^2 - 2)^3} + \dfrac{8}{(m^2 - 2)^2} + \dfrac{2}{m^2 - 2}$$

must be a cube, i.e. $\dfrac{2m^4}{(m^2 - 2)^3} =$ a cube.

Therefore $2m^4 =$ a cube, or $2m =$ a cube $= 8$ say.

Thus $m = 4$, $x = \dfrac{2}{14} = \dfrac{1}{7}$, and $x^2 = \dfrac{1}{49}$.

But for one side of the triangle we have to subtract 1 from this, which is impossible.

Therefore I must find another value of $x > 1$: so that
$$m^2 > 2 < 4.$$

And I must find a cube such that $\frac{1}{4}$ of the square of it
$$> 2 < 4.$$

Let it be n^3, so that $n^6 > 8 < 16$.   This is satisfied by
$$n^6 = \frac{729}{64}, \quad n^3 = \frac{27}{8}.$$

Therefore $m = \dfrac{27}{16}$, $m^2 = \dfrac{729}{256}$, $x = \dfrac{512}{217}$, and the square of this

> 1.   Thus the triangle is known.

24.   *To find a right-angled triangle such that its perimeter is a cube and the sum of its perimeter and area = a square.*

(1)   We must first see how, given two numbers, a triangle may be formed whose perimeter = one of the numbers, and whose area = the other.

Let 12, 7 be the numbers, 12 being the perimeter, 7 the area.

Therefore the product of the sides $= 14 = \dfrac{1}{x} \cdot 14x$.

Thus the hypotenuse $= 12 - \dfrac{1}{x} - 14x$.

Therefore from the right-angled triangle
$$172 + \frac{1}{x^2} + 196x^2 - 336x - \frac{24}{x} = \frac{1}{x^2} + 196x^2,$$

or, $172 - 336x - \dfrac{24}{x} = 0.$

This equation gives no rational solution, unless $86^2 - 24 \cdot 336$
    is a square.

But $172 = (\text{perimeter})^2 + 4$ times area, $24 \cdot 336 = 8$ times area multiplied by $(\text{perimeter})^2$.

(2)   Let now the area $= x$, the perimeter $=$ any number which is both a square and a cube, say 64.

Therefore $\left(\dfrac{64^2 + 4x}{2}\right)^2 - 8 \cdot 64^2 \cdot x$ must be a square,

    or, $4x^2 - 24576x + 4194304 =$ a square.

Therefore $x^2 - 6144x + 1048576$ is a square.⎫
Also $x + 64$ is a square.⎭

To solve this double equation, multiply the second equation
by such a square as will make the absolute term the same
as in the first. Then, taking the difference and factors,
&c., the equations are solved.

[In the text we find ἐξισώσθω σοι οἱ ἀριθμοί, which, besides
being ungrammatical, would seem to be wrong, in that
ἀριθμοί is used in an unprecedented manner for μονάδες.]

25. To find a right-angled triangle such that the square of its
hypotenuse = the sum of a square and its side, and the quotient
obtained by dividing the (hypotenuse)² by one side of the triangle =
the sum of a cube and its side.

Let one of the sides be x, the other x^2.

Therefore (hypotenuse)² = the sum of a square and its side,

and $\dfrac{x^4 + x^2}{x}$ = a cube + its side.

Lastly, $x^4 + x^2$ must be a square.

Therefore $x^2 + 1 =$ a square $= (x - 2)^2$ say.

Therefore $x = \dfrac{3}{4}$, and the triangle is found.

26. To find a right-angled triangle such that one side is a cube,
the other = the difference between a cube and its side, the hypotenuse
= the sum of a cube and its side.

Let the hypotenuse $= x^3 + x$, one side $= x^3 - x$.

Therefore the other side $= 2x^2 =$ a cube.

Therefore $x = 2$,

and the triangle is (6, 8, 10).

TRACT ON *POLYGONAL NUMBERS.*

1. All numbers, from 3 onwards in order, are polygonal, containing as many sides as units, e.g. 3, 4, 5, &c.

> "As a square is formed from the multiplication of a number by itself, so it was proved that any polygonal multiplied by a number in proportion to the number of its sides, with the addition to the product of a square also in proportion to the number of the sides, became a square. This we shall prove, first showing how a polygonal number may be found from its side or the side from a given polygonal number."

2. *If there are three numbers equally distant from each other, then* 8 *times the product of the greatest and the middle + the square of the least = a square whose side is (greatest + twice middle number).*

Let the numbers be AB, BG, BD (in fig.) we have to prove
$$8\,(AB)(BG) + (BD)^2 = (AB + 2BG)^2.$$

$$E \ldots A \ldots B \ldots D \ldots G$$

Now $\qquad\qquad AB = BG + GD.$

Therefore

$$8AB\,.\,BG = 8\,(BG^2 + BG\,.\,GD) = 4AB\,.\,BG + 4BG^2 + 4BG\,.\,GD.$$

and $4BG\,.\,GD + DB^2 = AB^2$ [for $AB = BG + GD$, $DB = BG - GD$],

and we have to seek how $AB^2 + 4AB\,.\,BG + 4BG^2$ can be made a square.

Take $\qquad\qquad AE = BG.$

Therefore $\qquad 4AB\,.\,BG = 4AB\,.\,AE.$

This together with $4BG^2$ or $4AE^2$ makes $4BE\,.\,EA$, and this together with $AB^2 = (BE + EA)^2 = (AB + 2BG)^2.$

3. *If there are any numbers in* A.P. *the difference of the greatest and the least > the common difference in the ratio of the number of terms diminished by* 1.

Let AB, BG, BD, BE...be in A.P.

$$B . A .. G .. D .. E$$

Therefore we must have, difference of AB, $BE =$ (difference of AB, BG) × (number of terms − 1).

AG, GD, DE are all equal. Therefore $EA = AG$ × (number of the terms AG, GD, DE) $= AG$ × (number of terms in series − 1).

Therefore &c.

4. *If there are any numbers in* A.P. *(greatest + least)* × *number of terms = double the sum of all.* $[2s = n\,(l + a).]$

Let the numbers be A, B, C, D, E, F.

$(A + F)$ × the number of them shall be twice the sum.

$$A . B . C . D . E . F$$
$$H . L . M . K ... G$$

The number of terms is either even or odd; and let their number be the number of units in HG.

First, let the number be even. Divide HG into two equal parts at K.

Now the difference of F, $D =$ the difference of C, A.

Therefore $F + A = C + D$, but $F + A = (F + A)\,HL$.

Hence $\quad C + D = (F + A)\,LM$, $E + B = (F + A)\,MK$.

Therefore $\quad A + B + ... = (F + A)\,HK$.

And $\quad (F + A)\,HG =$ twice $(A + B + ...)$.

5. *Secondly,* let the number of terms be odd, A, B, C, D, E, and let there be as many units in FH as there are terms, &c.

$$A . B . C . D . E$$
$$F . G . K . H$$

6. *If there are a series of numbers beginning with 1 and increasing in* A.P., *then the sum of all* × *eight times the common difference + the square of (common difference − 2) = a square, whose side diminished by 2 = the common difference multiplied by a number, which increased by 1 is double of the number of terms.*

[Let the A.P. be 1, $1 + a$, ... $1 + \overline{n - 1} . a$.

Therefore we have to prove

$$s . 8a + (a - 2)^2 = \{a\,(2n - 1) + 2\}^2,$$

i.e. $\quad 8as = 4a^2 n^2 - 4\,(a - 2)\,na,$

or $\quad 2s = an^2 - (a - 2)\,n = n\,(2 + \overline{n - 1}a)].$

Proof. Let AB, GD, EZ be numbers in A.P. starting from 1.

$$A \cdot K .. N ... B \qquad G \dotsc\dotsc\dotsc D \quad E \cdot L \dotsc\dotsc\dotsc\dotsc Z$$
$$H \cdot M \text{——} X - T$$

Let HT contain as many units as there are terms including 1.

Difference between EZ and 1 = (difference between AB and 1) × a number 1 less than HT [Prop. 3].

Put AK, EL, HM each equal to unity.

Therefore $\qquad LZ = MT \cdot KB$.

Take $KN = 2$ and inquire whether the sum of all × eight times KB + square on NB makes a square whose side diminished by 2 = KB × sum of HT, TM.

Sum of all $= \dfrac{1}{2}$ product $(ZE + EL) \cdot HT = \dfrac{1}{2}(LZ + 2EL) HT$,

and $\qquad LZ = MT \cdot KB$ from above.

Therefore the sum $= \dfrac{1}{2}(KB \cdot MT \cdot TH + 2TH)$,

or, bisecting MT at X, the sum $= KB \cdot TH \cdot TX + HT$.

Thus we inquire whether

$$KB \cdot TH \cdot TX \cdot 8KB + 8KB \cdot HT + square \ on \ NB$$

is a square.

Now $\qquad 8HT \cdot TX \cdot KB^2 = 4HT \cdot TM \cdot KB^2$,

and $\quad 8KB \cdot HT = 4HM \cdot KB + 4(HT + TM) KB$.

Therefore we must see whether

$$4 \cdot HT \cdot TM \cdot KB^2 + 4HM \cdot KB + 4(HT + TM) KB + NB^2$$

is a square.

But $\qquad 4HM \cdot KB = 2KB \cdot NK$,

and $\qquad 2KB \cdot NK + NB^2 = KB^2 + KN^2$,

and again $\qquad BK^2 = HM^2 \cdot BK^2$,

and $HM^2 \cdot BK^2 + 4HT \cdot TM \cdot BK^2 = (HT + TM)^2 BK^2$.

Hence our expression becomes

$$(HT + TM)^2 BK^2 + 4(HT + TM) KB + KN^2$$

$$A \cdot K .. N ... B \text{——} R$$
$$H \cdot M \text{——} X - T$$

or, putting $(HT + TM) BK = NR$, $\ NR^2 + 4NR + KN^2$

and $\qquad 4NR = 2NR \cdot NK$.

Therefore the given expression is a square whose side is RK,

and $\quad RK - 2 = NR$, which is $KB(HT + TM)$,

and $HT + TM + 1 =$ twice the number of terms.

Thus the proposition is proved.

7. Let $HT + TM = A,\ KB = B.$

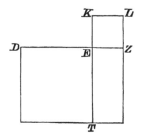

Therefore square on A × square on B = square on G, where

$$G = (HT + TM)\ KB.$$

Let $DE = A,\ EZ = B$, in a straight line.

Complete squares DT, EL, and complete TZ.

Then $DE\ :\ EZ = DT\ :\ TZ$, and $TE\ :\ EK = TZ\ :\ EL.$

Therefore TZ is a mean proportional between the two squares.

Hence the product of the squares = the square of TZ, and

$$DT = (HT + TM)^2,\ ZK = \text{square on } KB.$$

Thus the product $(HT + TM)^2.\ KB^2 = NR^2.$

8. *If there are any number of terms beginning from* 1 *in* A. P. *the sum is a polygonal number, for it has as many angles as the common difference increased by* 2 *contains units, and its side = the number of terms including the term* 1.

The numbers being represented in the figure, (sum of series multiplied by $8KB$) + $NB^2 = RK^2.$

$$O . A . K.. N ...B\text{———}R\ G\text{———}D\quad E . L\text{———}Z$$
$$H . M\text{———}X\text{———}T$$

Therefore, taking another unit AO, $KO = 2$, $KN = 2$, and OB, BK, BN are in arithmetical progression, so that

$$8 . OB . BK + BN^2 = (OB + 2BK)^2,$$

[Prop. 2], and $OB + 2BK - OK = 3KB$ and $3 + 1 = 2 . 2$, or 3 is one less than the double of the common difference of OB, BK, BN.

Now as the sum of the terms of the progression, including unity,

H. D.   16

242   DIOPHANTOS OF ALEXANDRIA.

is subject to the same laws as OB^1, while OB is *any* number and OB always a polygonal (the first term being AO [1] and AB the term next after it) whose side is 2, it follows that the sum of all terms in the progression is a polygonal equiangular to OB, and having as many angles as there are units in the number which exceeds by OK, or 2, the difference KB, and the side of it is HT which = number of terms, including 1.

And thus is demonstrated what is said in *Hypsikles'* definition.

If there are any numbers increasing from unity by equal intervals, when the interval is 1, *the sum of all is a triangular number: when* 2, *a square: when* 3, *a pentagon and so on.* And the number of angles = 2 + common difference, the side = number of terms including 1.

So that, since we have triangles when the difference = 1, the sides of them will be the greatest term in each case, and the product of the greatest term and the greatest term increased by 1 =: twice the triangle.

And, since OB is a polygonal and has as many angles as units, and when multiplied by 8 times (itself – 2) and increased after multiplication by the square of (itself – 4) [i.e. NB^2] it becomes a square, the definition of polygonal numbers will be :

Every polygonal multiplied 8 times into (number of angles – 2) + square of (number of angles – 4) = a square.

The Hypsiklean definition being proved, it remains to show how, given the sides, we may find the numbers.

Now having the side HT and the number of angles we know also KB, therefore we have $(HT + TM)\,KB = NR$. Hence KR is given $[NK = 2]$.

---

[1] This result Nesselmann exhibits thus. Take the arithmetical progression 1, $b+1$, $2b+1...(n-1)\,b+1$.

If s is the *sum*, $8sb + (b-2)^2 = [b\,(2n-1)+2]^2$.

If now we take the three terms $b-2$, b, $b+2$, also in A.P.,

$$8b\,(b+2)+(b-2)^2 = [(b+2)+2b]^2$$
$$= (3b+2)^2.$$

Now $b+2$ is the sum of the first two terms of first series; and $3 = 2.2 - 1$, therefore 3 corresponds to $2n-1$.

Hence s and $b+2$ are subject to the same law.

Therefore we know also the square of KR. Subtracting from it the square of NB, we have the remaining term which = number × $8KB$.

Similarly given the number we can find the side.

9. *Rule.* *To find the number from the side.*

Take the side, double it, subtract 1, and multiply the remainder by (number of angles – 2). Add 2 to the product, and from the square of the number subtract the square of (number of angles – 4). Dividing the remainder by 8 times (number of angles – 2), we find the required polygonal.

To find the side from the number. Multiply it by 8 times (number of angles – 2), add to the product the square of (number of angles – 4). We thus get a square. Subtract 2 from the side of this square and divide remainder by (number of angles – 2). Add 1 to quotient and half the result is the side required.

10. [A fragment.]

Given a number, to find in how many ways it can be a polygonal.

Let AB be the given number, BG the number of angles, and in BG take $GD = 2$, $GE = 4$.

$$A \, . \, T\text{——}B\text{——}E..D..G\text{——}K$$
$$Z\text{——}H$$

Therefore, since the polygonal AB has BG angles,
$$8AB \, . \, BD + BE^2 = \text{a square} = ZH^2 \text{ say.}$$

Take in AB the length $AT = 1$.

Therefore $\quad 8AB \, . \, BD = 4AT \, . \, BD + 4 \, (AB + TB) \, BD.$

Take $\qquad\qquad DK = 4 \, (AB + TB),$

and for $\qquad 4AT \, . \, BD$ put $2BD \, . \, DE.$

Therefore $\quad ZH^2 = KD \, . \, BD + 2BD \, . \, DE + BE^2,$

but $\qquad\quad 2BD \, . \, DE + BE^2 = BD^2 + DE^2.$

Hence $\qquad\quad ZH^2 = KD \, . \, BD + BD^2 + DE^2,$

and $\qquad\qquad KD \, . \, BD + BD^2 = KB \, . \, BD.$

Thus $\qquad\qquad ZH^2 = KB \, . \, BD + DE^2,$

and, since $DK = 4 \, (AB + TB)$, $DK > 4AT > 4$, and half $4 = DG$,
$$GK > GD.$$

Therefore, if DK is bisected at L, L will fall between G and K, and the square on $LB = LD^2 + KB \cdot BD$.

$$A \cdot T\text{——}B\text{——}E..D..G\text{——}L\text{——}K$$
$$Z\text{——}H\text{——}N\text{——}M$$

Therefore $ZH^2 = BL^2 - LD^2 + DE^2$,

or $ZH^2 + DL^2 = BL^2 + DE^2$,

and $LD^2 \sim DE^2 = LB^2 \sim ZH^2$.

Again since $ED = DG$ and DG is produced to L,

$$EL \cdot LG + GD^2 = DL^2.$$

Therefore $DL^2 - DG^2 = DL^2 - DE^2 = EL \cdot LG$.

Hence $EL \cdot LG = LB^2 \sim ZH^2$.

Put $ZM = BL$ (BL being $> ZH$).

Therefore $ZM^2 - ZH^2 = EL \cdot LG$; but DK is bisected in L,

so that $DL = 2 (AB + BT)$; and $DG = 2AT$.

Therefore $GL = 4BT$, and $BT = \dfrac{1}{4} GL$,

but also AT (or 1) $= \dfrac{1}{4} EG$ (or 4).

Therefore $AB = \dfrac{1}{4} EL$, but TB also $= \dfrac{1}{4} GL$.

Hence $AB \cdot TB = \dfrac{1}{16} EL \cdot LG$,

or $EL \cdot LG = 16AB \cdot BT$.

Thus $16AB \cdot BT = MZ^2 - ZH^2 = MH^2 + 2ZH \cdot HM$.

Therefore HM is *even*.

Let it be bisected in N.......

[Here the fragment ends.]

INDEX.

[The references are to pages.]

Ab-kismet, 41 *n*.
Abu'lfaraj, 2, 3, 12, 13, 41
Abu'l-Wafā Al-Būzjāni, 13, 25—26, 40—42, 148, 155, 157
Abu Ja'far Mohammed ibn Alhusain, 156
Addition, how expressed by Diophantos, 69; Bombelli's sign for, 45; Vieta's, 78 *n*.
Algebraic notation, three stages of, 77 —80
aljabr, 40, 92, 149—150, 158
Alkarkhī, 24—25, 71 *n*., 156—159
Al-Khārizmi, *see* Mohammed ibn Mūsā
almukābala, 92, 149—150, 158
Al-Nadīm, 39, 40 *n*.
Al-Shahrastāni, 41
Alsirāj, 24 *n*., 159
ἀναφορικός of Hypsikles, 5
ἀορίστως, ἐν ἀορίστῳ, 140
Apollonios, 4, 8, 9, 23
Approximations, 117—120, 147
Apuleius, 15
Arabian scale of powers compared with that of Diophantos, 70—71, 150— 151
Arabic translations, &c., 23, 24, 25, 39—42, 148—159
Archimedes, 7, 142, 143, 144, 146, 147
Aristoxenos, 14, 15
Arithmetic and Geometry, 31, 141— 142
Ἀριθμητικά of Diophantos, 33 and *passim*
ἀριθμητική and λογιστική, 18, 136, 145
ἀριθμός, ὁ; Diophantos' technical use of the word, 57, 150; his symbol for it, 57— 66, 137—138, 160
ἀριθμοστόν, 74

Ars rei et census, 21 *n*.
Auria, Joseph, 51, 56
Autolykos, 5

Bacchios ὁ γέρων, 14, 15, 16
Bachet, 49—53 and *passim*
"Back-reckoning," 85—86, 114; ex- amples of, 110, 111, and in the AP- PENDIX *passim*
Bhāskara, 153
Billy, Jacobus de, 3, 54
Blancanus, 3
Bombelli, 13, 14, 15, 23, 35, 36, 42— 45, 52, 134—135; his algebraic no- tation, 45, 68
Bossut, 32, 38, 90 *n*., 138—139 *n*.
Brahmagupta, 153
Brassinne, 221 *n*.

Camerarius, Joachim, 2, 42
Cantor, 55 *n*., 58, 59, 67, 141 *n*., 151, 152, 156, 157
Cardan, 43, 46, 70
Casiri, 41 *n*.
Cattle-problem, the, 7, 142—147
Censo, 70
Coefficient, 93 *n*.
Colebrooke, 12, 19 *n*., 33, 133, 136, 137 *n*.
Cosa, 45, 70
Cossali, 1, 3, 10, 12, 31, 35, 41 *n*., 43 *n*., 49, 51, 70, 71, 107 *n*., 133, 136, 140, 169 *n*., 220 *n*.
Çrīdhara, 153
Cubes: transformation of a sum of two cubes into the difference of two others, and *vice versâ*, 123—125
Cubic equation, 36, 93—94, 114

Data of Euclid, 140

Dedication to Dionysios, 136

Definitions of Diophantos, 28, 29, 57, 67, 74, 137, 138, 163

Determinate equations : *see* CONTENTS ; reduction of, 29, 149—150

Diagonal numbers, 142

Didymos, 14, 15, 16

Digby, 23

Diophantos, *see* CONTENTS

διπλῆ ἰσότης
διπλοϊσότης } 35, 98

Division, how represented by Diophantos, 73

Double-equations of the first and second degrees, 98—107 ; of higher degrees, 112—113

δύναμις and the sign for it, 58 *n.*, 62, 63, 66 *n.*, 67, 68, 140, 151 ; δύναμις and τετράγωνος, 67—68

δυναμοδύναμις and the sign for it, 67—68

δυναμοδυναμοστόν, 74

δυναμόκυβος and the sign for it, 65 *n.*, 67—68

δυναμοκυβοστόν, 74

δυναμοστόν, 74

εἶδος = power, 29 *n.*

Elements of Euclid, 4, 5, 142, 158

Epanthema of Thymaridas, 140

Epigrams, 2, 6, 7, 9, 142—147, 223

Equality, Diophantos' expression of, 75—76 ; Xylander's sign for, 76

Equations, classes of, *see* CONTENTS ; reduction of determinate equations, 29, 149—150

Eratosthenes, 5

Euclid, *Elements*, 4, 5, 142, 158 ; *Data*, 140

Eudemos, 67

Eunapios, 13

Fabricius, 1, 5, 14

Fakhrî, the, 24—25, 71 *n.*, 156—159

Fermat, 13, 23, 53, 54, 68, 123, 124, 125, 126, 128, 129, 130, 131, 221 *n.*

Fihrist, the, 39, 40, 41, 42

Fractions, representation of, 73—75

Gardthausen, 60, 64

Geminos, 18, 145—146

Geometry and algebra, 140—141, 151—153, 156, 158

Geometry and arithmetic, 31, 141—142

Girard, Albert, 3 *n.*, 55

Gow on Diophantos, 64—66 *n.*, 137 *n.*, 160

Hankel, 83—85, 129 *n.*

Harmonics of Diophantos, 14 ; of Ptolemy, 15

Harriot, 78 *n.*

Heiberg, 146—147, 160

Heilbronner, 3

Herakleides Ponticus, 16

Heron of Alexandria, 141, 153

Hipparchos, 5, 141

Hippokrates, 67

History of the Dynasties, see Abu'lfaraj

Holzmann, Wilhelm, *see* Xylander

Hultsch, 146 *n.*

Hypatia, 1, 8, 9, 10, 11, 17, 38, 39 *n.*

Hypsikles, 4, 5, 6, 135, 242

ι for ἴσος, 75

Iamblichos, 78, 79, 140

Identical formulae, 125

Indeterminate equations, 94—113, 144, 146, 147, 157, 158, 159

Irrationality, Diophantos' view of, 82

Isidoros, 5

Italian scale of powers, 70, 71

jabr, 40, 92, 149—150, 158

jidr, 150

John of Damascus, 8

John of Jerusalem, 8

ka'b, 71 *n.*, 157, 158

Kitâb Alfihrist, 39

Klügel, 11, 90 *n.*, 144

Kostâ ibn Lûkâ, 40

κυβόκυβος and the sign for it, 67—68

κύβος and the sign for it, 58 *n.*, 62, 63, 66 *n.*, 67—68

Kuster, 8

Lato, 70
Lehmann, 60
λεῖψις, and the symbol for it, 66 n., 71—73, 137, 163
λεῖψις ἐπὶ λεῖψιν πολλαπλασιασθεῖσα ποιεῖ ὕπαρξιν, 137 n.
Λεόφαντος or Λεώφαντος, 14
Lessing, 142, 143, 144, 146 n.
Limits, method of, 86, 87, 115—117; approximation to, 117—120
λογιστική and ἀριθμητική, 18, 136, 145—146
Lousada, Miss Abigail, 56
Luca Pacioli, 43, 70 n.
Lucilius, 9

"Majuskelcursive" writing, 64, 72 n.
māl, 71 n., 157, 158
Manuscripts of Diophantos, 19, 61
Maximus Planudes, 23, 38, 39, 51, 135
Meibomius, 14
Metrodoros, 10
minus, Diophantos' sign for, 66 n., 71—73; Bombelli's, 45; Tartaglia's, 78 n.; Mohammed ibn Mūsā's expression for, 151
Minus multiplied by minus gives plus, 137, 163
"Minuskelcursive" writing, 64
Mohammed ibn Mūsā Al-Khārizmi, 3, 40 n., 59, 92, 134, 148, 149—155, 156, 158
μονάδες, 69; the symbol for, 69
Montucla, 3, 11, 53, 71, 136
mufassirin, 40 n.
mukābala, 92, 149—150, 158
mūla, 150
Multiplication, modern signs for, 78 n.

nāqis, 151 n.
Nesselmann, 5, 10, 20, 21, 22, 23, 27, 31, 33, 34, 35, 36, 37, 44 n., 49, 51 n., 54, 55, 58, 59, 77, 78, 79, 85, 88, 91 n., 92, 108, 110, 114, 121, 125, 129 n., 133, 142, 143 n., 144, 145, 146, 147, 169 n., 212 n., 242 n.
Nikomachos, 6, 14, 15, 16, 38, 65 n., 135, 151

Notation, algebraic: three stages, 77—80; drawbacks of Diophantos' notation, 80—82
Numbers which are the sum of two squares, 127—130
Numbers which are the sum of three squares, 130—131
Numbers as the sum of four squares, 131—132

ὀργανῶσαι, 136—137
ὡρισμένοι ἀριθμοί, 140
Oughtred, 78 n.

Pappos, 11, 12, 17, 65 n., 139
παρισότης or παρισότητος ἀγωγή, 117—120
Peletarius, James, 2, 43
Pell, John, 56
Perron, Cardinal, 20
Phaidros, 14, 15
πλασματικόν, 169 n.
Plato, 18, 141—142, 145
πλῆθος, coefficient, 93 n.
plus, Diophantos' expression of, 71, 137 n.; Bombelli's symbol for, 45; Vieta's, 78 n.
Pococke, 2, 12, 41 n.
Polygonal Numbers, 31—35 and passim
Porisms, 18, 32—35, 37, 121—125, 210, 218
Poselger, 55, 120, 124 n.
Powers, additive and multiplicative evolution of, 70—71, 150—151
Proclus, 142
Progression, arithmetical, summation of, 239—240
πρότασις and πρόβλημα, 34
Ptolemy, Claudius, 9
Pythagoras, 141

Quadratic equation, solution of, 90—93, 140—141, 151—155; the two roots of, 92, 153—155

Radix, 68
Ramus, Peter, 10, 14, 15

Reduction of determinate equations, 29, 149—150

Regiomontanus, Joannes, 2, 20, 21, 22, 23, 42, 46, 78

Reimer, 32

Relati, 71

Res, 68

Riccati, Vincenzo, 27 *n.*

Right-angled triangle: formation of, in rational numbers, 115, 141, 142; use of, 115, 127, 128, 155, 156; examples, APPENDIX, especially Book VI.

ρίζη of Nikomachos, 151

Rodet, L., 29 *n.*, 59, 60, 61, 62, 75—76, 91 *n.*, 92, 134, 151, 155

Rosen, editor of Mohammed ibn Mûsâ, q. v.

Salmasius, Claudius, 19 *n.*, 224

Saunderson, Nicholas, 52 *n.*, 133

Scholia on Diophantos, 38, 39, 135

Schulz, 55 and *passim*

Series, arithmetical; summation of, 239—240

shai, 150

"Side-numbers," 142

Simultaneous equations, how treated by Diophantos, 80, 89, 113, 140

Sirmondus, Jacobus, 19 *n.*, 20

Square root, how expressed by Diophantos, 93 *n.*

Stevin, 3, 55

Struve, Dr J. and Dr K. L., 142 *n.*

Subsidiary problems, 81, 86; examples of, 97, 110, 111

Subtraction, Diophantos' symbol for, 66 *n.*, 71—73; Tartaglia's, 78 *n.*; Bombelli's, 45

Suidas, 1, 8, 9, 10, 11, 12, 13, 45

Supersolida, 71

Sursolides, 71

Suter, Dr Heinrich, 28 *n.*, 50, 53 *n.*

Symbols, algebraic: see *plus, minus,* &c.

tafsīr on Diophantos, 40

Tannery, Paul, 6, 7, 9 *n.*, 10, 13, 14, 15, 16, 133, 139, 142—146

tanto, Bombelli's use of, 45

Ta'rīkh Hokoma, 41

Tartaglia, 43, 78 *n.*

Theon of Alexandria, 8 *n.*, 10, 11, 12, 13, 38

Theon of Smyrna, 6, 135, 142

Thrasyllos, 15

Thymaridas, 140

Translations of Diophantos, *see* Chapter III.

Unknown quantity and its powers in Diophantos, 57—69, 139—140; in other writers, 45, 68, 70, 71 *n.*, 150, 151, 157, 158; Diophantos' devices for remedying the want of more than one sign for, 80—82, 89, 179

ὕπαρξις, 29 *n.*, 71, 137 *n.*

Usener, Hermann, 12 *n.*

Variable, devices for remedying the want of more than one symbol for a, 80—82, 89, 179

Vieta, 52, 68, 78 *n.*, 123—124

Vossius, 3, 21 *n.*, 56

Wallis, 70 *n.*, 71, 138

Wöpcke, 24, 25, 26, 155

Xylander, 45—51 and *passim*

Zensus, 68

Zetetica of Vieta, 52

CAMBRIDGE : PRINTED BY C. J. CLAY, M.A. AND SON, AT THE UNIVERSITY PRESS.

For EU product safety concerns, contact us at Calle de José Abascal, 56–1°,
28003 Madrid, Spain or eugpsr@cambridge.org.